Happy Abortions

OUR BODIES IN THE ERA OF CHOICE

Erica Millar

ZED

Happy Abortions: Our Bodies in the Era of Choice was
first published in 2017 by Zed Books Ltd, The Foundry,
17 Oval Way, London SE11 5RR, UK.

www.zedbooks.net

Typeset in Avenir and Haarlemmer
by Swales & Willis Ltd, Exeter, Devon
Index by ed.emery@thefreeuniversity.net
Cover design by Alice Marwick

A catalogue record for this book is available from the British Library

ISBN 9781-78699-131-7 hb
ISBN 978-1-78699-130-0 pb
ISBN 978-1-78699-132-4 pdf
ISBN 978-1-78699-133-1 epub
ISBN 978-1-78699-134-8 mobi

Printed and bound in Great Britain by CPI Group (UK) Ltd, Croydon CR0 4YY

CONTENTS

ACKNOWLEDGEMENTS

This book has been a long time in the making and, as such, I owe gratitude to just about everyone I know: so thank you! Many of the ideas in this book were developed in dialogue with friends and mentors, several of whom read drafts and offered astute and valuable feedback, helping to fill gaps and push my arguments to a further level of complexity. Jordy Silverstein has helped me see the value in my work, and her integrity and passionate engagement with the world has served as a model, motivating me to continue with and finish this book. I am incredibly grateful to Ann Genovese, who has offered me immense support and guidance in academia and beyond; her scholarship also provides endless inspiration. Maree Pardy gave invaluable advice on the manuscript and introduced me to theoretical frameworks that are fundamental to the book. Barbara Baird's work provided a platform upon which many of the arguments of this book developed, and conversations with her have helped refine its arguments immeasurably. Several other academic friends have carefully and perceptively read chapters and offered encouragement, and their excellent scholarship has extended my knowledge of the world in ways that have fed into the book in one way or another. Thanks especially to Cath Kevin, Claire McLisky and Ben Silverstein.

My students and colleagues in the School of Social Sciences at the University of Adelaide have made it a pleasure to come into work, and special thanks to Pam Papadelos, Anna Szorenyi and Megan Warin for offering me mentorship and friendship. My editor at Zed Books, Kim Walker, kept me to deadlines and provided encouragement through the process. My former editor, Kika Sroka-Miller, believed in the project and got it off the ground.

Parts of this book have appeared in earlier forms as follows; I thank the publishers for permission to reprint materials in this book and the editors and reviewers for their helpful feedback: (2014) Abortion, selfishness and happy objects. *In:* Brooks, A. and Lemmings, D. eds. *Norbert Elias, Emotional Styles and Historical Change.* New York: Routledge, 196–213; (2015) Choice-makers or failures: Providing a genealogy of abortion shame and shaming. *Law & History: The Journal of the Australian and New Zealand Law & History Society,* 2, 114–145; (2015) "Too many": Anxious white nationalism and the biopolitics of abortion in contemporary Australian history. *Australian Feminist Studies,* 30(83), 82–98; (2016) Mourned choices and grievable lives: How the anti-abortion movement came to define the abortion experience. *Gender & History,* 28(2), 501–519; (2017) Feminism, foetocentrism and the politics of abortion choice in 1970s Australia. *In:* Stettner, S., Ackerman, K., Burnett, K., Hay, T. eds. *Transcending Borders: Abortion in the Past and Present.* London & New York: Palgrave Macmillan, 121–136.

My parents, Jennifer and Alexander; my sisters, Meredith, Petra and Rachel; my neices and nephews; and my extended

Burgess and Robertson families have provided much needed encouragement and support; as have several dear friends, of whom I particularly thank Miranda, Vicki, Marina and Judith. Finally, I am deeply indebted to Shane, whose kindness, humour and brilliance helped me in innumerable ways to finish this book.

This book is dedicated to my grandmother, Dorothy Jean Bassett (1921–2016), whose warmth, care and affection sustained me for most of the time it took to research and write. Thank you.

INTRODUCTION: AN EMOTIONAL CHOICE

> Like a year ago I had an abortion at the Planned Parenthood on Madison Ave, and I remember this experience with a nearly inexpressible level of gratitude … Plenty of people still believe that on some level—if you are a good woman—abortion is a choice which should be accompanied by some level of sadness, shame, or regret. But you know what? I have a good heart and having an abortion made me happy in a totally unqualified way. Why wouldn't I be happy that I was not forced to become a mother? (Amelia Bonow cited in West 2015)

Pro-choice activists have recently begun to identify and challenge an emotional script that impinges upon women as they approach, experience and remember their abortions. The script depicts abortion as an incredibly difficult choice made in response to extraneous circumstances that are beyond the woman's immediate control; it requires women to justify their abortions, preferably by citing the best interests of their potential children, to grieve their lost children after abortion, and to keep their abortions secret out of a sense of shame or guilt.

This narrative belongs to the 'mushy middle' that dominates political debate about abortion and is at once 'pro-choice' and 'anti-abortion', professing support for abortion only through 'admission that abortion is a societal evil' (Freedman and Weitz 2012: 39). The idea that women can have abortions so long as they feel 'really, really bad' about them (Pollitt 2014: 37) balances the realisation that abortion is necessary (and women will have them regardless of the legislative context) with concern for foetal life and the corresponding view that abortion is morally problematic. The 2015 Twitter campaign *#ShoutYourAbortion* was a direct response to cultural expectations about how women should approach and experience their abortions. This campaign began after the US House of Representatives passed a bill defunding Planned Parenthood. Activist Lindy West retweeted the above abortion announcement from her friend Amelia Bonow, and called upon women to 'shout' about their abortions and, in so doing, reclaim the abortion narrative from those who wished to define it for them. West's call resonated with women worldwide; the hashtag *#ShoutYourAbortion* was used 100,000 times over a twenty-four hour period, trending in the USA, the UK, Australia and Ireland, where abortion remains illegal (Fishwick 2015).

The popularity of this hashtag attests to the widespread acknowledgment of a powerful set of expectations that burden women's feelings leading up to and after their abortions. Such expectations are not always articulated, but nevertheless, broadly shared and taken-for-granted. This book is the first sustained examination of the emotional common sense of abortion. It argues that particular emotions are repeatedly associated with abortion, and that these emotions powerfully delineate the cultural meaning of abortion for women and the community at large. Instead of designating abortion as explicitly wrong or sinful, emotions operate through the rhetoric of choice; they regulate abortion, not by calling explicitly for its prohibition, but by embedding anti-abortion sentiment into the shared meanings that script the experience and consequences of abortion. When we hear over and over again that women grieve and feel shame after their abortions, for example, abortion is produced as a procedure that is inherently productive of grief and shame. Such a positioning is perfectly compatible with the notion that women can choose to have abortions if they so desire, but nevertheless acts as a warning to women that an abortion will be a damaging experience.

The language of choice has become endemic to public discussions of abortion over the last fifty years. Abortion is widely considered to be a woman's choice and, in many contexts, pregnant women are lawfully entitled to access abortion. The possibility of a 'happy abortion', however, remains elusive. In labelling her abortion 'happy', we can assume that Bonow was being sincere; yet it was also, moreover, a political provocation: why wouldn't she 'be happy that I was not forced to become a mother?' This book addresses a similar question, asking why emotions that depict abortion as a positive and beneficial experience for women (for example, relief, happiness, hope and gratitude) are generally elided, foreclosed or disavowed in public discussions of abortion. Positive abortion narratives certainly exist, and have done since abortion began to be discussed publicly at the turn of 1970s. As with Bonow's, however, these narratives are usually set up on the defensive, responding to socially-acceptable means of talking about abortion, which emphasise emotions, such as grief, regret, guilt, shame and distress, that present abortion as an unfortunate and even harmful experience for women.

The repeated association of abortion with negative emotions is a means whereby an experience that women undergo routinely without complications or deleterious after-effects retains its status as an exceptional and abnormal occurrence. About one in three women will have an abortion in her lifetime (Chan et al. 2001; Jones and Kavanaugh 2011; Norman 2012; Royal College of Obstetricians & Gynaecologists 2011), and 25 per cent of all pregnancies worldwide end in abortion (Sedgh et al. 2016). Not only is abortion, therefore, very common, it is also rare for women to experience sustained, negative emotions after their abortions. Positive emotions are, in fact, more frequently reported in psychological and sociological studies of the abortion experience (Charles et al. 2008; Harden and Ogden 1999; Major et al. 2009; National Collaborating Centre for Mental Health [NCCMH] 2011; Romans-Clarkson 1989). Yet normative femininity prevents abortion from being widely perceived as the normal, routine and generally unproblematic procedure that it is.

Representations of abortion do not reflect women's experiences, but are in fact powered by norms surrounding gender, as they are refracted through other nodes of inequality such as race and social class; and because gender is inherently unstable and in need of constant reiteration and reinvention,

4

representations of abortion are one means by which norms pertaining to gender are naturalised and made to appear outside of culture. The ostensible freedom pregnant women have to control decisions about motherhood, a freedom that is often communicated through the rhetoric of choice, conceals the rigid emotional script of abortion. The emotional world of pregnant women is heavily circumscribed. It is widely supposed that women's lives are geared towards motherhood, and motherhood brings with it the only true promise of happiness for women, and for pregnant women most especially. Within this normative schema, happiness is generally reserved for motherhood alone, and abortion can only be imagined in negative terms. This is why we see abortion continually relayed through emotions that portray the experience as difficult, unpleasant and damaging. The emotional economy of abortion recuperates the procedure—which signals a woman's rejection of motherhood—to the norm of motherhood; it articulates the notion that pregnant women can decide whether or not to terminate or continue with their pregnancies while also producing abortion as a deviant and harmful choice for women to make. The rhetoric of choice presents pregnant women as free, self-determining subjects, disguising the effects of the emotions that attach to and regulate their choices.

This book focuses on the norms that act on women's abortion conduct, especially those that operate through particular emotions. Before turning to the various social and cultural forces that compete or converge to shape the shared meanings of abortion for women and the community at large,

I detail several other judicial and extra-judicial means that work to restrict women's access to abortion.

CHOOSING ABORTION

Choice has only become a central discourse regulating abortion in countries where women can access abortion lawfully. One quarter of the world's population live in sixty-six countries with laws that completely prohibit abortion or only permit it to save a woman's life. Most of these countries are in the Global South as well as central and eastern Asia. Of course, women have abortions regardless of whether or not it is legal and, in fact, proportionately more women have abortions in countries with restrictive legislative contexts than in those where abortion is lawful (Sedgh et al. 2016). Although the law cannot stop women from having abortions, it does affect the safety of abortion: approximately 5 million women are hospitalised and 47,000 women die from abortion each year, almost exclusively in countries where abortion is illegal (World Health Organization 2012).

Most Western countries moved away from the complete criminalisation of abortion at the turn of the 1970s. The Abortion Act 1967 (UK) expanded the definition of therapeutic abortion to explicitly permit medical doctors to perform abortion on the grounds of a woman's psychological (in addition to physical) health. Importantly, this act did not repeal existing legislation, but created a legal defence for abortion. Law reform in Britain helped ignite a worldwide trend. Between 1969 and 1982, forty countries liberalised

their abortion laws (and only three introduced more restrictive abortion legislation). New laws in Australia, New Zealand
and Canada were modelled on the UK Abortion Act. In the
USA, a Supreme Court decision of 1973 resulted in more
radical reform, conferring upon women the right to early
abortion on the grounds of privacy (Francome 2004: 1).

From this time onward, the USA has stood out from
other Western countries in terms of abortion law and politics.
This is in part because of differing legal trajectories. The
medicalisation of abortion was a 'compromise solution' to
abortion (Glendon 1987). Within jurisdictions that adopted
this model of law reform, abortion remained technically
illegal, and medical doctors or abortion committees determined whether individual women met the criteria to have a
therapeutic abortion; therefore, doctors rather than individual
women held decisional authority over abortion and abortion
was framed, at least in the law, as a 'medical issue', helping
to prevent its intense moralisation (Lowe 2016: 63–64). In
the USA, abortion law was reformed through the Supreme
Court, which determined that abortion was defined in law
as a constitutional right. A 'competing rights' framework for
abortion quickly developed—with pregnant women pitted
against foetuses—and a deeply polarised debate based on a
'clash of absolutes' (Tribe 1990), ensued (Condit 1990: 63;
Lee 2003: 96). The competing rights approach to abortion
was aided by the fact that abortion had been clearly defined
as a feminist issue by the time of the Supreme Court decision
of 1973; abortion politics are so passionate because, as
will become increasingly clear through this book, they are

also gender politics. In contrast, the Women's Liberation Movement had not altered the landscape of abortion politics when the Abortion Act 1967 (UK) provided its widely adopted model for medicalised abortion (Lee 2003: 98).

The growth of the New Right intensified the gender and moral politics of abortion in the USA. The New Right positions abortion as a key sign and symptom of the degeneracy brought about by the decline of Christian morality and the patriarchal nuclear family. This political development emerged in part from the anti-abortion movement of the 1970s and a historically unprecedented convergence between Catholic and evangelical Protestant denominations (Petchesky 1981). The lack of a sizeable evangelical community outside of the USA is one reason the New Right has not taken hold to the same degree elsewhere (Bean et al. 2008; Lee 2003: 99–100). Moreover, the abortion politics of the New Right and anti-abortion movement are closely aligned to the US Republican Party. In countries that medicalised abortion in the Anglophone West, major political parties have avoided platforms on abortion, affording their members conscience votes when debating the issue of abortion in parliament (for example, Overby, Tatalovich and Studlar 1998). In contrast, abortion is a partisan political issue in the USA; with few exceptions, Republican and Democratic officeholders since the Reagan Administration hold, respectively, anti-abortion and pro-choice positions (Sanger 2017: 12–14).

The highly politicised nature of abortion in the USA makes it an epicentre of abortion activism worldwide; anti- and pro-choice rhetoric and strategies often develop there before moving to other countries (see, for example, Lee 2003; McCulloch 2013). While anti-abortionists have remained marginalised in Britain (Lee 2003), Canada (Saurette and Gordon 2013), Australia (Baird 2017) and, to a slightly lesser extent, New Zealand (McCulloch and Weatherall 2017), they have enjoyed considerable political patronage and support amongst US Republican administrations—this was particularly true of the Reagan Administration. Trump has, once more, highlighted abortion as a defining issue of the political right. Trump's presidency has come after a period of unprecedented anti-abortion lawmaking in US states. A landmark Supreme Court ruling of 1992 enabled states to introduce measures aimed to, in the words of legal scholar Carol Sanger, 'persuade pregnant women against abortion' (2017: 32). More laws relating to abortion (205 in total) were introduced between 2011 and 2013 than in the entire preceding decade combined. Between 2011 and 2016, one-quarter of American abortion clinics closed because of the introduction of Targeted Regulation of Abortion Provider (TRAP) laws in many states, which, amongst other measures, require abortion clinics to meet the building and equipment requirements of ambulatory surgical centres (Redden 2016).[1] The Guttmacher Institute now classifies half of American states as being 'hostile' to abortion rights (Boonstra and Nash 2014). In contrast to the increasingly restrictive legislative context in the USA, Canada (in 1988) and, more recently, four Australian jurisdictions (the Australian Capital Territory, Victoria, Tasmania, and the Northern Territory) have decriminalised abortion and are presently the only places worldwide where abortion is no longer regulated by the criminal law (Baird 2017: 198). There are also organised campaigns in the UK and other Australian states to decriminalise abortion (bpas 2015; Waters 2016).

The criminalisation of abortion leaves it open to political and legislative contestation (McCulloch and Weatherall 2017). Laws also significantly determine the material practice of abortion. As mentioned, laws on abortion have a direct correlation to maternal morbidity and mortality rates. In countries with relatively liberal abortion laws, the law and its interpretation into policy can impede women's access to abortion in other ways. Laws on abortion, for example, were generally developed before the advent of medical abortion—a combination of mifepristone, which blocks the hormone progesterone so that the lining of the womb breaks down and shreds, with misoprostol, which causes a woman's uterus to expand, expelling the pregnancy. The two drugs are most effective when taken one to three days apart, and when taken in early pregnancy (to nine weeks), an abortion looks and feels much like heavy menstrual bleeding. Women could, in theory, get a prescription for early medical abortion from their local GP, collect it at their local pharmacist and take it at their own convenience—this method of provision is, for example, slowly becoming available to some Australian women (Children by Choice 2016). This practice is specifically prevented in jurisdictions where laws—developed in response to concerns about 'backyard abortions' and when abortion was only offered as a surgical procedure—specify that abortions must be performed by doctors at approved premises. Such laws can unnecessarily force women to travel long distances at significant cost (transport, childcare, time off work), and can result in women miscarrying while commuting back to their homes. In the UK, laws that restrict where abortion takes place have resulted in many providers offering women the choice of taking both medications within a day, which is less effective (Sheldon 2014). Such laws also hinder telemedicine's potential to offer women living in remote and rural areas with greater access to medical abortion. This is the case in three Australian jurisdictions, including one (the ACT) where abortion is decriminalised (Baird 2017).

Law reform does not, however, guarantee women freedom in the realm of abortion. For real choice, abortion would need to be accessible and affordable for everyone. In Britain, where abortions are fully covered by the National Health Service, health experts have nevertheless warned that abortion care is 'heading towards a crisis', pointing to 'inequitable access, inadequate numbers of appropriately trained staff, stigmatisation, and a culture of exceptionalism, or ghettoisation' (Goldbeck-Wood 2017). Women cannot have abortions in Northern Ireland (Sheldon 2016) and only secured the ability to have NHS-funded abortions on the mainland in June 2017 (Elgot and McDonald 2017). Also, women cannot generally have abortions in Scotland after the eighteenth week of their pregnancies despite the law allowing for abortion to twenty-four weeks (Purcell, Hilton and McDaid 2014). Women in New Zealand wait an average of four weeks between being referred for abortion and obtaining an abortion because of the long distances some women must travel or the time it takes for two certifying consultant physicians to approve of their abortion (McCulloch and Weatherall 2017).

Access and affordability remain key issues in countries where abortion has been decriminalised (Baird 2017; Rebouché 2014). After Canada became the first country with no criminal law on abortion in 1988, fewer hospitals began to provide abortions so that, today, the vast majority of hospitals have no abortion services. Combined with the absence of private clinics in many areas, women are often forced to travel long distances to have abortions. There were no abortion services on Prince Edward Island, for instance, from 1982 to 2016. Many provincial/territorial governments refuse to pay for abortions performed in private clinics or outside of their jurisdictions (Kaposy 2010; Sethna and Doull 2013). Furthermore, medical abortion, available to women in France since 1988, became available to Canadian women only in 2017; it is not covered under the majority of provincial drug plans and, because of strict regulatory guidelines, it is only offered in a few major cities (Vogel 2017). In most of Australia, the government rebate for abortion only covers about half of the cost of the procedure, the majority of abortions are performed in private clinics, and most abortion providers are in capital cities, meaning that women living in rural and remote communities must travel long distances to obtain an abortion (Baird 2017; Shankar et al. 2017). Despite the decriminalisation of abortion in Victoria in 2008, women's access to surgical abortion remains woefully inadequate in the state, and their access to later abortions has actually decreased in recent years (Keogh et al. 2017). In the USA (where abortion is at once lawful and, as explained, heavily restricted in many states under the law), 32 states and the District of Columbia follow the Hyde Amendment (1976) and only provide Medicaid funding for abortion in cases of life endangerment, rape or incest; as a consequence, many women (41 per cent in one study) find it 'somewhat or very difficult' to pay for abortions, and raising funds causes delayed care for many women (54 per cent in one study) (Guttmacher Institute 2016b). While a lack of financial resources can limit women's access to abortion, poverty can also drive women to terminate otherwise wanted pregnancies; as will be explicated below, the rhetoric of choice is meaningless when parenting remains financially unviable for many women.

For real choice, abortion would also need to be recognised as a legitimate choice, and one that pregnant women routinely and unproblematically make when they no longer want to be pregnant. Although abortion is statistically normal, it is far from normative. Even in countries where abortion is decriminalised, it is construed as a choice women make in exceptional circumstances after much agonising and soul-searching. Today, abortion politics are largely waged in terms of cultural politics—anti-abortionists frequently claim theirs as a struggle over 'hearts and minds' and academics often refer to abortion as a 'culture war' (Mouw and Sobel 2001). Originally focused on law reform, abortion activism now targets the 'shared meanings' of abortion (Condit 1990: 7). For example, the slogan of ProWomenProLife, the most visible anti-abortion blog in Canada (active since 1997), is 'A Canada without abortion, by choice'; it defines abortion as 'a moral, cultural and philosophical problem inextricably tied to our view about sexuality, motherhood and marriage' and aims, not to re-criminalise abortion, but to act on the 'culture of women' (cited in Saurette and Gordon 2013: 166). Pro-choice feminists have long insisted that abortion is a cultural and political debate about these same issues—sexuality, motherhood and, to a lesser extent, marriage—but view the gender roles contained therein as oppressive rather than the reverse (see, for example, Boyle 1997; Lowe 2016; Luker 1984; Petchesky 1984). The current cultural politics of abortion has material effects; it rationalises the lack of state investment in providing women with abortion services and stigmatises abortion providers, leading to an inadequate number of trained professionals able and willing to provide abortion care (Harris et al. 2011; Martin et al. 2014). Cultural meanings of abortion also shape how women experience abortion (Cockrill and Nack 2013; Major and Gramzow 1999), and how friends, family members and the broader community judge and evaluate women's choices (Lowe 2016).

Abortion cultures also shape legislative contexts. Moral and social codes that firmly tied women's sexuality to mother-hood upheld the criminalisation of abortion. Within the rigid normative bounds of chastity followed by motherhood upon marriage, a woman's desire to have an abortion, as a sign of unmarried sexual activity or a married woman's refusal of maternity, was virtually unspeakable—albeit widely practiced (Luker 1984: 15–16). In countries that medicalised abortion at the turn of the 1970s, a web of gendered power relations supported the concept that abortion should be a medical doctor's, rather than a woman's, decision. Within such laws, women were positioned as emotional, rash, and as potentially bad choice makers, coming under the paternal guidance and care of authoritative, knowing, rational (coded male) medical doctors (Sheldon 1993: 98).

The decriminalisation of abortion in Canada and several Australian jurisdictions represents a new stage in the legal regulation of abortion, consolidating a normative shift that had been under way for some time and can be discerned in other contexts where abortion remains criminalised. The decriminalisation of abortion removes formal obstacles that limited women's access to abortion (in the law if not in practice) and formally recognises women as subjects of decisions about abortion; as Barbara Baird recently observes, the 'reclassification of abortion from crime to health care is a longstanding goal of feminist and pro-choice activists ... [and] is surely a valuable achievement' (2017: 198). The decriminalisation of abortion also, however, reinforces a discursive context where, as I detail below, women are routinely addressed as free, individual, choosing subjects. The designation of aborting women as 'free' can veil the normative restrictions that continue to operate on and through women's abortion choices.

Scholars have examined such normative restrictions through the themes of abortion stigma and the 'awfulisation' of abortion, arguing that abortion is overwhelmingly represented in largely negative terms, ranging from unpleasant to abhorrent (Hadley 1997; Hanschmidt et al. 2016; Pollitt 2014). Even when abortion is considered necessary, it is routinely represented as something that should be avoided and the cause of inevitable distress for women. The awfulisation of abortion and abortion stigma present motherhood as the only unproblematic outcome of pregnancy, constructing abortion anew as a deviant and harmful choice for women. There is an emotional register to abortion stigma and awfulisation; shame is, for example, an internalisation of abortion stigma (Chapter 4), and the awfulisation of abortion is carried through particular emotions, such as the anguish and grief women are said to experience (Chapters 2 and 3).

This book examines how the meaning of abortion is produced across several 'public arenas of discourse' (Condit 1990: 6), including newspapers, activist literature, parliamentary debates, political speeches, and psychological and sociological studies of women's experiences of abortion. The international traction of the *#ShoutYourAbortion* campaign demonstrates the transnational purchase of the emotional narrative of abortion that centres this book. The materials I examine are drawn from the Anglophone West. Comprising Australia, Canada, New Zealand, the United Kingdom and the United States of America, this region shares a language and imperial history, has common legal and economic systems, and contains a network of political and economic relationships (Vucetic 2011: 2). Many of the arguments I make can extend to Western Europe, although this is certainly not a homogenous context—for example, restrictive legislative contexts prevail in Ireland, Malta and Poland (Lowe 2016: 20).

Postcolonial scholars and others have critiqued concepts such as the Anglosphere, 'the West', or the 'developed world' for reifying a hierarchical relationship between the 'West and the Rest' and the series of economic and geopolitical privileges that lie at its core. The Anglosphere is, for example, a profoundly racialised concept, forged through a constructed 'Angloness' and 'made up of the core and mostly white Self on the one hand and on the other the peripheral and overwhelmingly non-white Other' (Vucetic 2011: 6). 'The West' and the 'Anglophone West' are not geographical regions so much as ideological concepts that are continually reproduced through the process of reiteration (Hall 2006). The deployment of 'choice', especially in relation to women, is one mode whereby the 'West' is constructed as something different from, and superior to, 'the rest'. Women in the West are free, so it is claimed, and this can be measured through the choices to which they have access, particularly those surrounding sexuality and motherhood (Chapter 4). This book presents a critique of this discourse.

Within the broad area of the Anglophone West there is particular focus in this book on the context of Australia. Australia's abortion politics and discourses have always been transnational, with American and British influences most apparent. Moreover, the Australian case study provides a unique context for examining the normative assumptions that inform liberal laws relating to abortion. Speaking specifically to the (limited, if any) effects of law reform on the provision of abortion in the state of Victoria, Sally Sheldon (2017) has, for example, recently noted that '[t]hose considering legal reform in other jurisdictions, such as the UK, should take note' of developments there. In the USA, as we have seen, the past decade has seen restrictions on abortion increase, with activists and scholars fearing that the Trump Administration will, as Carol Joffe warns, usher in 'the most difficult period the reproductive rights/reproductive justice movement has faced since the Roe decision in 1973' (2017: 3; also see Girard 2017). In Canada, abortion was decriminalised through a Supreme Court Ruling; with the law based on the Canadian Charter of Rights and Freedoms, rather than a consequence of a protracted community or parliamentary debate, the discursive conditions for law reform are less generalisable to other countries, particularly those that do not have constitutional rights of their own (including Australia and the UK).[2] In the nearly thirty years since this historic pro-choice victory, the norms underpinning the meanings of abortion have also changed. Moves to decriminalise abortion are well under way in the UK and, given the shared legal traditions and cultural politics of abortion, the activist, media, and political contexts surrounding this campaign are very similar to those in Australia. In March 2017, the British Parliament voted to introduce a bill that would decriminalise abortion. The speaker who introduced the bill in a Ten Minute Rule motion, and the one who opposed it, both cited the Australian example as either proof of the benefits, or potential harm, of law reform (Johnson, MP and Caulfield, MP; United Kingdom 2017). The bill was expected to have its second reading debate in May, but fell when the parliament was dissolved in advance of the general election.

The Abortion Act 1967 (UK) is now fifty years old and has withstood a period of intense change in the provision and cultural politics of abortion. This book examines this historical period, beginning in the late 1960s, an era of abortion law reform that affected much of the Western world, to the present day, where the decriminalisation of abortion in Canada and four Australian jurisdictions represents the goal of many pro-choice activists and scholars worldwide and, so it would seem, the beginning of a larger trend. Significant change to the cultural meanings of abortion underpinned these legal developments; the rest of the introduction provides tools for mapping the shared meanings of abortion.

THE ABORTING WOMAN

This book examines how the 'choice' of abortion and the women who have abortions have been represented over a fifty-year period. The feminist concern with modes of representation derives from a political commitment to de-naturalise gender and, in so doing, open up entrenched gender roles, and the inequalities inscribed therein, to change. What it means to be a woman, this approach asserts, is not determined by biology or neurochemistry, but is constituted in the act of describing her (Butler 1993: 232).

Modes of representing the subject 'woman' often presume she is a fixed, natural entity that transverses across divergent cultural and historical contexts. Representations of abortion similarly fix the meaning of abortion and the women who have them. It is often presumed that women will experience abortion uniformly, and this is a means by which 'woman' is constructed as a natural, ahistorical subject. The assumption that all women grieve their abortions, for example, presumes there is something inherent in a woman that makes grief the only possible way to experience abortion. Modes of representing abortion, therefore, are a means by which the multiple ways women experience their abortions are reduced, and the subjects of abortion—women—are represented as sharing an inherent nature.

Established ways of thinking about abortion feed into women's experiences of abortion, although this is not a straightforward cause and effect relationship (Scott 1991). Jennifer Keys (2010) notes that women who are pro-choice tend to associate the abortion experience with relief, while those who are anti-abortion stress grief, regret, and maternal love for their foetuses. Such rules accompany women as they have abortions, but do not automatically produce the desired emotional states. Women, she argues, deploy several emotional management techniques in order to better mould their experiences into the desired emotional script; one example would be to personify the foetus as their baby (anti-abortion women) or, alternatively, to view the contents of pregnancy as an embryo, foetus or as pregnancy tissue (pro-choice women). Multiple and contested emotional scripts of abortion co-exist, and any script does not automatically program women's experience of abortion.

The dominant emotional narrative examined in this book is remarkable, however, because it bears little correlation to studies of women's emotional experiences of abortion, which, as mentioned, overwhelmingly paint abortion as a positive and beneficial experience for women. This is because the 'aborting woman', as she appears discursively, is a socio-cultural type that reflects, not the women who have abortions, but broader cultural anxieties. Such anxieties ensure she is, as Imogen Tyler writes of similar discursive figures, 'publicly imagined ... in excessive, distorted, and caricatured ways' (2008: 18). The aborting woman is analogous, for example, to other cultural figures, such as the 'asylum seeker' or the 'Muslim', produced at the axes of social concerns, such as those pertaining to gender, race and the nation. In the case of abortion, such concerns cluster around women's sexuality and motherhood. Representations of abortion are performative (Austin 1975); they do not merely describe women who have abortions, but bring them into being as gendered subjects. Because gender is a process and not a fixed ontology, it requires constant iteration and maintenance (Lorber 1994). Representations of abortion are a means by which gender is made and remade.

Normative accounts of pregnancy, and norms of gender more broadly, determine that abortion is a hugely problematic choice for pregnant women; abortion is, in fact, as Carol Sanger has recently observed, 'the antithesis of all that women are traditionally understood to be and do' (2017: 189). Within a normative schema Lauren Berlant terms 'foetal motherhood', pregnant women are already viewed as mothers to autonomous children, embarked on a life trajectory that positions all girls and young women on a path towards motherhood:

> The narrative of natural development from gendered womanhood to pregnancy and motherhood has provided one of the few transformational lexicons of the body and

identity we have. It has framed womanhood in a natural narrative movement of the body, starting at the moment a child is sexed female and moving to her inscription in public heterosexuality, her ascension to reproduction, and her commitment to performing the abstract values of instrumental empathy and service that have characterised norms of female fulfilment. (1997: 99)

The repeated representation of pregnancy as entailing a 'mother' and her 'unborn baby' works to naturalise a historically and contextually specific view of pregnancy; one that, as we shall see, has emerged over the past fifty years in response to the convergence of several historical developments, including the liberalisation of abortion laws and the Women's Liberation Movement and its aftermath. Due to the proliferation of foetal screening technologies and images of the 'public foetus' over this time period, the foetus has also emerged as an 'important cultural player' (Duden 1993; Petchesky 1987; Sanger 2017: 71). The foetus is read through multiple and irreconcilable conceptual frames (Gibson 2004). The meaning attributed to foetal life is also historically contingent, so that as Sara Dubow writes:

[a] fetus in 1870 is not the same thing as a fetus in 1930, which is not the same thing as a fetus in 1970, which is not the same thing as a fetus in 2010. Although multiple and competing fetuses have always coexisted, particular historical circumstances have generated and valorized different stories about the fetus. (2010: 3)

In contemporary modes of depicting abortion and pregnancy more generally, the embryo often merges with the foetus and, frequently, the viable foetus, the perinatal foetus and, even, the baby. This is despite the fact that, technically, the embryo only becomes a foetus in about the tenth week of pregnancy. The vast majority of abortions occur within the first trimester of pregnancy, and very early abortion (before nine weeks of pregnancy) is on the rise alongside the increasing use of medical abortion (Peterson 2010; Sheldon 2015: 12–13). The meaning of foetal or embryonic life also changes according to context. Thus, for example, the discarding of embryos in the process of *in vitro* fertilisation (IVF) is granted different significance to that in abortion, and this is largely because of the presumed intent and actions of the woman who is pregnant (Lupton 2013: 70–90). In the case of abortion, the embryo is in a woman who has had sex without reproductive intent and who does not want to nurture it to birth or afterwards; with IVF, the embryo is in a freezer and the product of a procedure intended to result in motherhood (Pollitt 2014: 91).

Definitions of the embryo and foetus always involve the pregnant woman, in either extreme as a body for herself (an autonomous subject) or, as the regime of foetal motherhood would have it, a body for another (with limited or no autonomy). The centrality of gender, and particularly motherhood, to the politics of abortion is well established. In the mid 1980s, Kristen Luker influentially defined the abortion debate as a 'referendum on the place and meaning of motherhood' (1984: 193). Abortion rights were so prominent in the Women's Liberation Movement of the 1970s because activists believed they were necessary to free women from a social and cultural world that limited their activities and ambitions to motherhood (Chapter 1). Anti-abortion activists, in contrast, generally reassert traditional family values and the gender roles contained therein (Chapters 1 and 3). As Reva Siegel observes, 'The entrance of feminists into the abortion debate [in the early 1970s] both increased support for liberalization of abortion laws and energized opposition', and in the minds of anti-abortionists 'the wrong of abortion is gender trouble, not murder' (2014: 1369, 1373).

The valorisation of motherhood drives cultural representations of abortion, with the women who have abortions frequently depicted as the negative other to the 'good mother' (Baird 1998b: 6; Boyle 1997: 27–28; Sheldon 1993). Abortion politics also articulate whether women's sexuality should be tied to reproduction (Sanger 2017: 10–11). In anti-abortion logic, in Katha Pollitt's words, 'when a woman has sex she is contracting to carry any resultant pregnancy to term, no matter what … The notion of sex as a contract is just another way of asserting that women shouldn't be sexual beings' (2014: 91). When I talk about foetal motherhood in this book, I refer to an encompassing schema, where women's sexuality is fused with reproduction, motherhood is taken to be a woman's anchoring point, and pregnancy is conceived of as a relationship between mothers and their autonomous children. Importantly, to flag an argument I extend below, foetal motherhood also differentiates women through axes such as race and class, designating some as good and responsible mothers, and others as bad and irresponsible. An aborting woman claims for herself the position of subject in her pregnancy, choosing not to mother the embryo or foetus she is carrying. The choice of abortion thereby threatens to fracture the norm of foetal motherhood and its myriad cultural investments. This is why abortion remains such a contested social issue.

There is a notable exception to the general schema I am mapping here, where it is normatively imagined that pregnant women, cast always and already as mothers, will act in their 'children's' best interests by continuing with all conceived pregnancies. Namely, women who terminate foetuses with severe foetal abnormalities are often presented through, rather than in opposition to, the trope of the 'responsible mother'. Opinion polls demonstrate that people consider terminating pregnancies for foetal abnormalities more acceptable than for other reasons, and many legislative contexts include different (more permissive) regulations for abortions under these circumstances (Sheldon and Wilkinson 2001). Termination rates for some foetal abnormalities are also incredibly high: in Australia, for example, 93 per cent of pregnancies diagnosed with Down syndrome are terminated; in the USA, this figure is somewhere between 61 and 93 per cent (Stephenson, Mills and McLeod 2017: 74). Some disability rights advocates have presented a critique of routine prenatal screening and selective abortion, arguing that the termination of pregnancies for foetal abnormalities is a form of eugenics that perpetuates discrimination. The social model of disability argues that the vast majority of inconveniences disabled people face are due to the lack of investment in forms of support (in terms of healthcare and public infrastructure, for example) that would best enable their participation in public life (Saxton 2006). The selective termination of disabled foetuses does nothing to address, and arguably increases, forms of disability discrimination, and the belief that some children should be spared from disability can devalue the lives of those living with such disabilities. In a model of abortion that focuses on the pregnant woman rather than the foetus, however, it is also important to recognise that mothers currently do the majority of primary care work for children with disabilities, and this care is often expensive and can be a lifetime commitment (Pavalko and Wolfe 2016). We can support women's choice while also arguing that the creation of a better support network for disabled people would enhance women's options when considering whether to terminate foetuses with disabilities.

Another exception to my focus on foetal motherhood is the critique levelled by some trans activists and allies of the taken-for-granted claim that only women have abortions; it has been argued, for example, that political slogans such as 'trust women' (which leads Irish and British calls for abortion law reform) are discriminatory because they exclude the experiences of gender diverse or trans men who also have abortions. When Lauren Rankin (2013) wrote that 'We must acknowledge and come to terms with the implicit cissexism in assuming that only women have abortions', Katha Pollitt (2015) responded by arguing that: 'Once you start talking about "people", not "women", you lose what abortion means historically, symbolically and socially. It becomes hard to understand why it isn't simply about the right to life of the "unborn"'. The critique of gender-specific language in the context of abortion poses several questions for pro-choice activists and scholars: can and should activism and scholarship use gender-neutral language when talking about abortion, when thinking about the politics of abortion, and when addressing the people who have abortions? Is it possible or desirable to envisage gender-neutral subjects of experiences, such as pregnancy, that are so firmly attached to gendered subjects? Progressive politics certainly need to account for the marginalisation of and failure to recognise the gender identity of trans and gender non-conforming people. While recognising such critiques, and the fact that people who do not identify as women have abortions, I nevertheless refer to 'woman' as the subject of abortion throughout this book. This book focuses on dominant modes of representing abortion, which invariably assume 'woman' as the subject and are only intelligible within cultural meanings ascribed to femininity. The argument that cultural representations of abortion are gendered feminine is not the same as pronouncing that only women have abortions; and, in fact, the gendering of abortion is precisely why trans and non-binary people are so often excluded from abortion discourse and services. While my use of the subject 'woman' runs the risk of reifying her as the only subject of abortion, I also aim to denaturalise this subject, opening the way to conceptualise the people who have abortions as multiple and heterogeneous, whether they identify as women, men or neither.

The norm of foetal motherhood determines that, at present, a 'happy abortion' is anathema to discourses constituting the viable female subject. The norm of foetal motherhood closes down possibilities for abortion and burdens the experience with negative affect; within it, women cannot approach abortion willingly or experience abortion positively. Instead of representing abortion through the schema of foetal motherhood, I argue in this book that we need to approach abortion from the position of the women who have them. As Barbara Baird writes:

> It is from this woman's perspective that it is so demeaning, and ridiculous, to suggest that abortion is by definition a negative and unfortunate experience. While an unwanted pregnancy would probably be an experience that few unpregnant women would choose, for the woman who is pregnant and not wanting to be so, an abortion could easily and logically be understood as a Godsend. (Baird 1998b: 40)

The figure of the 'unwillingly pregnant woman' involves framing pregnancy as an interdependent relationship with women as its subjects and foetuses as part of (not distinct from) their bodies. This accords with feminist depictions of the pregnant body as 'neither one nor two' (Irigaray 1985: 207). The pregnant body defies Western ontology, which presumes a bounded, autonomous self, and is thus misrepresented when she is depicted as either one or two people—she is neither. The legitimacy of abortion stems not merely from the condition of pregnancy and, in Carol Sanger's words, 'the messy business of birth but the social consequences of motherhood—the obligations of child raising [that] mark women's adult lives as different from men's' (2017: 188). Although this book focuses on the unwillingly pregnant woman as a discursive aspiration, she is also a material one. Women can only choose abortion willingly when parenting is an economically and socially viable option, and measures such as paid parental leave and state-funded childcare need to be fought for alongside abortion (Price 2010; Ross 2006; Smith 2005; Zavella 2016).

This book considers why and how the subject position of the unwillingly pregnant woman is so often occluded or foreclosed in public discussions of abortion. The short answer to this question is foetal motherhood and the cultural investments contained therein. The regime of foetal motherhood is now normalised for women through the meanings ascribed to their pregnancy choices, rather than through explicit prohibitions on these choices. The discourse of choice has become central to the regulation of abortion in the contemporary era. The normative effects of emotions would not operate without the illusion of freedom that choice affords.

A SUBJECT OF CHOICE

Critique of the rhetoric of choice has existed since it became attached to abortion. When abortion is reduced to an issue of women's choice, it can figure purely as an individual decision. Women do not become pregnant, mother or have abortions in a vacuum, however, and the decisions they make about pregnancy and parenting, as well as the consequences of such decisions, cannot be isolated from how factors such as their gender, class and race position them in ways that give them access to some choices, close others off, and shape the broader socio-cultural meaning ascribed to their choices (Solinger 2001). The reduction of freedom to choice also obscures the socio-political factors that make abortion one of the defining moral, social and political issues of our times.

Rickie Solinger (2001) shows in the US context that pro-abortion activists turned towards the rhetoric of choice in the 1970s in order to soften the 'abortion rights' approach and make the idea of pregnant women's autonomy more palatable to the political mainstream; at the same time, anti-abortionists began deploying the language of choice to rationalise moves to absolve the government from responsibility for ensuring women can access abortion. Hastened by the Hyde Amendment (1976), which prohibited the use of federal funds for abortion, anti-abortionists transformed the politics of abortion into a question of whether or not the state should pay for women's abortions. They argued that poor women have fewer choices available to them, and just as the state does not provide money to poor women in order to expand their consumer choices, it should not support women in their demands for greater reproductive choice. In countries that medicalised abortion and have relatively extensive public health services (such as Australia, the UK, Canada and New Zealand), abortion has not been framed as a privately-funded consumer choice, at least to the same degree. Nevertheless, Solinger's analysis cautions against using 'choice' as short-hand for 'freedom' in the realm of abortion.

Women of colour and black and Indigenous feminists have been at the forefront of revealing the forms of structural inequality elided in the rhetoric of choice. They show that 'choice' became prevalent in the abortion rights movement, which was and continues to be led by middle-class white women and focused on their concerns, often oblivious to the structures, particularly economic, that prevent women from exercising choices they formally have access to (Nelson 2003). Eugenic and other population control policies have often rewarded and encouraged the motherhood of white, middle-class women (hence their pre-occupation with abortion rights), while preventing, discouraging or stigmatising the motherhood of marginalised women. The promotion of contraception and abortion purely in terms of women's choice and empowerment obfuscates how these technologies have been used to control the fertility of women who have been deemed undesirable breeders by virtue of their race, class or disability (Nelson 2003; Roberts 1997; Ross 2006; Smith 2005). Restrictions on abortion are one of many obstacles to women's reproductive freedom, and the right to 'not have a child' needs to be considered alongside 'the right to have a child … [and] the right to parent the children we have, as well as to control our birthing options' (Ross 2006: 14).

Choice disguises forms of structural inequality and, in the contemporary world, is also a technique of regulating subjects, producing them as though they are free. The regulative effects of 'choice' need to be seen in terms of the ascendency of neoliberal political rationality over the last forty years. Neoliberal political rationality can be roughly characterised as the generalisation of the economic order onto the social and political spheres, resulting in 'depoliticisation on an unprecedented level' (Brown 2006: 704). Neoliberalism reconfigures society as a group of individuals, so that each individual is imagined to be free from external constraints on their actions and is endowed with entrepreneurialism and capacity. Free from the normative and legal barriers and incentives that previously channelled their lives in particular directions, the contemporary subject is believed to be someone who literally 'chooses him- or herself' (Salecl 2008: 171). Neoliberal subjects are impelled to see their lives as a series of choices made and to be made, and to take personal responsibility for the socio-economic consequences of these choices (Rose 1999: 85–89). Within the regime of personal responsibility, 'a "misman-aged life" becomes the new mode of depoliticising social and economic powers' (Brown 2003: 6).

The positioning of young women as free from gender is central to the contemporary illusion that individuals are wholly responsible for their own life circumstances. A 'post-feminist sensibility' has accompanied neoliberalism; within this sensibility, feminism (defined in its liberal guise as focused on formal equality and complicit with capitalism) is taken into account, celebrated as a finished project, and claimed to have no relevance in the present day. Angela McRobbie terms this exchange of formal equality for a rejection of feminist politics the 'post-feminist sexual contract' (McRobbie 2007: 718). The mirage of gender equality has provided the conditions whereby young women can embrace femininity—normatively consti-tuted as white and based on heterosexist norms of physical attractiveness, marriage, and reproduction—as a personal choice. At the same time, 'demarcated pathologies (leaving it too late to have a baby, failing to find a good catch, etc.) … carefully define the parameters of what constitutes liveable lives for young women without the occasion of re-invented feminism' (McRobbie 2009: 22). Women are now regulated through their choices rather than through prohibitions on certain choices; this makes the workings of power and inequality much more elusive and difficult to analyse because, as Rosalind Gill observes, 'the mode of power is not external oppression but regulation and discipline that take up residency in the psyche by, quite literally, producing new subjectivities' (2008: 46).

The aborting woman as a subject of choice is one such 'new subjectivity'. She is constructed through several 'demarcated pathologies' that designate which women should have children or more children, those who should delay or forgo childbearing, and those women who have 'too many' children already. Normative femininity is regulated *through* the choices that aborting women make, in large part through the emotions that construct how the viable female subject should approach abortion and feel after the procedure.

AN EMOTIONAL SUBJECT

I want to bring a bit of sanity back into what is an emotional issue. (Tony McKenzie, MP; Australia 1973: 1969)

[T]he tableau of considerations—medical legal, theological and psychological—needed before a decision is taken are often twisted or forgotten in the height of emotion. (Stephens 1987)

> Abortion is an emotional issue, which is why it is best
> discussed with cool heads and open hearts. (*The Age*,
> 2005)

One of the most frequently circulated statements made about abortion is that it is an inherently emotional experience and political issue—the designation of abortion as 'emotional' has reached the status of common sense. The category 'emotion' is, however, too broad to have any concrete meaning, containing, as it does, numerous and disparate feeling states. A study of emotions and their effects must therefore identify the specific emotions referenced and elicited in discourse on abortion. When emotions are interpreted as personal feelings alone, and abortion construed as inherently emotional, the politics of abortion also manifest as not entirely rational and beyond cogent critique. Abortion is thereby transported from the political domain—beyond, for example, struggles over norms of femininity—to the private realm of feelings. Feminists have long contested the distinction between the private (experience and emotion) and the public (the law, the political), for public worlds are 'affect worlds at least as much as they are effects of rationality and rationalisation' (Berlant 2004a: 450). This book places emotion at the heart of the politics of abortion.

In the 1970s, when considering emotions, pro-choice activists and scholars focused on abortion guilt and shame, predominantly viewing these emotions as a consequence of normative expectations regarding women's sexuality. Contemporary work on abortion stigma develops several of these themes (Chapter 4). In response to the increasing centrality of grief to anti-abortion activism since the mid-1980s (Chapter 3), scholarship has also moved to examine the regulative effects of this emotion. Ellie Lee's (2003) comparative study on Post-Abortion Syndrome (PAS) in America and the UK traces the emergence of the claim that abortion harms women psychologically and emotionally in the American anti-abortion movement, showing how it moved, with far less legislative or political success, into the British context. Legal scholars have traced how claims that abortion is emotion-ally and psychologically damaging to women have resulted in legislation that severely restricts women's access to abortion in several American states under the guise of protecting them from harm (Madeira 2014; Siegel 2008; Suk 2010). The most notorious example of the translation of an emotional common sense pertaining to abortion into protectionist legislation was when the Supreme Court upheld the Partial-Birth Abortion Ban Act (2003) with the reasoning that: 'While we find no reliable data to measure the phenomenon, it seems unexcep-tionable to conclude some women come to regret their choice to abort the infant life they once created and sustained' (cited in Siegel 2008: 1694). Another important strand in abortion scholarship uses surveys and interviews with women to quan-tify and measure the emotional experience of abortion (Foster et al. 2013; Goodwin and Odgin 2007; Major et al. 2000; Russo 2000). Abortion scholars and activists tend to refer to emotions as descriptive words that communicate (or miscom-municate) how women experience their abortions or how others represent women's experiences. The cultural turn in the understanding of emotions shows us, however, that emotions do not merely describe their objects, but actually produce subjectivities, materialise communities, and powerfully bind individuals to social norms.

Attention to the productive nature of emotions turns around the commonly-received view that emotions are 'touchstones of personal reality' (Reddy 2001: 43). As Sara Ahmed writes, emotions usually appear as 'a form of positive residence ... something that belongs to a subject or object, which can take the form of a characteristic or quality' (2004b: 119). There is, as Lauren Berlant asserts, a 'fantasy that the emotional event tells a simple, clear, visceral truth about something'. Emotions, she continues, are now taken to represent the "truth" of the modern subject'—conjectures about the emotional world of individuals are a primary means by which their inner realities are normatively constructed (Berlant et al. 2012). Because emotions are seen to emerge from deep within the subject, unaffected by the social world they inhabit, depictions of women as having a particular emotional experience before and after their abortions convey the 'truth' about abortion and the characters and desires of the women who have them in a particularly efficient and potent way. It is extremely common to generalise the emotional life of aborting women through assertions such as there are 'aspects of regret in all women. Abortion for any woman is a tragedy' (Professor Chris Healy, cited in Curtis 1996). The emotional register of such statements binds aborting women together as members of a pre-cultural group; the assumption that women experience abortion in a uniform way secures and reinforces a naturalised, depoliticised rendering of abortion and the subject 'woman'.

The designation of emotions to the realm of nature has historically associated emotions with femininity to the degree that, as Elspeth Probyn writes, 'it can now go unqualified' (2005: 81). The cultural turn in emotions challenges their consignment to the natural and the feminine, positing instead that emotions are produced in, and productive of, the social world, forming communities, moulding social relationships, and driving historical change (Clough 2008). As Barbara Rosenwein, a leading historian of emotions, explains:

> *[E]very* culture has its rules for feelings and behavior; *every* culture thus exerts certain restraints while favoring certain forms of expressivity … emotions are not pressing to be set free; they are created by each society, each culture, each community. (2002: 837)

Historically and contextually-specific 'feeling rules' (Hochschild 1979) govern the experience of abortion. Particular feelings are encouraged, or even compelled, and others are discouraged or disavowed.

Emotions can be thought of as circuits—or, as Derek Hook (2005) avers, a pulse in a circuit—between individuals and the social norms that give their life meaning and bind them to the communities in which they live. The emotions that carry, infuse, and are elicited by discourses on abortion constitute, in Hook's words, '*an affective grounds of belief* which feels deeply singular and individualised despite that is comes from an Other place'. The feeling of abortion shame, for example, registers a woman's failure against deeply internalised social values, such as motherhood. With this profound sense of personal failure thoroughly interiorised, the experience isolates women from the socio-cultural production of abortion shame and the normative expectations, values, and subjectivities it issues from and secures. Abortion is thereby made inherently shameful, and the women who have abortions are oriented towards shame as a natural response to abortion.

Berlant (2007) argues that social norms contain a 'cluster of promises', pertaining to future happiness and social inclusion in particular, that compel subjects to follow the scripts of fulfilment laid out for them. We often act, she insists, through our affective attachment—an optimistic attachment—to socially-mediated fantasies, such as those contained in motherhood. This insight is particularly useful when thinking about pregnant women's subjectivities, for normative pregnancy orients pregnant women towards their future roles as mothers and to the fantasy of maternal happiness. At the level of biopolitics, pregnancy also orients the nation towards the foetus as a future citizen (Chapter 5). Both motherhood and abortion contain promises often communicated through anticipated emotional fulfilment or dissatisfaction that, at least in the sphere of representation, invest pregnant women in motherhood while repelling them from abortion.

The aborting woman is further generated through her relationships with others, including those with her foetus and broader community. Emotions shape and determine the intensity and dynamic of such relationships. Sara Ahmed views emotions as orienting devices. Emotions draw individuals towards and away from other individuals, a process that produces normative bodies and communities through attaching them to, or distancing them from, others. This is why the specificity of emotions is important, for 'naming emotions involves different orientations towards the objects they construct' (2004b: 14). For example, fear draws subjects away from and against its objects, while love draws its subjects and objects together. Emotions, then, create the 'us' and the 'them' and the force of our attraction to or repulsion away from others.

Individuals, practices and objects get produced as containing or causing particular emotions in the socio-cultural realm. Emotions are produced through the exchange and circulation amongst and between discourses and bodies, across social and psychic fields, and exchanges of emotion are bound up with other exchanges—social, discursive and material. Emotions can be thought of as effects of circulation, where words for feeling and objects of feeling circulate in *'relationships of difference and displacement without positive value'* (Ahmed 2004a: 118). They move sideways, so that some objects get stuck to other objects through chains of association, and backwards and forwards, so that what 'gets stuck' together depends on histories of associated signs and objects: 'emotions work as a form of capital ... [and are] produced only as an effect of its circulation' (Ahmed 2004a: 120). The more objects of emotion circulate, the more affect is seen to reside in objects, thus erasing the socio-cultural and political forces through which they were produced. Drawing on Judith Butler, Ahmed argues that the repetitive stickiness of emotions to objects is the way 'boundary, fixity and surface' are produced

(Butler cited in Ahmed 2004b: 3). This process of repetition turns 'feelings' into 'fetishes', 'qualities that seem to reside in objects … through an erasure of the history of their production and circulation' (2004b: 11). The more that abortion is represented as a shameful choice, for example, and the more the figure of the aborting woman is attached to other figures of shame, such as the irresponsible sexual subject or the 'teen mum', the more shame is seen to emanate inherently and automatically from abortion. The emotion of shame is, thereby, naturalised in the context of abortion and the social norms that produce shame (including those pertaining to responsible sexuality and motherhood) are simultaneously produced as outside of politics and culture.

Emotional economies are effects of circulation that in turn affect individual subjectivities and social worlds. Emotions 'do things' and the doing of emotion always relates to social norms; to whether individuals are excluded from them, reach them, or are held back from doing so. An individual's emotional life is said to emanate from deep within the subject, and there is a certain truth attached to emotions that, in the language of common sense, rules 'if I feel this it must be true'. The good and bad of choices—particularly in this case, motherhood and abortion—are conveyed through specific emotions. The promises of emotional satisfaction (happiness) or dissatisfaction (grief) orient pregnant women in normative directions. Our investment in normativity is affective, imprinting socio-cultural aspirations at the level of personal desire, further directing individuals through their choices. Emotions also invest the community in women's abortion choices.

Emotions circulate in public speech on abortion, generating the figure of the aborting woman in a very specific way. Although women have ready access to abortion in many contexts, the meanings given to choices pertaining to pregnancy, and the women who make particular choices, are heavily circumscribed. Aborting women are now regulated, not so much by restrictions on their choices, but through the meanings given to their choices, meanings largely communicated and produced through emotions. The emotions through which women's abortion choices are made meaningful are produced by a historical process of repetition so they appear to have no history in the present. This book unpacks the historical and cultural processes by which certain emotions have become embedded in the meanings we ascribe to abortion and the women who have them. In this way, this book de-naturalises 'abortion common sense'— those every day statements made about abortion that, while seemingly benign, carry hugely potent normative weight, producing idealised female subjects and re-producing abortion to be a deviant choice made by, and resulting in, problematic women.

CHAPTER PLAN

Abortion is frequently represented in a way that restores the women who have abortions to foetal motherhood through their choices. The discursive rehabilitation of aborting women to foetal motherhood contains the fragmenting effects of abortion, securing the fantasy of a naturalised maternal desire despite the significant number of pregnant women who have abortions.

This book unravels the assumptions about abortion that circulate as truths through particular emotions. It considers why and how it has become so commonplace and uncontroversial to view abortion as a shameful and grievable choice, while the possibility that abortion could be an emotionally benign, or even happy, choice is simultaneously disavowed. By unravelling the process whereby certain emotions have become entangled with abortion, we will see that such emotions have histories and are a consequence of struggles over the requirements of normative femininity. This historicisation reveals the restrictions that operate on and through women's abortion choices, while opening up the possibility that such restrictions can and will change over time.

The surge in abortion activism that affected much of the Western world from the late 1960s through the 1970s dramatically altered the legislative and discursive contexts of abortion. Chapter 1 examines how three transnational activist organisations framed the issue of abortion in the 1970s—Right to Life, the Abortion Law Reform Association (ALRA), and the Women's Liberation Movement (WLM)—and how each influenced the broader cultural politics of abortion. I argue that by the end of the decade there was broad agreement with the principle of 'women's choice', but the meanings through which choice was rationalised disavowed WLM's emphasis on women's autonomy, ceded significant discursive terrain to anti-abortionists, and drew largely on the compromise position of ALRA, which viewed safe, medical abortion as the unfortunate but necessary alternative to 'backyard' operations. This normative position reinforced the view that foetal life was inherently valuable and framed the morality of abortion in terms of whether the law should protect foetal life; viewing abortion as a 'necessary evil', this approach garnered support for abortion on the basis of compassion for 'desperate women' who, it supposed, were forced to terminate their pregnancies because they lacked the necessary social or economic resources required to parent their potential children effectively. The normative 'pro-choice' but 'anti-abortion' position lay the foundations for the contemporary era, where, as subsequent chapters show, the idea that abortion is a 'woman's choice' co-exists with a decidedly anti-abortion common sense.

Chapter 1 establishes the centrality of choice to cultural frames of abortion and demonstrates the limits of choice when used to communicate the goals of reproductive justice. The remaining four chapters each focus on a particular emotion through which the choice of abortion is commonly communicated: maternal happiness, abortion grief, shame, and nationalist fear and anxiety.

Chapter 2 examines how abortion is repeatedly repre-sented in relation to a framework that posits motherhood as the only authentic happy choice for pregnant women; with motherhood so positioned, abortion emerges as a counter-intuitive and unnatural choice for women to make. The chapter begins by tracing a shift in a dominant articula-tion of pro-choice activism away from arguments for self-determination to a maternal ethics of care. Proponents of this 'maternal pro-choice' approach contend that women decide to terminate their pregnancies, not to satisfy their own desires, but to benefit those around them, particularly their potential children. I argue that this is a postfeminist iteration of pro-choice politics, and its emergence aligns with a broader shift in normative femininity. While motherhood was once seen as a woman's destiny, it has been re-positioned as a choice women make to be happy. Yet women's maternal happiness only manifests as normatively selfless (as opposed to selfish) if they can guarantee the happiness of their potential children; class, race and age act as guarantors for this happiness. Advocates of the maternal pro-choice position represent women as inevitably oriented towards their potential children as 'happy objects' (Ahmed 2010b), but as driven to abortion for the wellbeing of their future children. They therefore incorporate abortion into women's maternal identities. The chapter moves to a close analysis of a series of parliamentary debates in Australia in the 2000s that resulted in legislation affording women greater abortion choice. I argue that parliamentarians did not support fewer legal restrictions on abortion because they believed it was a social good; rather, they drew on maternal pro-choice politics to contend that women always, inevitably, monitor their own abortion conduct in relation to the emotional script of maternal happiness, making restrictive abortion laws unnecessary.

On the reverse side of the economy whereby motherhood manifests as the only truly happy choice for pregnant women is the expectation that abortion is emotionally harmful to women. Chapter 3 provides a genealogy of foetocentric grief, an emotional framework that permeates accounts of abortion across multiple discursive sites. Foetocentric grief represents women as indelibly mourning their 'unborn children' after abortion. The emotion first came to prominence in anti-abortion activism of the mid-1980s. Focus on the purported consequences of abortion for women enabled anti-abortionists to respond to charges that they were unsympathetic towards the women who have abortions. Foetocentric grief also transcribes the primary claim of the anti-abortion movement—that abortion entails a mother's destruction of her unborn child—onto the very experience of abortion. Since the mid-1980s, foetocentric grief has moved outside the anti-abortion movement to dominate accounts of the abortion experience more generally, even amongst some prominent pro-choice activists and feminists. This chapter maps the convergence of these trends and examines the political and regulatory effects of foetocentric grief. Foetocentric grief is a culturally enforced emotion that discursively recuperates the figure of the aborting woman to normative regimes of pregnancy and femininity, where pregnant women are envisaged as already mothers to autonomous foetal-subjects.

Chapter 4 examines abortion shame. A fear of shaming, or an internalised feeling of shame, leads women to routinely conceal their abortions from other people: the silence of aborting women is one of the most salient features of public discussions about abortion and helps explain the consistency in the emotions through which abortion is made meaningful. Abortion is represented, more often than not, by people who have not had abortions themselves, meaning that such representations are infused with assumptions about how women would *and should* experience the procedure. Although abortion is incessantly linked to shame, abortion shame can be historicised, and thereby de-naturalised, by looking at shifts in the norms that trigger shame (as a sign of failed femininity). Abortion shame previously emanated from a normative trajectory whereby women were expected to remain chaste and then marry and have children. Today, the emotion is triggered by the expectation that women will control their reproductive potential through diligent and effective contraceptive use so that all foetuses conceived go on to be born. Thus, although women can have abortions, women who experience unwanted pregnancies are always already positioned as irresponsible 'failures' and 'losers' for getting pregnant unintentionally. After examining abortion shame, the chapter moves to consider abortion shaming. While shame is a deeply internalised feeling of failure against social expectations and norms, shaming is a political weapon used to mark individuals as failing their communities. By bringing the discussion from shame to shaming, the book shifts attention away from considering how aborting women are represented as individual gendered subjects to their representation as members of a community. Different modalities of shaming attach to pregnant women depending on how the community measures the value of their potential children. Whereas some women are shamed for abortion, others are shamed for having too many children. Modes of shaming target pregnant subjects differentially with regard to several axes of identity, including those of race and class.

Women who have abortions are caught in a web of emotions that either address her as a pregnant woman, a member of the national community or both. Chapter 5 examines the aborting woman's constitution as a national object, unpacking one of the most frequently articulated statements made about the procedure: that there are 'too many' of them. Abortion politics are also nationalist politics, concerned with attempts to manage the size and constitution of the nation's population, which is imagined in racialised terms. After outlining this theoretical framework, the chapter turns to the specific case study of Australia to examine two periods of intense worrying over the abortion rate (1979 and 2004 through 2006). It argues that in times of national crisis, debates over abortion can become a site where politicians, journalists and other influential social commentators attempt to manage the size and constitution of the future population. The statement that there are 'too many abortions' carries the imperative for white women to reproduce the nation. This demand is made perceptible through a history of maternal citizenship for white women, which reverberates in the present, and the articulation of the desire to eradicate abortion alongside other key biopolitical technologies: the disavowal of Indigenous sovereignty and the exclusion of non-white immigrants from the nation. The association of (white) aborting women with other threats to the security of white socio-cultural hegemony produces her as an object of fear for the nation, re-affirming the goal of white reproduction as a national duty and social good.

In the conclusion, I bring the arguments that run through the book together to advocate for a rethinking of pro-choice politics and scholarship. Freedom in the realm of abortion requires a new subjectivity for pregnant women; one that neither centres on motherhood, nor constructs pregnancy as involving two autonomous subjects. Some pregnant women do not want to be pregnant, and in order to recognise the subject position of the unwillingly pregnant woman there needs to be a disruption in the emotions through which abortion is currently made intelligible.

Behind the rhetoric of women's choice and the claims of freedom contained therein lies a framework that normalises motherhood for all women (but pregnant women most especially), imagines foetuses as autonomous subjects (as the woman's baby and future citizen of the nation) and determines the value of pregnancies and foetuses differentially according to axes of identity including those of race and class. In this way, the high number of women who terminate their pregnancies does not threaten to unravel normative, maternal female identity and the series of privileges this identity is organised by and naturalises. When the politics of abortion are reduced to women's choice, and it is presumed that the choice of abortion inevitably holds certain emotional consequences for women, then abortion is de-politicised and the subject of abortion— woman—is presumed to hold a natural, ahistorical, character and temperament. It is through such processes that gender and gendered experiences such as abortion are abstracted from power and structures of inequality. While unpacking the emotional intelligibilities of choice that produce aborting women as maternal subjects, this book is also a history of a critical period of change in the regulation of abortion. This era of change began with the law reforms and abortion activism of the late 1960s through the 1970s. Chapter 1 explores this period in detail.

CHAPTER 1

THE POLITICS
OF CHOICE

Abortion is sought as a drastic remedy, often in desperation and with distress, to an unwanted pregnancy ... The
Right to Life movement serves a valuable purpose raising
public concern for the unborn, but without a balanced
respect for the rights of others, [and] compassion for the
desperate. (Claude Forell [1978], journalist for *The Age*,
Melbourne)

In his weekly political column, entitled on this occasion
'Abortion: Rights and Wrongs', the Australian journalist
Claude Forell summarised what was, at the time, a developing
common sense on abortion. Forell ceded ideological terrain
to the anti-abortion movement, using its language to describe
the foetus as 'the unborn'. He also framed the morality of
abortion in gender-neutral terms, labelling abortion a 'public'
issue, rather than one of particular relevance to women. Forell
also, however, called for 'compassion' for the 'desperate'
and distressed women forced to endure the 'drastic remedy'
of abortion. In the pro-choice position Forell articulated,

women did not have abortions willingly, but only in extraordinary circumstances, and abortion was a dramatic rather than routine or normal procedure. This was very different to the abortion politics of the Women's Liberation Movement (WLM), which viewed abortion as an act of self-determination, enabling women to escape the strictures of compulsory motherhood.

Forell's comments came towards the end of a decade of significant worldwide change in the legal and cultural regulation of abortion. In the mid-1960s through the 1970s, abortion began to be discussed publically on a scale never before witnessed, and with these public articulations came new, and increasingly stylised, modes of representing abortion, which increasingly circumscribed the meanings ascribed to abortion and the women who had them. Several transnational abortion activist campaigns emerged or re-energised during this period; their political slogans reverberated across the globe, carrying divergent, sometimes antagonistic, messages about abortion. Popular slogans included: 'Abortion—a right; Contraception—a responsibility'; 'Abortion is a woman's right'; and 'Abortion: A Choice to Kill'. This chapter begins by examining how three large campaigns framed the issue of abortion and the women who had them: the civil liberties arguments for abortion forwarded by the Abortion Law Reform Association (ALRA), the gender politics of WLM's abortion campaign, and the foetal-rights agenda of Right to Life (RTL).[1] I identify the cultural narratives and characterisations (Condit 1990: 13–14) that drove these three activist movements before examining their respective influence on the formal governing of abortion.

I argue that the choice of abortion was increasingly normalised during the 1970s. By the end of the decade, politicians and the general public largely accepted that women should have the choice of abortion in many instances, and abortion was widely available, virtually (if not lawfully) on request, at least in major metropolitan areas. The incorporation of the language of choice into public discourse on abortion coincided and did not conflict, however, with a morality that understood abortion to singularly entail the cessation of human life. Abortion was integrated into the discursive framing of pregnancy decision-making as an exceptional choice, and one absented from the radical gender politics of the WLM. The framing of abortion as an exceptional choice enabled, as Celeste Condit has argued, abortion to be constructed as a 'problem without engaging the powerful value sets that surrounded it'; primary amongst these value sets were ideologies about sex and motherhood which, for nearly a century prior to this time, 'had coded "abortion" as a subject that should not be articulated' (1990: 23–24). The exceptionality of abortion recuperated abortion to the trope of motherhood; with motherhood restated as the norm for women generally, and pregnant women most acutely, abortion gained legitimacy, somewhat paradoxically, through its coding as a deviant choice. As we will see in further chapters, the incorporation of the 'awfulisation' of abortion into an ostensibly 'pro-choice' framework lay the groundwork for a contemporary paradox, where the abortion choices of women are simultaneously accepted as necessary and admonished as morally dubious (Pollitt 2014).

The organising principle of this chapter is choice rather than, as with subsequent chapters, particular emotions. While, as other chapters detail, emotions saturate abortion politics today, anti- and pro-abortion discourses of the 1970s rarely cited women's experiences of abortion as a rationale for their political positions; following this, abortion politics were not, as a rule, articulated alongside any particular emotional framework. I do, however, highlight an emotional register that was important to each of the examined movements and continues to resonate within abortion activism today. This will start us thinking about how particular emotions can inflect or bend the meaning of abortion choice and represent the women who have abortions in particular ways.

THE CHOICE OF ILLEGAL ABORTION

By the reforms at the turn of the 1970s, abortion had only been illegal for about one hundred years in North America, Western Europe, Australia and New Zealand. The official morality coded in the law never predominated in the larger population, however, where there existed, in US historian Leslie Reagan's words, an 'unarticulated, alternative, popular morality, which supported women who had abortions' (1997: 6—for contexts other than the USA, see Brookes 1988; Finch and Stratton 1988; McCulloch 2013: 146; McLaren and McLaren 1997: 32–44). Abortion was an 'open secret' that was widely practiced in underground medical practices or female networks of provision; yet it was rarely prosecuted and seldom spoken about in public forums, largely because it was illegal, and partly because it was excised from the public domain, relegated instead to the private world of women. The reluctance to talk about abortion in public forums also related to a taboo on discussing issues relating to sex and the strong attachment of women's sexuality to reproduction. Women were expected to remain celibate until marriage and then dedicate married life to bearing and raising children. Against this normative life trajectory, women who had abortions were frequently stereotyped as sexually immoral, hedonistic, and selfish, refusing their maternal instinct as well as their duty to reproduce citizens for the nation (Chapter 5). The women who received sympathy in public texts (such as popular fiction) were considered to be victims of male licentiousness or poverty. If they were single, depictions of their vulnerability to male sexual coercion could provide some excuse for their transgression; if married with several children, their poverty could provide a rationale for not wanting further children (Baird 1998b; Moore 1996, 2001).

Because cultural understandings of abortion were enmeshed with norms pertaining to femininity and sex, abortion activism entailed normative claims across these domains. The abortion politics of early reformers in the UK and other contexts, including Canada and the USA, were embedded in a broader gender politics, which celebrated women's sexuality and critiqued the regime of compulsory motherhood (Brookes 1988: 83, 121; McLaren and McLaren 1997: 69, 75; Roberts 1997: 56). The Abortion Law Reform Association (ALRA) in the UK, for example, was established in 1936 by radical women who fought for abortion law reform on the grounds that it was 'the right of every woman ... to decide what should happen to her body' (cited in Brookes 1988: 95).

The Thalidomide crisis of the early 1960s, which affected much of the Western world, reinvigorated movements for abortion law reform. The association of the sedative, used to treat morning sickness amongst other conditions, with birth defects reinvigorated abortion activism in many countries, lending abortion an air of respectability because, in part, it was recognised that middle-class, married women sometimes terminated wanted pregnancies. Abortion was thereby removed from its association with sexual immorality and placed within the domain of public health (Condit 1990: 28–31; Hindell and Simms 1971: 111–112; Nelson 2003: 11–12).

Within this context, ALRA dampened its radical, woman-centred approach to emphasise instead the deleterious public health impact of illegal abortions, the important role medical doctors played in offering safe abortions and the class-based inequities of access to safe, medically performed abortions. The framing of abortion as a medical issue intensified when the British Medical Association officially supported law reform on the grounds that the law should not interfere with a medical doctor's judgement about a medical decision and procedure (Brookes 1988: 154–155). The public health approach to abortion, which permitted doctors to perform abortions for reasons of psychological and physical health, was also the dominant strand of activism in the USA, embedded in the American Law Institute's model for law reform (Reagan 1997: 221), as well as in Australia (Petersen 1993), Canada (Tatalovich 1997: 31–34) and New Zealand (Leslie 2010).

The arguments leading to law reform at the turn of the 1970s were not premised on the idea that abortion was a social good or routine experience. Reformers argued instead that abortion was an inevitable consequence of a range of factors, including poverty and inadequate access to effective contraceptive devices. Rather than being unregulated and dangerous, campaigners argued that abortions should be safe and monitored by medical doctors (Gregory 2005: 132–137). These campaigns and their consequent reforms led to an intense politicisation of abortion, where, for the first time, a broad range of social actors—including politicians, journalists, churchmen, activists and doctors—were granted an enhanced capacity to speak openly about the practice. With this public articulation came new ways of thinking about abortion. The rest of this chapter examines the prominent narratives and character types to emerge during in this era.

FREEDOM OF CONSCIENCE

A prominent argument in support of liberal abortion legislation focused not on the women who needed abortions so much as the moral status of foetal life. In Australia, this position was articulated most strongly by ALRA, which emerged in several states following the Abortion Act 1967 (UK) and continued to campaign for further reforms after many states changed their laws at the turn of the 1970s.

Like strands of abortion activism elsewhere (Nelson 2013: 12; Hindell and Simms 1971), ALRA drew on liberal political philosophy to argue that legal prohibitions on abortion represented an unwarranted incursion of the state into the individual consciences of its citizens. ALRA (1970c) framed abortion as a moral issue relating to foetal life—'[t]he most complex and emotive aspect of the abortion reform debate'; it contested claims that the foetus was objectively knowable, by religious tenet or scientific fact, arguing instead that one's 'personal values and beliefs' determined their opinion regarding foetal life. Abortion morality was therefore variable and subjective, and restrictive abortion laws unjustly imposed a minority, Catholic morality onto the entire population. ALRA initially emphasised the consciences of doctors, whose medical judgement was obstructed in laws that set guidelines as to when abortions could be performed. From 1972, the association began placing equal emphasis on women's consciences and changed its name from the Abortion Law *Reform* Association to the Abortion Law *Repeal* Association to reflect its new campaign for the complete repeal of statute laws criminalising abortion (ALRA 1972a).

A striking aspect of ALRA's politics was its depiction of abortion as 'unpleasant' (McMichael 1972b), and the recurring idea that, in the words of one of the association's presidents, '[n]o-one actually likes the idea of terminating pregnancies' because of 'a natural respect for life in any form' (McMichael 1972a: 5). As noted above, abortion law reform had not been achieved in Australia, or elsewhere, through presenting abortion as a social or moral good. Reformers argued instead that regulated medical abortion presented the better alternative to illegal, unregulated 'backyard' operations. ALRA continued to rationalise abortion by presenting it on a sliding scale of desirable options. Abortion, it argued, was more desirable than the birth of unwanted children—'every child should be a wanted child', so a leading slogan exclaimed. The association reproduced scientific studies demonstrating that unwanted children experienced greater levels of emotional and physical abuse than wanted children and frequently became 'social misfits', 'inadequate parents' and 'deprived and inadequate citizens' (ALRA 1970b; 1970d; 1970c). Support for abortion on the basis of the poor quality of children born from unwanted pregnancies was the closest ALRA came to advocating for abortion on eugenic grounds, a rationale that plagued the transnational birth control movement through the first half of the twentieth century (Ziegler 2013). Although more desirable than the birth of unwanted children or unsafe 'backyard' operations, ALRA asserted that abortion was less desirable than other modes of contraception and placed a moral obligation on women to prevent unwanted pregnancies. Its leading slogan in the early 1970s was 'Abortion—a right; Contraception—a responsibility'. This slogan differentiated abortion from other modes of contraception and clearly presented abortion as the 'second best' (McMichael 1972a) method of birth control and '*the last resort*' (ALRA 1972b) after other contraceptives had failed. The framing of abortion as an issue involving the status of foetal life, which should be granted 'natural respect' in some form, prevented ALRA from depicting abortion in positive terms.

COMPASSION FOR THE DESPERATE

ALRA generally assumed that women required abortions because they were unmarried and wanted to avoid the shame of unwed motherhood or they were married with several children, living in poverty or in volatile and sometimes abusive relationships. As Celeste Condit observes of the US context, the trope of the 'helpless victim' with 'culturally potent' reasons for abortion was a discursive form that attracted support for abortion through recuperating it within the key social symbols of the 'family' and 'motherhood' (1990: 25–36). Of the three case studies of women seeking abortion presented in ALRA's 1972 publication *Abortion: The Unenforceable Law*—written by a social worker, psychiatrist and general practitioner—all three women were married with children, two accounts dwelt on the woman's financial hardship, and two women had abusive husbands (Boas 1972; Gold 1972; McMichael and Wynn 1972). Such representations worked to present aborting women as distressed victims of unfortunate circumstances beyond their control. The circumstances that ALRA believed led women to seek abortion implicitly circumscribed the conditions under which women were believed to mother effectively: being middle-class and in a secure relationship. Such characteristics constituted the stability ALRA (1974a) evoked in its description of law reform as amounting to 'willing mothers, wanted children, [and] stable families'. The figure of the desperate aborting woman also aligned a woman's want of abortion with her desire to be a 'good mother', who acted to protect her children or potential children from (further) poverty and/or from being born without a permanent father figure.

By depicting women who had abortions as victims of poverty or men (either their licentiousness or inability/unwillingness to care for their family), they appeared as, in Condit's words, '"good", or, at the least, unable to control her own destiny', compelling the public 'to feel sorry for the agent and angry with the forces that bring her suffering' (1990: 25). ALRA accused those who did not support progressive law reform, or trivialised women's reasons for having abortions, of 'lacking in compassion … [for] the anguish, desperation and degradation of thousands of Australian women' (Wainer 1969). The emphasis on women's suffering provided a useful rhetorical defence to the image of the 'selfish aborting woman' evoked by opponents of law reform; however, ALRA's call to legitimate abortion on the grounds of compassion presented abortion, not as a woman's unassailable right, but as a gift that society (through its laws) and medical doctors gave pregnant women as a means to alleviate their suffering and, by implication, rescue potential children from immature, impoverished or overburdened mothers. Lauren Berlant asserts that a politics based on compassion organises a relationship 'between spectators and sufferers, with the emphasis on the spectator's experience of feeling compassion and its subsequent relation to material politics' (2004b: 1). The compassion driving ALRA's activism established a hierarchical relationship between the suffering victims who had abortions and the spectators (ALRA members, politicians and medical doctors), who possessed the knowledge, skill or influence to alleviate their misery, and thus have their capacity to alleviate another's suffering, and their benevolence for doing so, confirmed (Kennedy 2011: 268). The relationship between victim and saviour was articulated through gender paternalism and social class, with male doctors helping their female patients (doctors were invariably male in ALRA publications), male parliamentarians forming better laws, and middle-class ALRA members (Gregory 2005: 242–244) protecting the less privileged. In ALRA publications, it was often suggested that aborting women should feel grateful rather than deserving; for example, doctors who referred women for abortions were depicted as 'professional martyrs' (Anonymous GP 1972) who should receive thankfulness in exchange for this generosity because 'women look to doctors for help' (ALRA 1974b). As a gift, compassion can be withheld. Compassion generates a 'hierarchy between "good" versus "abject" suffering' (Berlant 2004b: 1). ALRA (1974c) equated worthiness to 'the suffering of women with acute physical and mental distress, [and] economic hardship', thereby sustaining the middle-class, 'selfish abortion' as a silenced other.

Some aspects of ALRA's politics were undoubtedly progressive for the time. The demand for abortion with no legal restrictions is a goal yet unrealised in most of the world. The non-judgemental assertion that single women should have access to abortion also represented a morality that broke with the then prevalent ideology of female sexual virtue (Reekie 1997). In the main, however, ALRA argued for the decriminalisation of abortion by integrating the practice into the dominant social and political values of the time; values that reaffirmed abortion as a negative practice and motherhood as the only unproblematic outcome of pregnancy. Abortion was viewed as a deviant choice—an undesirable, albeit necessary procedure required when other forms of contraception had failed. Women who terminated their pregnancies were generally depicted as victims of circumstance rather than subjects of an autonomous choice, who did not necessarily aim to reject motherhood, but acted to protect their existing or potential children from either intensified poverty or the economic and social status of having an unwed mother. By appealing to the compassion of legislators and the public at large, they were transformed into the subjects of the abortion debate, with the 'desperate women' who had abortions materialising as objects to be rescued by other peoples' goodwill.

'A WOMAN'S RIGHT TO CHOOSE'

Within ALRA publications of the early 1970s, a women-centred approach was increasingly articulated alongside the dominant, foetocentric position. In a radio interview transcribed in *Abortion: The Unenforceable Law*, Germaine Greer (1972), an Australian feminist on an international tour after the publication of her acclaimed *The Female Eunuch* in 1970, criticised the staunch paternalism embedded in laws that had medicalised abortion for forcing a woman 'to claim that she'd go off her rocker if she had a baby ... We've got to argue ... as idiots—as moral cripples, who are not able to make decisions for themselves'. By permitting abortion only in cases where women were medically (and, more often than not, psycho-logically) 'at risk', the law reinforced a gendered binary that presented women as 'irrational' victims and doctors as their 'rational' saviours (Sheldon 1997). Greer and other liberation-ists argued instead that abortion should be recognised in law as a rational decision made by psychologically stable women.

Abortion politics were central to the new wave of femi-nist politics that swept much of the western world in the 1970s. Feminist intervention into abortion politics, in turn, significantly altered the terms of the abortion debate (Siegel 2014). First-hand experience with illegal abortion mobilised many women into action. Activists pointed out that restric-tive abortion laws led to unnecessarily high mortality and morbidity rates; they made it difficult for women, especially poor women, to access abortions, and they compelled women to view their abortions as the consequence of individual moral transgressions. Consciousness-raising was key to the political awakening and agitation of liberationists, and the theoretical tools developed at the time enabled women to connect their personal experiences of abortion to broader structures of power (Nelson 2003: 27–28, 34–35).

The Women's Liberation Movement (WLM) viewed legal prohibitions on abortion, and the system of values that upheld such laws, as an exemplary example of the patriarchal system whereby men indirectly (through social mores) and directly (through laws) controlled women's lives for their own benefit. Restrictive abortion laws also highlighted the sexism of the sexual revolution of the 1960s, which had expanded men's sexual access to women while freeing them from the obligations of marriage or economic support. Without legal access to abortion and with limited access to contraceptives, women could be left alone to carry the consequences of unwanted pregnancies and, if they chose to give birth, were often unable to provide sufficiently for their children (Nelson 2003: 21–54). The WLM's campaign for abortion communicated the movement's goal for women's autonomy, as sexual subjects, from men, and from the institution of 'compulsory motherhood'; activists forwarded, in activist and academic Rosalind Petchesky's words, 'the powerful idea that restricting abortion means compelling motherhood, [and] that motherhood is a social relationship and not a punishment or a destiny' (1984: 131). Other key campaigns—for equal pay and childcare and against sexual objectification—also pivoted around these central themes.

In Australia, the WLM established a single-issue campaign for the repeal of all abortion laws in 1972, the Women's Abortion Action Coalition (WAAC). Australian liberationists believed they were part of an international struggle with 'our sisters overseas' against patriarchy and specific issues, such as abortion. WAAC was a conscientiously global movement. Its political slogans, including 'Women unite: Abortion is our right' and the title of its magazine, *Abortion Is a Woman's Right to Choose (Right to Choose!)*, were echoed across the Western world (McCulloch 2013; Petchesky 1984; Rebick 2005). Activists also shared campaign strategies. These included consciousness-raising activities, including mass demonstrations, 'speak outs' and 'self-incrimination' campaigns (Nelson 2003: 33–38). For example, in 1973 Melbourne activists took inspiration from the manifesto signed by Simone de Beauvoir and hundreds of other well-known French women confessing to their abortions, marching on the police head-quarters demanding to be arrested for breaking abortion laws (Gregory 2005: 255–256).

Liberationists believed that abortion rights translated into nothing less than 'the right to control their own bodies and lives' (WAAC 1974b). WAAC's magazine, *Right to Choose!*, was a major forum for WLM's critique of the 'image of a mother who is always giving … who never puts herself first' (1979: 5). Restrictions on abortion, activists argued, ensured women's attachment to the twin institutions of marriage and the family, 'which make women inferior to men—which make women the possession of men—which keep women from being free' (WAAC 1978b). Without access to abortion, women remained 'in biological bondage and tied to the nuclear family' (WAAC 1975c: 10); they were mere 'child producing units' (WAAC 1974c: 4), imprisoned in 'a twenty-year sentence of enforced motherhood' (WAAC 1977). The coalition insisted that women 'cannot be free to use their talents and skills fully unless they know their lives will not be interrupted by unplanned pregnancy and child rearing' (WAAC 1975d: 9). Women's inability to completely control their fertility compromised their educational achieve-ments, provided justification for employers to keep women in low-status and poorly remunerated careers (WAAC 1978c) and formed a psychological barrier, preventing women from seeking fulfilment outside the roles of wife and mother (WAAC 1975b: 5).

WAAC asserted that men controlled every aspect of abortion: Catholic priests framed abortion as a moral issue based on foetal life; male politicians and judges delineated its legal position; and laws on abortion, in turn, gave the abortion choice to male medical doctors. *Right to Choose!* was littered with images of gagged pregnant women, exhausted mothers with demanding children at their feet, and passive pregnant women, standing in judgement before men in their roles as doctors, judges, politicians, and priests. Alongside slogans such as 'Get your rosaries off my ovaries' and 'Not the church, not the state, women must decide our fate', such images forcefully depicted women's subordination in decisions with profound implications for their lives.

WAAC maintained that the dominant view of abortion as a moral tragedy derived from 'the reactionary media, churchmen and politicians who daily intimidate women into believing they have no right to control their own bodies' (WAAC 1973). The male-oriented representational system defined women as mothers and compelled women to view abortion as a shameful, guilty secret they had to hide from others (WAAC 1975a: 18; 1978d: 2). WAAC insisted that mainstream abortion morality, which viewed abortion in terms of foetal life and contraceptive failure, was a 'club to beat us [women] with' (1978c: 2), reframing the issue of abortion as one 'about political power, power over women's lives' (1978c: 5). Although campaigning for safe, free and widely available contraceptives, WAAC also warned women of the health consequences of many contraceptive devices, reframing contraception as a woman's choice rather than obligation (1977: 21) so that, in part, women who had abortions were not compelled to feel 'embarrassment at having "failed" with their contraception' (1978a: 3). In order to 'overcome the terrible stigma attached to abortion', WAAC believed it was 'necessary for women to get up in the streets and state they have had abortions and that they believe that it is every woman's right to decide' (Schnookal 1974).

For the WAAC, therefore, abortion was a social good and political necessity; an essential precondition for the ability of women to live as independent subjects, free from the shackles of compulsory motherhood. The autonomous, liberated subject of the abortion choice in WAAC publications was a direct challenge to ALRA's desperate aborting woman; she was a subject seeking to define her own life path and, in so doing, assert her own wishes and desires in a world that too readily conspired to define these for her.

ABORTION RELIEF

WAAC (1979) believed that abortion shame and guilt were 'socially conditioned … [by] the patriarchal structure'. Although recognising a 'very wide range of emotions', the coalition also represented abortion as 'a liberating experience for women. There is often a new self and social awareness with positive validation of experiences, and new-found strength to hopefully enable future self-determination in society' (1980–1981: 21–22). Liberationists forwarded the view that abortion was more emotionally benign than motherhood: 'you are far more likely to end up in a psychiatric clinic as a result of having a baby, than of having an abortion' (1976a: 8). Reversing the commonly reviewed view, where abortion was equated with death, they represented abortion as a 'life-giving act', and contrasted abortion with unwanted childbearing, which 'could be said to be the death of dreams or the failing of a creative spirit' (WAAC 1981–1982: 15). By conceptualising abortion as a positive resolution of an unwanted pregnancy, the WLM replaced guilt and shame with the emotion of relief (for example, WAAC 1978a: 3; 1986: 15).

Relief involves contrasting a current positive state with a previous negative one; the subject of relief employs 'counter-factual thinking' to weigh 'what is' against 'what could have been' (Sweeny and Vohs 2012: 465). In the context of abortion, a woman could thus weigh her current, non-pregnant state positively in relation to the alternative of continuing with a pregnancy and mothering the child in the future. In contrast to the dominant mode of representing women who had abortions in ALRA publications (as suffering objects of compassion), abortion relief afforded a new subject position for pregnant woman: the woman who did not want to be pregnant, did not want to mother, and who acted in order to realise her desires for autonomous self-determination. By positioning 'not-mothering' as a major source of women's liberation, however, WLM elided a class- and race-bound history that constructed motherhood as a privilege that only some women should enjoy.

THE LIMITATIONS OF CHOICE

The WLM's focus on abortion rights as a means of liber-ating all women is exemplary of a broader failure to properly acknowledge the gross inequalities that exist between women and to address the concerns of women whose experiences did not converge with those of the white, middle-class, heterosexual women who dominated the movement and for whom gender was their primary mode of oppression (Burgman 2003: 141–147).

In focusing on 'women's choice', activists obfuscated the inequities that differentially determined, and continue to determine, women's access to abortion. The importance of considering class-based inequities in accessing abortion services was brought home to activists internationally after the US Hyde Amendment (1976) cut federal funding to most abortion services. A bill introducing similar legislation (the Lusher Motion) was introduced, only to fail, in Australia in 1979.[2] In response to threats to the state funding of abortion, many WAAC members, like activists overseas, pushed to replace the slogan 'right to choose' with 'free abortion on demand' (Abortion Campaign Committee n.d.; Nelson 2003). Even if women secured the legal ability to choose abortion, they argued, abortion needed to be readily available and affordable before women could exercise this choice (WAAC 1976b: 16).

Lesbians critiqued the heterosexism of WLM's activism. In proclaiming that 'there is hardly a woman alive who has not been faced with the problem of an unwanted pregnancy' (WAAC 1975b), for example, liberationists reinforced the assumption of women's heterosexuality, one that worked to marginalise other sexual identities. Some activists for abortion and lesbian rights, however, sought an alliance based on the shared goal of recognising a non-procreative sexuality for women (Nelson 2003: 175).

Women of colour were at the forefront of pushing for an approach that would come to be termed 'intersectional', developing a distinct political consciousness and theoretical framework in response to racism within the WLM and sexism within black activist movements. In the USA, African-American women were primary agitators in pushing for a class critique of abortion access. Because black women were disproportionally poor, they constituted, in their words, 'the vast majority' of women 'who died at the hands of incompetent practitioners' when abortion was illegal; they were also disproportionately affected by the Hyde Amendment (cited in Nelson 2003: 77). In contrast to the regime of compulsory motherhood that propelled liberationists to define reproductive freedom in terms of access to abortion and contraceptives, the motherhood of women of colour was routinely denigrated or prevented through impelled regimes of foster care, adoption and programs of forced or coerced sterilisation (Chapter 5). As a consequence of programs aimed to limit the reproductive potential of black and Latino populations, male activists within these communities at the beginning of the 1970s generally likened birth control to racial genocide and were opposed to fertility control, assigning to women the role of the revolution's breeders. Women successfully worked within the majority of these movements to change their policies pertaining to contraception and abortion, while also pushing the issues of forced sterilisation and coercive contraception programs onto the WLM's agenda (Nelson 2003).

In the Australian context, Aboriginal women, often aligning themselves with black feminists overseas, were at the forefront of critiquing the whiteness inherent in the WLM. In the 1970s, the primary political demand of Aboriginal women stood in stark contrast to WLM's aim to delegitimise the norm of the family. They called instead to be recognised as legitimate mothers and to keep their families and communities together. Racist state policies in Australia tore Indigenous communities apart and separated children from their mothers. In the 1970s, medical services in Indigenous communities were also using Depo Provera, banned in the USA because of its carcinogenic side effects and not approved for use as a contraceptive in Australia, on Aboriginal women (Daylight and Johnstone 1986: 64; Moreton-Robinson 2000). By focusing on patriarchy as the explanatory framework for oppression and power, WLM was unable to account for why one of the biggest obstacles to white women's reproductive choice was abortion, when for many Aboriginal women it was the ability to have children and keep their children after birth. WLM needed to consider the discriminatory effects of colonisation and race to comprehend this contrast. The movement failed to do this because, as many Aboriginal women have argued, it would have entailed recognition of white women's role as oppressors of Aboriginal women. Aboriginal women noted the primacy of race when understanding why they were fighting to 'stop *forced* sterilisation on our black women … while white women campaign for the right to abortion' (Vashti Collective 1973: 15).

In response to criticism of the movement's ready conflation of reproductive choice with abortion choice, liberationists worldwide included the demand for 'no forced sterilisation' alongside calls for abortion rights. They did not generally communicate this demand using the nascent intersectional tools offered by Indigenous women and women of colour, however, but through the language of autonomous choice and self-determination that they used to describe women's liberation from patriarchy (Nelson 2003). Since the 1970s, the demands of women outside the white, middle-class, heterosexual norm have witnessed the growth of an encompassing reproductive justice framework, which aims to support the capacity of women to have children as well as decide when and whether to do so (Silliman et al. 2004).

The introduction of feminist arguments for abortion fractured the rhetorical landscape that would come to be called 'pro-choice' by the end of the 1970s; the increasing demands for feminist activists and scholars to think of gender as it intersects with race, sexuality and class fragmented this further. The emergence and growth of an organised anti-abortion movement in the early 1970s saw an additional proliferation in ways of speaking about abortion and the women who had them.

'A CHOICE TO KILL'

Before abortion laws were liberalised, the Catholic Church were the only organised opposition to abortion. With funding and guidance from the Church, the US National Right to Life Committee formed in 1973 months after *Roe v Wade* (Munson 2010: 85). Following America's lead, Australia's first and largest anti-abortion organisation, Right to Life (RTL), was established in 1973 with the financial backing of the Catholic Church (Coleman 1988). With American activism at its core, the anti-abortion movement is a global franchise (Wyatt and Hughes 2009: 236). Strategies and 'archetypal' narratives pertaining to foetal life and the women who have abortions are shared internationally, a transnationalism that helps construct the movement's underlying values as universal truths (Hopkins et al. 1996: 543; Wyatt and Hughes 2009: 224). In countries like Australia, where there are very few committed anti-abortion activists, the movement's internationalism allows it to appear much larger. The Australian anti-abortion movement has also wielded media and political influence far greater than its small size (Wyatt and Hughes 2009: 236). This is largely due to the influence of a handful of politicians, all Catholic men, who have enjoyed disproportionate political influence by holding government ministries or the balance of power in parliament (see, for example, Gleeson 2011).

In the 1970s and early 1980s, RTL's politics were exclusively foetocentric, communicated through slogans including 'Choose life' and 'Every abortion kills a baby' (RTL 1977b). Framing abortion as murder, the organisation petitioned governments to extend the protection of human life to foetuses. RTL has continually used graphic images to 'clearly show that "unborn babies are people, too"' (1976b). These images include pictures purportedly showing babies and baby body parts in rubbish bins and its 'precious feet' insignia, which pictures two adult fingers gently holding miniature feet (Condit 1990: 79–89; Sanger 2017: 81–87). Foetal imagery and the testimony of anti-abortion doctors were key strategies in the global anti-abortion effort to translate arguments that were theological in origin into a purportedly objective pseudoscience (Franklin 2014; for an example, see Professor Liley in RTL 1981a).

Depictions of the foetus always entail representations of the pregnant woman. When the foetus is imagined to be an autonomous, baby-like entity, pregnant women are assumed to be already mothers, and when activists argue that foetal life needs to be protected regardless of the desires of pregnant women, women are reduced to passive carriers for the lives of others (Petchesky 1987). In the foetal imagery that pervaded RTL publications of the 1970s and early 1980s, pregnant women were generally erased from the scene, with baby-like foetuses magically appearing outside of women's wombs. Alternatively, their bodies were blackened to highlight their luminescent foetuses. RTL's logo from the 1970s and 1980s featured a child-looking foetus, replete with piggy tails, standing, with no umbilical cord, in a blackened and faceless woman's body. Another pictorial theme in its newsletters was that of motherhood; images of mothers holding their children with captions such as 'mother love' or 'we do love babies' were common (for example, RTL 1976a, 1979, 1980a). In sharp contrast to such images of maternal nurturance, RTL activists represented women who had abortions as mothers who killed their babies—'Don't kill me, Mommy' (Faludi 1991: 409), so one anti-abortion slogan read—and they committed infanticide for, in the words of longstanding President Margaret Tighe, 'purely selfish reasons' (cited in Gregory 2005: 165).

In RTL publications, women who had abortions figured as 'affect aliens' (Ahmed 2010b); as selfish killers rather than selfless nurturers of their children, they were out of alignment with the proper emotional script for women—that of maternal love. The aborting woman's perceived absence of maternal affection aligned her with a world turned upside down, the revolutionary order threatening to emerge with the coalition of social movements collectively known as the New Left. Writing in 1981, in the wake of Reagan's presidential victory, Rosalind Petchesky labelled the anti-abortion movement a 'backlash movement' aimed to 'turn back the tide of the major social movements of the 1960s and 1970s' (1981: 234). As she observed, 'the abortion issue resonates many social and political meanings—the family, sexuality, the position of women—that go far beyond the status of the fetus; and thus *the organized opposition to abortion has never, in fact, been a "single-issue" movement*' (1981: 220). RTL was not merely a response to the New Left, particularly the WLM, but also to a series of demographic trends suggesting that the institutions feminists targeted were in a state of demise. By the mid-1970s, families with men as the sole breadwinner were in stark decline (constituting just 13.5 per cent of households in the USA), the birth rate was decreasing, and there were increases in divorce, the employment rate of married women with children, and amongst young, unmarried women giving birth (Petchesky 1981: 235–236). Within a context of stark demographic and cultural change, the erosion of women's access to abortion held the hope of restoring a gender order based on the patriarchal nuclear family, procreative sexuality for women, and women's innate role as mothers and carers—this is why Jennifer Somerville (2000) terms organised opposition to abortion 'the other women's movement' (also see Luker 1984; Petchesky 1981; Wyatt and Hughes 2009: 236).

The gender politics driving WLM's abortion activism meant it was also never concerned with abortion alone. RTL and the WLM were opposing movements. WLM often represented women who had abortions through the figure of the 'liberated woman'—free from men, compulsory motherhood and reproductive sexuality—with this figure representing aspirations for a more equitable future. For RTL, the figure of the 'liberated woman' who terminated her pregnancy was profoundly unnatural, with her deformed, pathological and harmful orientation towards her 'children' symbolic of a world order heading in the wrong direction. For RTL, the threat to the social order that abortion represented was more than a loss of privilege amongst those whose identities were previously 'unmarked' (the white, male, middle-class heterosexual); it was also about the loss of secure identities (such as the natural mother or family patriarch) in which activists were deeply invested. Liberationists were also deeply invested in seeking alternative identities and lives for themselves and other women (Coleman 1988; Luker 1984; Petchesky 1981).

The discursive frames of the WLM and RTL were often in dialogue with one another. While for the WLM, patriarchal power relations and social values produced a conservative abortion morality, RTL argued that abortion morality was

a product of 'truth' and 'science'. Placards used in demonstrations, for example, rebuked the slogan 'Abortion: a
woman's right to choose' by crossing out and replacing the
word 'choose' with 'kill'. Others demanded that individuals
'Choose life' and proclaimed that 'It's a baby, NOT a choice'
(RTL 1977c). RTL viewed abortion as murder and aborting
women as denying their motherhood and unnaturally, and
criminally, elevating their own self-interest above the welfare
of their 'babies'. For the WLM, in contrast, abortion was
a choice that liberated women from patriarchal sex roles.
ALRA's politics stood somewhere in between these two
extremes. ALRA viewed abortion as a morally dubious act
that took the life of a nascent human being and championed
contraception as a means of preventing the need for abortion;
it also argued that safe and legal abortion was necessary in
order to prevent unsafe 'backyard' practices as well as the
birth of unwanted children to mothers unable to look after
them for social (the lack of a male partner) or economic
reasons. ALRA's abortion politics did not carry an explicit
gender politics, but by representing abortion as a choice that
only desperate women made in exceptional circumstances, it
consolidated the normalcy of motherhood for all pregnant
women and did nothing to displace a maternal-centred norm
of femininity.

This chapter moves to consider how activist language
translated into mainstream political debate about abortion.
My intention here is to show how anti-abortion sentiment
was embedded in the choice of abortion at the very time that
this choice became a topic of public conversation.

A POLITICISED CHOICE

In the 1970s, governments attempted to respond and adapt, in various ways, to the changing landscape of abortion brought by the era's law reforms. In the UK, the 1970s witnessed one parliamentary committee (the Lane Committee) and seven (ultimately unsuccessful) bills tabled in parliament (Keown 1988: 138–158). Canada and New Zealand also held major government inquiries into abortion (McCulloch 2013: 131–143; McLaren and McLaren: 138–139). In Australia, where abortion law is a matter of state jurisdiction, the Commonwealth government attempted to intervene in abortion politics where it could: territorial law, a royal commission and government funding for abortions.

The first Commonwealth debate concerning abortion in the 1970s was over a pro-abortion bill sponsored in 1973 by Tony Lamb and David McKenzie, two ALRA members and MPs elected for the first time with the victory of the progressive Labor government led by Gough Whitlam in 1972. The Medical Practice Clarification Bill (commonly termed the McKenzie-Lamb Bill) sought to remove legal restrictions on abortions performed by medical doctors to the twenty-third week of a woman's pregnancy in the Australian Capital Territory (ACT). Lamb and McKenzie forwarded the bill to begin a national discussion on the abortion issue. If adopted, the bill would have resulted in one of the most liberal abortion laws worldwide at the time (Henshaw and Morrow 1990); and, indeed, it proved too progressive for the government and failed decisively.

The debate over the bill did, however, lead to the establishment of the Royal Commission on Human Relationships, which reported in 1977 (Gregory 2005: 302–303). A royal commission is the highest form of Commonwealth inquiry into matters deemed to be of public importance, thus its establishment reflected government acknowledgement that social mores regarding abortion were changing and may require some policy or legislative response. The establishment of the Lane Committee in the UK was a major impetus behind its formation, and the final report drew heavily on the Lane Report but was more progressive in its recommendations. While the Lane Report recommended retaining laws that medicalised abortion, the Commission recommended that abortion be regulated like any other medical procedure until foetal viability, conservatively measured to commence when a woman was twenty-two weeks pregnant (Evatt 1977, v1: 105). This recommendation did not, however, lead to any Commonwealth or state action on abortion. Instead, in 1979, Stephen Lusher, an anti-abortion Catholic and member of the socially-conservative Country Party, moved a motion to cease Commonwealth funding for abortion except in cases where a medical doctor certified that the aborting woman was suffering from a 'pathological condition' or the abortion was required to save a woman's life (Stephen Lusher, MP; Australia 1979a: 693). The Lusher Motion represented the first anti-abortion intervention into Australia's formal politics. Unlike the US Hyde Amendment (1976) upon which it was based, the motion failed by an overwhelming majority.

The Royal Commission authoritatively affirmed that the abortion debate hinged on 'whether the life of the foetus should be protected by the criminal law [and whether] society [can] condone the destruction of the foetus without at the same time diminishing the value of human life' (Evatt 1977, v3: 147). It further represented abortion as an 'issue of serious concern to everyone' because it 'brings that new life to an end' (Evatt 1977, v3: 149). The foetocentric framing of abortion foreclosed WLM's position on abortion, which centred on each pregnant woman's willingness to remain pregnant and become a mother. The Commission thanked RTL for helping them appreciate that the 'foetus is certainly human life', expressing no equivalent gratitude to 'pro-choice' organisations.[3] Yet it also concluded that foetal life was of a 'different quality' to life after birth, a conclusion informing its recommendations to decriminalise most procedures (Evatt 1977, v1: 54).

Parliamentarians debating the McKenzie-Lamb Bill and Lusher Motion reinforced an abortion common sense that viewed abortion through the lens of a foetocentric morality. The idea that the abortion debate hinged on the moral status of foetal life was built into the very structure of the debates, where parliamentarians were granted the ability to vote according to their individual consciences rather than any party affiliation. Conscience votes are rare, and usually only extended to members when debating 'life-or-death' issues (Warhurst 2008). The narrowing of the abortion debate to 'one's assumption or otherwise that a foetus becomes a human being at the time of conception' was noted by one Member of Parliament (Richard Klugman, MP; Australia 1979a: 1004). Parliamentarians who supported women's access to abortion argued that the value one ascribes to foetal life was 'a matter of conscience ... primarily for the woman and her doctor' (David McKenzie, MP; Australia 1973: 1963). Anti-abortionists argued that foetuses were the moral equivalent of born humans and, as such, pregnant women were not autonomous subjects under the law: 'another person is involved in this question of choice—the unborn child' (Peter Shack, MP; Australia 1979b: 1104).

Parliamentarians and the Royal Commission unanimously presented abortion to be a profoundly disturbing and undesirable practice. McKenzie claimed that his bill was 'not a matter of whether one agrees with abortion—I do not, and very few people do' (Australia 1973: 1964). The Commission referred to abortion as 'repugnant ... to the conscience' (Evatt, 1977, v3: 153), and an opponent of the Lusher Motion asserted that 'I do not believe that any honourable member believes that abortion is morally a good thing' (Neal Blewitt, MP; Australia 1979a: 1113). Parliamentarians who supported fewer or no restrictions on abortions performed by medical doctors emphasised the need for contraception and social welfare services to alleviate the need for abortion: a clause in the McKenzie-Lamb Bill, for example, required doctors to provide women having abortions with contraceptive counselling (David McKenzie, MP; Australia 10 May 1973: 1963). The Commission was similarly directed to investigate how education and contraceptive services could reduce the number of abortions (Evatt 1977, v3: 153). 'Pro-abortion' politicians viewed abortion as 'the lesser of two evils' when placed along-side its alternatives: not forced pregnancy and motherhood, but dangerous, 'backyard' abortion practices and the birth of unwanted children (Harry Jenkins, MP; Australia 1979a: 982). Politicians, therefore, accepted abortion only by framing it as an exceptional and 'terrible choice', pleading with 'people who are so loud in their criticism to show real compassion for women' forced to have abortions (David McKenzie, MP; Australia 1973: 1968). The object of their compassion was the desperate aborting woman and the related figure of the neglected, unwanted child, character types articulated in one MPs description of 'the tired and overworked mother of a poor man's clutch of children' (Clyde Cameron, MP; Australia 1979a: 988).

The use of the term 'pro-choice' to describe politics that, in the 1970s, the media and parliamentarians usually termed 'pro-abortion' was not commonplace until the 1980s. Rickie Solinger (2001) notes of the American context that activists increasingly adapted the liberal principle of choice to avoid condoning abortion as a social or moral good. The same is true of Australian activists and politicians. The emphasis on choice stemmed in part from the discomfort many advocates for abortion law reform had with the practice of abortion itself, and the accompanying sentiment that 'I do not know anyone who is pro-abortion' (Ian MacPhee, MP; Australia 1979a: 1081). A 'pro-choice' position enabled individuals to support liberal abortion laws without also, explicitly, supporting abortion. RTL (1980b) capitalised on the ambiguity of the 'pro-choice' yet 'anti-abortion' approach. A cartoon printed in its newsletter after the failed Lusher Motion, for example, depicted a politician outside parliament with two faces; one pointed to the sign 'pro-abortion' and the other to an 'anti-abortion' sign. It was captioned 'I am personally opposed to abortion, BUT ...' (1980b). The implication here was that individuals must be either for or against abortion.

Women-centred arguments had little impact on political debate in the 1970s. With the exception of a few MPs that expressed discomfort over discussing a 'women's issue' with no women in parliament, MPs generally argued that abortion was 'one of the most sensitive and controversial issues facing the Australian community' (Phillip Lynch, MP; Australia 1973: 1979). The presentation of abortion as a 'community' rather than 'women's issue' authorised a range of social actors—including journalists and politicians, almost exclusively male—to speak authoritatively about the issue, foreclosing the idea that women held a particularly important speaking position in the debate.

CONCLUSION

The majority of parliamentarians, the media and the general community held Lusher's defeat to settle the issue of how the state should regulate abortion, and there were very few legislative debates over the issue of abortion in Australia over the ensuing decades. Abortion would remain technically illegal and administered by doctors, whose broad interpretation of the mental health risks of continuing with unwanted pregnancies ensured that first trimester abortions were virtually available upon a woman's request (Crespigny and Savulescu 2004: 202). As I outlined in the introduction to this book, Australia—like the UK, New Zealand and Canada—lacks the political and demographic conditions that have fuelled the contested nature of abortion in the USA. Instead, political and public opinion on abortion has been broadly 'pro-choice' since the 1970s. By the end of the decade, more than three times as many Australians believed abortion should be available on demand (30 per cent) than banned entirely (8 per cent), with the majority supporting abortion for women's health or social hardship (Betts 2004). Importantly (and this will be explored further in Chapter 2), these opinion polls suggest that most Australians supported abortion as an exceptional choice made under desperate circumstances—i.e. under the same terms ALRA and pro-choice politicians emphasised when speaking about abortion.

During the 1970s, the rhetoric of abortion choice gradually entered into the public vocabulary; as it did so, the meanings ascribed to this choice were narrowly circumscribed, so abortion was normatively framed as the death of a foetus, and the women who had abortions stereotyped as either self-ishly refusing their maternal duties or desperately seeking relief from circumstances that compromised their capacity to mother effectively. The ascendency of a foetocentric framing of the abortion choice in the 1970s was the consequence of a political struggle largely involving the status of women. When parliamentarians, activists and others spoke about abortion, they were, regardless of whether they explicitly acknowledged it, discussing whether pregnant women were already mothers, whether they should be compelled to become mothers and, frequently, which women made the best mothers. They were also discussing whether or not women's sexuality should remain fused with reproduction.

The competing definitions of 'choice' and the 'choosing subject' outlined in this chapter begin to unravel the ready equation of freedom with choice, a project this book develops in further chapters. The concept of choice can carry quite specific and diverse political aspirations, and, as individual capacity, it can construct its subjects in precise yet varying ways. RTL likened the choice of abortion with infanticide and, by implication, depicted the women who had abortions in opposition to the selfless images of 'mother love' adorning the pages of its newsletter. On the reverse side of this discourse, WAAC's women-centred abortion politics asserted that a male-centred representational system produced the foetocentric morality of abortion, which infused abortion with secrecy and shame in order to bind women to the mothering role. Although ALRA argued for the complete repeal of abortion laws, it also ceded significant terrain to ideologies that buttressed anti-abortion politics. Choice materialised in ALRA's rhetoric as a consequence of despair rather than self-determination, and one, albeit horrific, required to alleviate women's suffering and deliver children from overburdened and potentially negligent mothers.

The prevalence of the 'desperate woman' stereotype offered a rhetorical defence to the figure of the 'selfish aborting woman' that existed prior to the liberalisation of abortion law and flourished in anti-abortion rhetoric. The defence, however, reified the notion that self-interest in the context of abortion was abnormal or deviant. The WLM attempted to claim for women the ability to be selfish and also introduced an alternative view of motherhood and pregnancy, communicated in part by the emotion of abortion relief. In contrast, RTL exaggerated selfishness in the context of abortion, representing the abject affective state of aborting woman as representative of the more encompassing threat to the political and social order that abortion was taken to represent. Although the valorisation of foetal life over the rights of pregnant women for 'first-trimester' abortions has never gained significant traction in the majority of countries that liberalised their abortion laws at the turn of the 1970s (with the prominent exception here being, arguably, the USA), we will see in future chapters that recourse to women's selfishness has remained central to legitimating restrictions on women's access to the procedure.

Lawful access to abortion is crucial to women's reproductive freedom. Although they did not achieve this goal, ALRA and WAAC improved and transformed women's access to abortion, ensuring that the new laws introduced at the turn of the 1970s were applied as liberally as possible (Gregory 2005: 278). There was also political expediency in ALRA's framework, which aligned the notion of 'abortion choice' with existing cultural values; perhaps, as Celeste Condit suggests, this change-seeking discourse formed a necessary bridge between 'old' belief sets and new political aspirations, making the political, legal and cultural changes of the 1960s and 1970s possible (1990: 32). But arguments for law reform were too often advanced through, rather than in opposition to, the presumption of abortion's illegitimacy, meaning that the exceptionality of abortion was written into the rhetoric of choice from the moment it became attached to abortion. In the 1970s, mainstream pro-choice politics represented abortion to be a fundamentally illegitimate choice that required justification in reference to women's desperation and, implicitly at least, their status as potentially unfit mothers. Politicians, activists and others appealed to 'compassion for the desperate' (Forell 1978) as a trope to justify the unpleasant and morally dubious choice of abortion, transforming the women who have abortions into the objects of public debate and other people's goodwill, rather than subjects of an autonomous decision. The virtual absence of a feminist voice in public discourse of abortion meant that, as Rosalind Petchesky observed of the US context of the mid-1980s, 'feminists won the battle [but] they did not win the war' (1984: 131). Although abortion remained lawfully available, the framing of abortion as, in Celeste Condit's words, 'a matter of "socially good excuses" rather than a consequence of the wishes and desires of women' (1990: 33, 35) placed abortion activists and women who had abortions on the defensive, requiring them to explain and justify each woman's abortion decision.

The ambiguity of abortion I have historicised here, where abortion is recognised as a necessary yet also an imperfect and undesirable choice, is at the heart of contemporary abortion politics, and manifests in what scholars call the stigmatisation or 'awfulisation' of abortion (Hadley 1997; Kumar et al. 2009). Although abortion laws have been liberalised, it is commonsensical to refer to abortion as a terrible and morally suspect practice with damaging effects on women (Chapter

3). The framing of abortion as a 'necessary evil' in the 1960s and 1970s also paved the way for future political and legal contestations. The use of women's bodies as a surface upon which broader ideological and political battles are waged was, for example, on full display in the weeks after the inauguration of the US president Donald Trump in January 2017. Within a couple of weeks, Trump reinstated an extended version of the 'global gag rule', which prohibits US aid from funding NGOs involved in abortion or abortion counselling, the Congress passed a bill that would turn the Hyde Amendment (1976) into permanent law and Trump nominated an anti-abortion appointment to the Supreme Court with the explicit goal of working towards overturning *Roe v Wade* (Chuck and Silva 2017). In the UK, debates about abortion counselling and 'sex-selective' abortions have retained and intensified focus on women's motives for abortion and the 'problem' of abortion more generally (Hoggart 2015; Lee 2017). In Australia after decades of relative calm, in 1996, the newly elected Howard Government, in a political deal with an anti-abortion Independent MP, introduced a global gag rule for Australian international aid and effectively prohibited the use of medical abortion in the country (both measures have since been repealed) (*The Age* 2006a; Heath 1996).

The next two chapters examine the development of pro- (Chapter 2) and anti- (Chapter 3) abortion activism since the 1970s. In the ensuing decades there has been a proliferation of anti- and pro-choice movements (Freedman and Weitz 2012: 38). Rather than providing comprehensive histories of these movements from the 1980s onward, I pick up on dominant strands of activism. Chapter 2 also introduces a more focused examination of emotions, concentrating on maternal happiness. Selfishness is a charge levelled against women who fail to exhibit this normative emotion. As an act where women are commonly viewed to place their own interests above those of their potential children (and, indeed, where many women consciously do so), nowhere is selfishness in women more admonished than in the context of abortion. The form of pro-choice rhetoric examined in Chapter 2 combats the pernicious stereotype of the selfish aborter with the depiction of abortion as a choice women make selflessly in the best interests of their potential children. In doing so, it reifies a maternal identity for women, reproducing abortion anew as an exceptional, incredibly difficult, and potentially harmful choice.

CHAPTER 2

HAPPY CHOICES

[The pro-choice movement has] kind of gotten stuck in the 1970s' 'biology is destiny' [arguments, which don't] … sit quite as comfortably in a world that has a better idea that you can't necessarily be that individualistic, you can't necessarily say, 'well, this is my right and this is what I'm going to do', if it adversely impacts on other people. (Lindsay Beaton, Australian Reproductive Health Alliance, 1998, cited in Cannold 2000: 57)

[W]omen who assert themselves as self-interested individuals confront the reproach of 'selfishness', itself a metonymy of failed femininity. Accused of organising themselves around the self they are not supposed to have, they are figured as monstrous in their departure from a (selfless) nurturing nature. (Wendy Brown 1995: 165)

In this passage, Wendy Brown describes the 'selfish woman' as a monstrous 'metonymy of failed femininity', so designated because of the continued centrality of motherhood to normative femininity. As we saw in Chapter 1, the abortion politics of the Women's Liberation Movement (WLM) attempted to displace the regime of compulsory motherhood and the selflessness this mandated. Liberationists argued that as long as motherhood remained normative for women, abortion would materialise as an abject choice. The norm of female selflessness and conservative abortion politics are mutually reinforcing. Given this, it may seem surprising that a spokesperson for the Australian Reproductive Health Alliance characterised WLM's abortion politics as selfishly individualistic, advocating a shift to an other-centred pro-choice position. Beaton's comments make sense, however, when located within a broader trend. From the early 1990s onwards, many prominent pro-choice activists began to explicitly distance their politics from the WLM, arguing that women required abortions, not to realise their own wants and needs, but to uphold their responsibilities to others, particularly their potential children. They argued that abortion was a fundamentally selfless rather than selfish choice, and concepts such as self-determination, bodily integrity and compulsory motherhood forward a distorted view of the relationship that exists between pregnant women and their foetuses. This mode of pro-choice rhetoric, which I term 'maternal', depicts women who have abortions as mothers acting in the best interests of their potential children.

Maternal pro-choice politics realign the figure of the aborting woman with normative femininity. This realignment has been enabled, I will argue in this chapter, through the postfeminist contract (McRobbie 2007), where women are perceived to have endless choices available to them (including abortion), making the radical gender politics of the WLM appear irrelevant and antiquated. As we shall see, many maternal pro-choice activists deploy this logic in their rejection of WLM's abortion politics. Instead of freeing femininity from motherhood, I will demonstrate in this chapter that the interpellation of young women as subjects of choice has in fact re-naturalised motherhood for women through choice. Maternal pro-choice politics is one of many instances where this has been achieved discursively. It is commonly supposed that, despite having a range of choices available to them, women generally choose to centre their lives and identities on motherhood because motherhood promises to bring them happiness. Motherhood, in its association with happiness, is no longer considered a woman's destiny (as it was in the early 1970s), but a woman's desire. As destiny, choices other than motherhood, including abortion, were deemed inconsequential to women's life paths. In contrast, the availability of choices, particularly that of abortion, is critical to the sustainability of the motherhood-as-desire fantasy. Normative presumptions regarding women's happiness—in diverse contexts, including the media, government policies and political speeches—have re-naturalised motherhood through the idiom of choice. When motherhood is installed as the only happy choice for pregnant women, abortion manifests as an agonising and heart-breaking choice for women to make.

By emphasising how happiness orients women towards motherhood, this chapter turns more explicit attention to the emotions articulated alongside cultural representations of abortion. Specifically, I trace representations of abortion in terms of how happiness circulates around all women, and pregnant women most acutely, in a way that orients them towards the figure of the foetus or child as a 'happy object' (Ahmed 2010b). The selfish woman, and in particular the selfish aborting woman, is disoriented, refusing (through wilfulness or misjudgement) to find happiness in her future children. Maternal pro-choice politics rationalise abortion through re-orienting women who have abortions in the normative or 'right' direction.

I begin this chapter by summarising the major arguments characteristic of the maternal pro-choice approach to abortion. I then introduce a theoretical framework to elucidate how this approach reifies a maternal identity for pregnant women, thereby articulating ideas about abortion, and the women who have abortions, that ultimately serve to bolster anti-abortion ideologies. The chapter then examines the language parliamentarians used when debating whether or not to liberalise women's access to abortion under the law. I argue that parliamentarians did not remove restrictions on women's access to abortion because they believed pregnant women are or should be autonomous subjects. Rather, they represented abortion through an emotional economy, viewing motherhood as the only choice that can guarantee pregnant women's happiness. Drawing on a larger cultural narrative, parliamentarians represented abortion as a 'difficult choice' that women endure out of a sense of love or duty to their potential children. Within this narrative, pregnant women inevitably make choices as mothers, even when they, paradoxically, choose to have abortions.

MATERNAL PRO-CHOICE POLITICS: KILLING FROM CARE

The stereotype of the 'selfish aborting woman' has existed since at least the turn of the twentieth century (Baird 1998b: 144). Women's Liberationists of the 1970s argued that women who had abortions were labelled 'selfish' because they failed according to 'the cultural definition of women as other-determined' (WAAC n.d.). Feminists themselves were quickly stereotyped as 'selfish' in popular culture because of their arguments for women's self-determination (Tyler 2007). WLM's push for abortion rights is often invoked to exemplify the movement's more general narcissism; as Rebecca Klatch notes, the 'equation of feminism with total self-gratification interprets abortion as the ultimate selfish act, the placement of a mother's desires above a baby's life' (1988: 129).

The 'selfish aborting woman' stereotype is constructed today through the repeated characterisation of abortion as, in the words of one US Justice, an 'arbitrary decision based on convenience' (cited in Sanger 2017: 10). The concept of the 'convenience abortion' implies that women terminate their pregnancies for frivolous reasons. A predominant theme in British print media's coverage of abortion in 2010 was, for example, the depiction of abortion as a 'lifestyle choice' (Purcell et al. 2014). Such characterisations rationalise measures that aim to restrict or monitor abortion. As we saw in Chapter 1, activists campaigning for increased abortion access have responded to the stereotype of selfishness in various ways. The Abortion Law Reform Association

(ALRA) emphasised the trope of the 'desperate woman' and the social and economic circumstances that forced women to make the ultimately undesirable choice of abortion. The WLM, in sharp contrast, claimed for women the right to escape the strictures of compulsory motherhood and claim a self-centred, or selfish, identity. Maternal pro-choice advocates developed a further defence, arguing that abortion was not necessarily a desperate choice, and it was never a selfish one; rather women, they argued, terminated their pregnancies for the benefit of those around them, particularly their potential children.

Maternal-pro-choice rhetoric attempts to acknowledge or even celebrate the 'value' that should, so it is claimed, rightfully be afforded foetal life in all its forms (Manninen 2013). The position differs from ALRA's activism (Chapter 1) because it responds directly to the gender politics of the WLM; it also appeals to women's embodied and emotional experiences of pregnancy to authenticate the foetal framing of pregnancy choice. In the first major publication belonging to this tradition, US writer Linda Francke wrote in *The Ambivalence of Abortion* that 'any woman who has had children knows that certain feeling in her taut, swollen breasts, and the slight but constant ache in her uterus signals the arrival of life' (1978: 5). Another early example of this trend is the Canadian writer Kathleen McDonnell, who claimed in *Not an Easy Choice: Re-examining Abortion* that 'women's experience of abortion is not being addressed [in pro-choice politics] ... Nobody *likes* abortion ... what abortion inspires more than anything else is a profound ambivalence, which finds a particular expression in women' (1984: 23, 28). Appeals for a more foetocentric pro-choice politics continued into the 1990s and beyond with the writings of celebrity feminists Naomi Wolf and Germaine Greer (Chapter 3) as well as several academics (Cannold 1998; Little 2003; Shrage 2003).

Although pro-choice activists have been responding to WLM's abortion activism with calls for greater acknoweldgement of foetal life since the late 1970s, this history is often erased in iterations of maternal pro-choice politics, which are generally presented as fresh critiques on a movement that is frequently represented as morally deficient, misguided in its women-centredness, and outdated in its focus on gender. In 2005, for example, the president of Catholics for Choice, Frances Kissling, claimed that 'There is a strong distaste of the prochoice community in many facets of society because of the inability or unwillingness to acknowledge one iota of value in fetal life' (2005: 15). US bioethicist Bertha Alvarez Manninen extends on Kissling's critique, asserting that the idea that 'the fetus is just a "clump of cells" or mere "tissue"' hails from an era when women's 'predestined role ... as mothers and homemakers' made it strategically necessary for feminists to make a distinction between the moral statuses of foetuses and pregnant women. Young women today, she continues, 'are far removed from the concerns and oppressions suffered by the generations of women before them' (2013: 665), and consequently, it is time for the pro-choice community to acknowledge the 'moral complexities, and at times ambiguities, of abortion' (669). Manninen further claims that the women who have abortions 'pine for ... acknowledgment of their emotions, and they desire to ground their abortion decision not via a dismissal of the worth of fetal life, but, rather, by acknowledging its value and still defending abortion rights through its lens' (668). Manninen reifies the familiar claim that pro-choice politics are not 'pro-abortion' (Chapter 1), endorsing Ronald Dworkin's guarded support for abortion as 'a waste of a human life and … therefore, a bad thing to happen, a shame' (cited in Manninen 2013: 679). Thus although Manninen views abortion as 'a right', she argues that it is one that should be 'exercised with less frequency' (676). This is a reinscription of the common depiction of abortion as an unpleasant necessity (Chapter 1) and another way of articulating the logic that carried the slogan made famous internationally by the Clintons in the 1990s—that abortion should be 'safe, legal and rare' (Weitz 2010). There are several points of Manninen's argument I want to highlight here, the significance of which will soon become apparent: firstly, she implies that women are free from the rigid gender roles of the previous era, characterising a feminist focus on these as anachronistic; secondly she infers that all women experience abortion similarly, and that these feelings are a response to the 'value' of foetal life and antiethical to its 'dismissal'; and, finally, her pro-choice politics are forged through an explicit distaste for abortion.

Maternal pro-choice activists and scholars repeatedly call for acknowledgement of the morality of abortion, which they define in purely foetocentric terms. Kathleen McDonnell's critique is typical: 'we [feminists] have largely abdicated any role in the moral discussion of abortion, and Right-to-Life ideology has filled the vacuum' (1984: 47). The framing of abortion morality solely in terms of foetal life cedes significant discursive terrain to the anti-abortion movement. The view that pregnant women should not be forced to continue pregnancies to term is a moral precept. The framing of abortion as a 'bad thing' or 'shame' privileges the foetus in imaginings of pregnancy, so erasing the subject position of the unwillingly pregnant woman, for whom abortion could be considered a life-affirming 'good thing'.

With abortion singularly framed as an act that destroys the life of a nascent human being, maternal pro-choice politics turns attention, like ALRA did before it (Chapter 1), to the reasons that compel women to terminate their pregnancies. These reasons congregate around the view that abortion is an act of maternal sacrifice, where women act selflessly for the wellbeing of their potential children. This approach is clearly articulated in Leslie Cannold's *The Abortion Myth*, published in 1998. *The Abortion Myth* begins, as so many maternal pro-choice texts do, with the premise that the pro-choice movement has no solid moral foundation (1998: xiii, 15–18). It then attempts to forge such a morality by dispelling the myth of the 'selfish abortion'. Arguing against the view of abortion as an act of self-determination, Cannold claims that women terminate their pregnancies 'thoughtfully, sorrowfully and with respect for the sacredness of pregnancy and with love for their could-be child' (1998: 127–128). Decisions where women 'act responsibly' and 'kill from care' fall within the 'moral circle' (1998: 127–128); in contrast, decisions that are 'just plain wrong' do 'not reflect a woman's "feelings" and "love" for her could-be child and other significant people in her life, and [are] not motivated by care and protective concern for all those she loves' (1998: xiv).

Cannold's approach drew heavily on the feminine 'ethic of care' developed by psychologist Carol Gilligan. Gilligan's research into abortion decision-making in the early 1990s led her to conclude that, for women, 'abortion can be justified only as an act of sacrifice, a submission to necessity where the absence of choice precludes responsibility' (Gilligan 1993: 86; Cannold 1998: xxxii–xxxiii). Here, Gilligan represents abortion, not as an autonomous choice, but as an act of self-sacrifice and 'submission to necessity', which women endure because of their responsibilities towards other people. Gilligan argues that this other-centred reasoning is peculiarly feminine, and she has been duly criticised for essentialising gender roles, albeit through the discourse of developmental psychology rather than biology (Weisstein 1993). Cannold similarly suggests that women are inherently maternal, observing that '[t]he idea that the desire for motherhood is completely culturally constructed undermines the accountability women must hold for their choices and, therefore, diminishes the respect and power that ought to be bestowed upon women's choices' (1998: 96–97). By arguing that women's choices should be respected because they are, at least in part, internally wired for motherhood, Cannold implies that abortion is an agonisingly difficult, counterintuitive and perhaps even unnatural choice, legitimated only when each woman acts out of 'love for their could-be child'.

MOTHERHOOD AS CHOICE

By setting itself up as distinct from the radical gender critique of feminism and citing the principle of choice while also reaffirming motherhood as the only authentic choice for pregnant women, maternal pro-choice politics is a postfeminist iteration of the movement. Rosalind Gill and Christina Scharff describe postfeminism as a sensibility that characterises 'large parts of contemporary culture ... where feminism is both "taken into account" and repudiated' (2013: 4). Postfeminism entails hostility towards a radical gender politics, which constitutes more than a simple backlash against feminism (Faludi 1991). Rather, feminism is widely celebrated as a successful movement that has given women an unprecedented opportunity to determine their own lives, free from previous constraints. Feminism is considered to have done its work, and gender and gendered power relations are no longer seen to structure women's (or men's) lives. Instead, young women are constructed as subjects of choice. This interpellation has, however, justified a renewed attachment to heavily circumscribed prescriptions of femininity (McRobbie 2009). Youthful femininity is embossed with norms of whiteness and heterosexuality and focused on being sexually attractive and in pursuit of a husband. Yet women are seen to follow this normative script, not because they are forced to by social custom or prohibitions on their actions, but because they freely choose to do so (McRobbie 2009: 22).

Normative, youthful femininity is one preparing for the role of mother: finding a good partner, attaining qualifications, and beginning a career to ensure her future motherhood will not pose a burden on the state in terms of the provision of welfare (McRobbie 2013: 131). Women's choices, then, are normatively constructed as pivoting around motherhood. Motherhood is also the standard upon which women's choices are evaluated; as Pam Lowe observes, '"proper" women' are expected to 'put the welfare of children, whether born, *in utero*, or not yet conceived, over and above any choice or desires of their own. The idea of maternal sacrifice acts as a powerful signifier in judging women's behaviour' (2016: 3). The importance of female labour to the post-industrial economy, and women's desires to work, has meant that the highly gendered roles of housewife and breadwinner are not as pronounced as they were before the WLM (McRobbie 2013: 121). Motherhood nevertheless remains central to femininity; the ideology of maternal sacrifice regulates women's behaviour (Lowe 2016), and the cultural meanings of parenthood differ along gendered lines. In the mass media, for example, there remains a celebration of 'opting-out' and 'stay-at-home mothers'—only, however, for the white middle- and upper-class elites whose partners can afford to support them financially (Kuperberg and Stone 2008; Orgad and De Benedictis 2015). In other contexts, women are expected to adapt their working lives to accommodate the demands of parenting, as evinced in the repeated circulation of phrases such as 'work/life' balance and 'flexible workplace arrange- ments', used to describe the working lives of mothers (but generally not fathers). And, indeed, women are significantly more likely than men to reduce their work hours to care for small children (Dieckhoff et al. 2016; Treas and Lui 2013). A recent Australian study (Australian Institute of Family Studies 2017) has shown that women also do slightly more child caring (two hours per week) in the small number of families where mothers work full time and their male partners stay at home (4 per cent of families have stay-at-home fathers in Australia, compared to 31 per cent with stay-at-home-mothers).

The ideologies and practices of parenthood remain heavily gendered, a gendering often hidden behind the rhetoric of 'choice'. Choice is the most frequently deployed explanatory schema used to describe why women have children and alter their work patterns to care for them. For example, the British sociologist Catherine Hakim argues that the large majority of women prefer to sacrifice their paid employment to focus on motherhood upon the birth of a child, and that mothers were therefore satisfied with 'lower grade and lower paid jobs' in exchange for flexible workplace arrangements (Hakim 1995: 534). Hakim's work is heavily criticised within the social sciences (Ginn et al. 1996; McRae 2003). Nevertheless, in Australia, the conservative Coalition Government led by Prime Minister John Howard (1996–2007) cited Hakim's 'realistic and compelling' research in several policy speeches and sponsored her tour of Australia in 2003 (Campo 2009: 101–102). Armed with Hakim's 'preference theory', Howard (2005) proposed that policies favouring stay-at-home mothers adhered to 'the principle of choice and freedom of choice for Australian women'; such policies included the refusal to grant women maternity leave and the introduction of income splitting, which gave significant tax breaks to heterosexual couples with children on a single or primary income (Hill 2007: 241). Two key policy documents in the UK from the early 2000s similarly emphasised 'choice' in titles such as 'enhancing choice' and 'choice and competitiveness', even though the policies effectively opened up, facilitated, or closed down the choices available to women so that lone parents were coerced into finding employment, and partnered women were given tax credits so that, as one document put it, 'mothers who wish to leave work ... will find it easier' (cited in Himmelweit and Sigala 2004). The rhetoric of personal choice conceals the structural barriers and cultural norms that position women and men differentially when it comes to work and family life. Such obstacles include the gendering of care work, the high cost of childcare and shortage of childcare places, the gender wage gap, and the continued model of the 'ideal worker' as a person unencumbered by domestic and reproductive responsibilities (Friedman 2015; Hill 2007; McRae 2003; Pocock 2003).

The disavowal of the explanatory power of gender for understanding patterns in men and women's labour has been achieved through the dismissal of feminism's radical gender politics. From the mid-1990s onward, feminism has been characterised as a movement concerned solely with individual career advancement (Campo 2009), as redundant because women enjoyed formal equality and freedom of choice (McRobbie 2009), and as out of touch with the maternal-centred desires of most women (Henderson 2006). These interrelated claims reached a height of cultural expression with the so-termed 'mummy (mommy) wars', a transnational, media-generated narrative that blamed feminism, in Chilla Bulbeck's words, 'for telling women they could "have it all"—combine career and motherhood—producing a genera- tion of childless career women, stressed out working mothers and denigrated housewives' (2010: 27; also see Campo 2005; Milkie et al. 2016). As an example of this discourse, Australian journalist Virginia Haussegar (2002, 2005) wrote a book and series of newspaper articles where she accused her feminist foremothers of persuading her that 'female fulfilment came with a leather briefcase' instead of motherhood: 'I am childless and I am angry. Angry that I was so foolish to take the word of my feminist mothers as gospel' (2002). Other prominent Australian women joined Haussegar's offensive. Ita Buttrose, one of Australia's best known 'career mums', attributed 'the guilt mothers felt regarding their children … to the gaining of "choices" at the time of Women's Liberation'; these choices, she implied, distracted women from stay-at-home mother- hood, which was 'every woman's dream' (Adams and Buttrose 2005: 4, 207). In a favourably reviewed book and several journal articles, journalist Anne Manne (2005) added that children need the full-time care of their mothers. To make this argument, Manne drew on Gilligan's ethic of care, as Cannold had done, to claim that most feminists devalued femininity, a natural sentiment geared towards the selfless nurturing of other people.[1]

Choice for women is often represented as entailing two incompatible options: motherhood or a career, with the choices made expressing whether or not women hold properly oriented, selfless sensibilities, or disoriented, unfeminine, self-interested ones (Hays 1998: 16). With women's life paths reduced to a series of choices, the convergence of women's choices around motherhood has amounted to a re-naturalisation of motherhood through choice. Claims about women's happiness are central to this new femininity; feminism, so it is frequently claimed, orients women towards the wrong happy object, the career, and away from the only authentic source of women's happiness in motherhood. The availability of the choice of abortion has been integral to this overall, postfeminist reinscription of maternal identity. This chapter develops a theoretical framework for thinking about how happiness orients women in normative directions, which will provide a lens through which to understand how motherhood can materialise as a woman's choice even when she chooses abortion.

HAPPY CHOICES

It has become a commonsense dictum to declare that happiness is the ultimate measure of individual success and personal satisfaction. Happiness orders our lives, giving them purpose and meaning (Ahmed 2010a: 572). Following Sara Ahmed, I argue that this conceptualisation of happiness does not relate to what happiness actually is, but gives happiness its normative authority. Happiness is not a quality that resides in people or objects, but a force that pulls us towards objects perceived to ensure our happiness. Happy objects are designated as such before individuals experience them as happy. Happiness can therefore operate as a promise that directs individuals through the belief that 'if you do this or if you have that, then happiness is what follows' (Ahmed 2010a: 576). Ahmed describes happiness scripts as 'straightening devices, ways of aligning bodies with what is already lined up' (2010b: 91). This 'already' is a profoundly normative vision of the world that animates our conformity to predetermined life paths; the promise of happiness transforms social norms into social goods and socio-cultural normativity into personal desire, individualising and depoliticising social, structural, and cultural mechanisms of power (Ahmed 2010a: 572).

Ahmed singles out marriage and reproduction as key happy objects for women, focusing on the figure of the 'happy housewife'. The housewife performs domestic tasks, so it is imagined, not because others direct her to, but because domesticity promises to bring women happiness. The promise of happiness impels women towards marriage and motherhood; and the 'claim that women are happy and that this happiness is behind the work they do functions to justify gendered forms of labor, not as products of nature, law, or duty, but as expressions of a collective wish and desire' (Ahmed 2010a: 572–573).

The norms of women's happiness that circulate in the postfeminist discourses discussed above position a child of one's own as *the* happiest object for women, and particularly for pregnant women. In this way, for pregnant women, the foetus (as it is discursively inscribed) is a fantasy figure that contains a 'cluster of promises' (Berlant 2007) relating to women's happiness, individual success, and personal fulfillment. Happiness, and the conceptualisation of children (and foetuses) as happy objects, provides the momentum that aligns women with the 'narrative of natural development' that, as the introduction to this book outlined, positions girls and young women on a trajectory towards motherhood and designates pregnant women as already mothers (Berlant 1997: 99). In pointing out the labour that this happiness script disguises, feminists are represented as 'kill joys' (Ahmed 2010a), accused of refusing to share an orientation towards children as sources of happiness and, in narratives such as Haussegar's, literally diminishing the happiness of women by orienting them towards the wrong happy object—the career.

Maternal pro-choice rhetoric presumes that all women are oriented towards their children as happy objects, yet in some circumstances, a woman's desire to parent must be put on hold for the benefit of her 'could-be-child'. As Bertha Alvarez Manninen expresses this formation: 'Many women have a precise idea of what it means to be a good mother and they are honest that, at the present time, they fall short of this ideal' (2013: 665). The idea that a woman can express her maternal desire through the seemingly paradoxical choice of abortion involves a judgement about which women should defer their own happiness for their potential children. Such judgement is predicated on the stratification of maternal happiness along several axes, including those of race, age and class.

FAMILIAL HAPPINESS

> The good woman is good in part because of ... how she aligns her happiness with the happiness of others. (Sara Ahmed 2010b: 55)

Sara Ahmed writes of a link between happiness and virtue—the happy person is also the virtuous person because '[i]deas of happiness involve social as well as moral distinctions insofar as they rest on ideas of who is worthy as well as capable of being happy "in the right way"' (2010b: 13). The repeated attribution of happiness to the figure of the child/foetus orients all women towards motherhood. In the social imaginary, the compromised happiness of the children of certain mothers means, however, that women occupy the fantasy of maternal happiness differentially. Mothers are only deemed to be truly happy, virtuous (selfless) and 'good' when they are perceived to bring their children happiness; markers such as social class and age distinguish the virtuous mother from other mothers, who are positioned as undeserving, immature, bad or selfish. Within the economy of female happiness, therefore, the foetus features as a happy object, orienting women towards motherhood, as well as a happy subject, productive of the figure of the 'good mother'.

With the rise of neoliberal political rationality in advanced liberal democracies, 'welfare mums' have become particularly visible exemplars of bad motherhood (McRobbie 2013: 120; Tyler 2008a). The individualisation of reproductive and domestic labour, which is often, as described above, operationalised through the rhetoric of 'choice', scripts individuals on welfare support as failures, as evinced in coercive state policies that compel mothers on welfare 'back to work' (Blaxland 2010; Hill 2006; Shaver 2002). Discriminatory and coercive policies targeting single mothers are rationalised through the belief that mothers who depend on welfare orient themselves towards happiness in a deformed way because they cannot, it is widely presumed, ensure their children's happiness. The negative characterisation of 'teen mums'—another abject maternal figure with transnational purchase—also needs to be seen in the context of the more general derision of welfare (Lowe 2016: 52–55; Simic 2010). As McRobbie asserts '[m]iddle class respectable status requires the refusal of early motherhood', for young women are expected to 'postpone early maternity to accrue the economic advantages of employment and occupational identity and thus contribute to the solving of the crisis of welfare' (2007: 731–732).

Legislation that denies lesbian and single women access to *in vitro* fertilisation (IVF) technologies has also been rationalised through recourse to the happiness of children that, ironically, such legislation aims to prevent from being conceived (Smith 2003). Until 2008, 'the need of a child for a father' (McCandless and Sheldon 2010) was the rationale behind such discriminatory legislation in the UK, and this was the argument forwarded when the Australian government attempted, unsuccessfully, in 2000 to change the Sex Discrimination Act 1984 (Cth) to prevent states from providing lesbian and single women access to IVF services (Baird 2004; Johnson 2003).

In settler-colonial contexts, representations of the 'good mother' are built into the colonial project; she is constructed as non-Indigenous (white) through the discourse of maternal and parental neglect in Indigenous communities (Jacobs 2009; Kline 1993). In a recent, particularly notorious example of this more general trend, in 2007, the Australian government responded to a report detailing the physical and sexual abuse of children in seventy-three Indigenous communities in the Northern Territory with a series of emergency legislations that breached its obligations under International Law and the Racial Discrimination Act 1975 (Cth), including the forceful inspection of children under the age of sixteen for signs of abuse. The government cited the breakdown of 'normal community standards and parenting behaviours' (Brough 2007) as justification for this intervention.

The discourse of child neglect has also been used to legitimate the dehumanising treatment of asylum seekers (Leach 2003). To return to the context of Australia, in 2001, the Commonwealth government falsely claimed that asylum seekers arriving by sea had thrown their children overboard in an attempt to gain political refuge. Then Prime Minister John Howard notoriously declared on radio that 'I certainly don't want people of that type in Australia', thus powerfully differentiating 'that type' from the Australian 'us' via the shocking imagery of children being abandoned by their parents to the ravages of the open sea (cited in Grove and Zwi 2006: 1937). 'Our' happy children were thereby distinguished from 'their' unhappy ones, with the figure of the 'unhappy child' joining Aboriginal and asylum-seeker families together, providing 'the moral justification for government policy that denies human rights' (Baird 2008a: 295).

Within the economy of female happiness, then, a woman's happiness in her children can only be deemed normatively selfless (virtuous and good), as opposed to selfish, when she can guarantee her children's happiness. The economy of maternal happiness enables us to see how a woman's maternal desire can lead her to choose abortion: she wants children, but nevertheless selflessly terminates her pregnancy in order to protect her existing children or gather the resources deemed necessary for her to ensure her children's happiness in the future (Lowe 2016: 47). Reverberating with the stereotype of the 'desperate aborting woman' introduced in Chapter 1, the economy of familial happiness provides the conditions that can legitimate the otherwise illegitimate choice of abortion.

The rest of this chapter applies the concepts I have sketched thus far, those of maternal pro-choice politics and the economy of familial happiness, to parliamentary discussions of abortion. This involves unpacking an 'abortion common sense' that transverses several national contexts and includes a preoccupation with why women have abortions and stereotypes such as the 'selfish abortion' and the 'difficult choice'.

NEOLIBERAL ABORTION

Parliamentary debates provide a snapshot of discourses through which abortion is made meaningful in the broader community. Parliamentarians must construct the subjects of law—for example, the women who have abortions and the figure of the foetus—in order to justify their position on legislative change, and legal discourse 'marshals the coercive power of the state behind certain vocabularies instead of others' (Condit 1990: 97). The relationship between legal and public discourses means that parliamentary debates provide insight into the modes of rationale that underpin the two primary forms of power in the contemporary world: juridical—the imposition of external restrictions on individuals that work to coerce particular behaviours through the threat of punishment; and productive—the normative codes of behaviour that incite individuals to monitor their own behaviour according to social expectations and the rewards that accompany those who aspire towards such expectations (Butler 1990: 2).

Scholars of the contemporary, late-modern era argue that there has been a shift from juridical to productive modes of power (Rose 1999). This insight urges us to consider what, if any, productive modes of power have moved in to replace the law as a mode of regulating women's abortion conduct. I argue here that abortion laws were liberalised in Australia because parliamentarians were confident that women would only 'resort' to abortion in exceptional cases. Their confidence was based on the presumption that pregnant women are inevitably oriented towards their foetuses as happy objects and, therefore, abortion is an incredibly difficult choice for women to make. Parliamentarians widely believed that women, to put this differently, regulated their own conduct in relation to abortion, making restrictive laws unnecessary.

As stated in the introduction to this book, the Australian case study provides a unique context for examining the normative assumptions that inform liberal laws relating to abortion; the language parliamentarians have used when discussing abortion in Australia is also echoed elsewhere. For example, Ellie Lee notes that British parliamentarians debating the Human Fertilisation and Embryology Act of 1990 presented women who had abortions as 'deserving of sympathy ... [or]

women's need for abortion was justified through an appeal to their desire to be good mothers' (2003: 88). Parliamentarians described abortion as a 'tragedy' (V. Bottomley, MP), a decision women 'agonise about' (Mahon, MP), 'a desperate measure for desperate situations' (Primarolo, MP), and something women 'suffer' and 'endure' (Doran, MP) (cited in Lee 2003: 88). When forwarding her bill to decriminalise abortion in the British parliament in 2017, Diana Johnson asked her fellow MPs to prioritise the interests of 'the vulnerable women who are ill-served by our current laws' (United Kingdom 2017). Australian parliamentarians deployed similar tropes of vulnerability and a 'difficult choice' to justify their support of liberal abortion laws.

When considering parliamentary debates on abortion it is important to emphasise that the state (through its laws) cannot actually control whether women have abortions. The law does not affect the frequency of abortion, but only whether they are safe and affordable, and, to a degree, the methods employed (Finer and Fine 2013). In the debates discussed here, many parliamentarians implicitly acknowledged the law's limited hold over the practice of abortion, arguing that current laws were out of step with clinical practice. Alternatively, the opponents' seeming attachment to the law may betray a delusion of control over a process that, through virtue of their bodies, they would never fully control (Brown 1995: 141). Support and opposition for the two bills was heavily gendered—the vast majority of female parliamentarians supported the two bills, and the significant majority of opponents were men.[2] Restrictions on abortion place abortion decisions (formally if not in practice) under the control of (traditionally male-dominated) social institutions, particularly medicine and the law, instead of with individual women (Baird 1996; Sheldon 1993). Yet the law is not merely a system that imposes punishment for wrongdoing, it prescribes and formalises a society's normative morality (Cook 2014; Smart 1990). Thus instead of debating whether or not women should be prohibited from having abortions under the law, parliamentarians debating abortion are often concerned with how and whether abortion fits into a normative or idealised worldview.

A SELFLESS DECISION

In Australia, the 2000s witnessed a period of intense public discussion on the issue of abortion on a scale not witnessed since the 1970s (Baird 2013). The parliamentary debates examined here were legislative responses to a growing conservative tide in the nation's abortion politics (explored in Chapter 5). In 2006, a Private Member's bill in the Commonwealth parliament overturned legislation enacted in 1996 that had effectively banned the importation of the medical abortifacient RU486 into Australia. Since 2002, four state and territory parliaments—the Australian Capital Territory (2002), Victoria (2008), Tasmania (2013) and the Northern Territory (2017)—have also decriminalised abortion. I focus here on the Commonwealth and Victorian debates—the first because of its national scope, and the second as an example of the rhetoric used when politicians are debating the decriminalisation of abortion.[3] Of the four jurisdictions where abortion is now legal in Australia, Victoria is the most populous and its debate was by far the most expansive. These bills are examined together to emphasise the synergy in the representation of the women who had abortions between parliamentarians debating the two bills and, more surprisingly, between those who opposed and supported them.

Parliamentarians who supported the bills placed great emphasis on the reasons women terminate their pregnancies. While they unanimously condoned abortions performed to preserve a woman's physical and psychological health, in cases of severe foetal abnormality, or when the pregnancy was a consequence of rape or incest, the majority expressed uneasiness over the practice of abortion for so-called 'social' reasons. As one Member of the Victorian Legislative Council stated, 'I wish it [abortion] did not happen except in cases of emergencies or difficult circumstances. The majority of people with whom I have discussed the bill share this view' (Eideh, MLC; Victoria 2008e: 4149). Another went so far as to state that for reasons 'such as incest or rape or where scanning of the foetus shows severe abnormalities that mean the foetus will not survive', abortions are 'easy to talk about' (Leanne, MLC; Victoria 2008d: 4008). In the context of abortion, rape and incest are designated as 'easy' discussion points because women's desires and self-interests are removed from the sexual intercourse that led to pregnancy. Abortions performed for foetal health can be rationalised through recourse to the happiness of future children, and, along with those performed for maternal health, descriptions of such abortions generally represent women as terminating much wanted and desired pregnancies, ensuring that the child/foetus remains in place as a happy object.

Supporters also represented abortions for so-called 'social' reasons in a way that maintained a woman's orientation towards her foetus or future child as a happy object, claiming that desperate circumstances drove women to terminate their pregnancies. Supporters deemed such circumstances to be 'desperate' (Theophanus, MLC; Victoria 2008e: 4092), 'traumatic' (Nairn, MP; Australia 2006d: 69), 'terrible' (Barber, MLC; Victoria 2008: 4151), 'tragic' (Pennicuik, MLC; Victoria 2008e: 4161; Gibbons, MP; Australia 2006d: 153), 'unfortunate, regrettable' (Albanese, MP; Australia 2006c: 94), 'frightening' (Gibbons, MP; Australia 2006d: 153), and 'never envisaged and not necessarily of their own making' (Koch, MLC; Victoria 2008e: 4157). They routinely framed the conditions compelling women to terminate their pregnancies in terms of lack: aborting women, for example, had not completed their education, did not have sufficient social support, lacked the necessary financial resources, their contraception failed or they 'just cannot cope with one more child—they cannot cope physically, emotionally, mentally, financially or for some other reason' (Plibersek, MP; Australia 2006c: 46).

By emphasising the reasons that women terminate their pregnancies, pro-choice parliamentarians drew on a long tradition in public health research concerned with the 'type' of woman who terminates her pregnancy—charting factors such as her age, marital status and religion—and the reasons women give for terminating their pregnancies (Abigail et al. 2008; Nickson et al. 2004; Rowe et al. 2009). As others have argued (Baird 2006a: 142; Ryan, Ripper and Buttfield 1994: 10), such research works to construct women who terminate their pregnancies as deviations from the norm and aim, explicitly or otherwise, to locate those women most 'at risk' of abortion in order to alter the variables leading them to abortion. Not surprisingly, a major theme in both debates was the need for more support services to enable women to continue with their pregnancies: '[i]nstead of applying penalties to women facing an abortion, this parliament should be working hard to alleviate the problems and concerns that can force women to the point where they have to make a decision about an abortion' (Lundy, Senator; Australia 2006b: 42).

More support services are certainly required to ensure that women do not terminate otherwise wanted pregnancies for economic reasons. In the context of these debates, however, parliamentarians emphasised contextual reasons for abortion not to advocate for the expansion of health and welfare services, but to present women as 'compelled' (R. Smith, MLA; Victoria 2008a: 3362) or 'forced' (Lindsay, MP; Australia 2006c: 96) to terminate their pregnancies because they 'see no option but abortion' (G. Howard, MLA; Victoria 2008a: 3385). The trope of compulsion blurred the distinction between women who would like to continue with pregnancies if circumstances were different and those who, regardless of circumstance, no longer want to be pregnant and do not want to be mothers now, at all, or to another child. The suggestion that the state could alleviate the 'problems and concerns' that compel pregnant women to terminate their pregnancies left no room for the possibility that some pregnant women do not want to remain pregnant and become mothers to the embryos or foetuses they are carrying. In this context, a freely desired and chosen abortion was an impossibility, an impossibility communicated by one MLA who declared in her support of abortion that '[t]here is no way a person would choose to have an abortion … just because her pregnancy was unwanted' (Powell, MLA; Victoria 2008a: 3349–3350). Abortion was not framed as a choice equal to continuing with a pregnancy, therefore, but as 'a last resort for all women' (Viney, MLC; Victoria 2008d: 3928), and the 'awfulisation' of abortion remained firmly in place.

By affirming that a woman's abortion decision 'must be based on her own circumstances and life situation' (Johnson, MP; Australia 2006d: 30–31), parliamentarians afforded women formal choice on the condition that they approach this choice after 'careful consideration' (Lindsay, MP; Australia 2006c: 96). Drawing on the 'killing from care' ethic voiced by Leslie Cannold, supporters trusted women to make appropriate and responsible decisions. Tanya Plibersek, one of Australia's best known female politicians, described pro-choice politics as the belief 'that for most women it is a terribly difficult thing to decide to terminate a pregnancy, but we respect women enough to believe they have the ability and the right to make such decisions for themselves' (Australia 2006c: 46). By suggesting that, for most women, abortion was a 'terribly difficult' decision, supporters made suffering the only intelligible position from which to approach the abortion decision. The reasons they emphasised when depicting the women 'forced' to terminate their pregnancies also produced a 'type' of woman most suitable for motherhood. Abortions among teenagers or women who would require state support to raise a child were hyper-visible, while those among post-teen, middle-class women in stable, heterosexual relationships were invisible.

The parameters of an acceptable social abortion were set by the economy of familial happiness, although talk of race was muted, subsumed to discussions of welfare dependency.[4] The differentiation between social abortions and those performed for rape, incest, and foetal or maternal health in one instance, and within social abortions for those performed for 'legitimate' (hypervisible) and 'illegitimate' (invisible) reasons accord with attitudes towards abortion amongst the general population. Opinion polls consistently show that, while most Australians broadly support a 'woman's right to choose', just over 50 per cent support abortion in cases outside of threats to maternal health, foetal deformity, relationship status and poverty (Baird 2006b: 207). Opinion polls in the USA (Pollitt 2014: 47–48), Britain (YouGov 2011), and Canada (Angus Reid 2013) show a similar pattern: not only do those polled generally view themselves as capable of judging the legitimacy, or otherwise, of a woman's abortion choice, but this legitimacy is granted on a scale where, as Pam Lowe observes, 'good abortions' are those when women are perceived to delay motherhood until she is able to 'put any child's interest first' (2016: 69) and 'bad abortions' are those where women are seen to place 'their own lives above that of the foetus and thus failing to act as appropriate women' (2016: 67).[5] Katha Pollitt unpacks the logic of such attitudes, stating that 'If you really mean what you tell pollsters, your respect for "life" is entirely conditional. It depends not on any quality of the embryo or fetus—you're willing to dispose of it if the reason meets your approval—but on your judgment of the pregnant woman' (2014: 49).

In the debates, poverty, youth and relationship instability formed the boundaries of an acceptable 'social' abortion. The narrative of acceptability was reconfirmed in the language two female parliamentarians used to describe their personal experiences of abortion in support of the Victorian bill for decriminalisation. Senator Lyn Allison (2008) described the abortion she had when she was eighteen years old thus: 'I had a boyfriend, but I wasn't interested in marrying him ... Neither of us had any money. And being pregnant outside of marriage was not acceptable in my family'. MLC Colleen Hartland had an abortion when she was twenty-two years old to escape a 'cycle of poverty' (cited in Nader 2008), and stressed the undesirability of abortion in her contribution to the Victorian debate:

> I do not believe pro-choice advocates like abortion; women who have had abortions do not like abortion. Abortion is never an easy choice for a woman, but we want it to be safe and we want it to be legal so that women no longer feel they are some kind of criminal. (Victoria 2008c: 3915–3916)

Parliamentarians who supported reducing the legal restrictions on abortion did not represent women as autonomous subjects of choice, but as vulnerable and powerless victims of circumstance. Their speeches thus show similarity with the paternalism inherent in ALRA's activism (Chapter 1). Supporters justified the abortion choice through the somewhat paradoxical claim that, in some circumstances, women had no choice but to terminate their pregnancies: abortion, thus, figured as a necessity rather than a choice made to realise a (non-maternal) desire. The social directive placed on women to justify their abortions in terms of financial, social or some other lack is a variation on the test of necessity prescribed in laws that medicalised abortion at the turn of the 1970s. Parliamentarians did not argue that abortion should be a woman's choice without justification, but presumed that women only had abortions under extreme circumstances; and because 'people's circumstances will always be unique', women were best positioned to determine whether they should have abortions (Linsday, MP; Australia 2006c: 96). By placing external circumstances as the cause of a woman's abortion, 'pro-choice' parliamentarians represented aborting women as temporarily 'held back' from doing what would make them happy. Aborting women stray from the ideal—they are disoriented. Sentiments such as 'women often stray through no fault of their own' and they 'don't *choose* to stray' are technologies of re-orientation, realigning aborting women with what is already 'lined up' (Ahmed 2006: 92)—a norm where pregnant women are oriented towards their foetuses as happy objects.

A SELFISH ABORTION OR DIFFICULT CHOICE

The emphasis on women's reasons for abortion was a defence against the stereotype of the 'selfish aborting woman', the strength of which placed supporters on the defensive, making expressions such as 'I genuinely believe it is not a procedure that is sought on a selfish whim' commonplace (Shardey, MLA; Victoria 2008a: 3928). The emphasis on selfless abortions, however, amounted to a reverse discourse that recapitulated the connection between abortion and selfishness it attempted to displace (Foucault 1990: 101). The rhetorical association between abortion and selfishness framed the major questions of the debates: would the respective pieces of legislation make abortion easier for women, lead to more abortions, to abortion 'on demand' or to 'convenience abortions'?

The goals of 'abortion on demand' and 'abortion rights' have carried negative connotations since activists began campaigning for them (Pollitt 2014: 29; Solinger 2001: 406). The use of the word 'demand' to communicate the political goal of removing legal restrictions on abortion implies an unwavering and stubborn desire that sits uncomfortably with normative femininity. For this reason, those advocating for abortion rights with no explicit gender politics have generally avoided the phrase. The Abortion Law Reform Association (1971), for example, advocated for 'abortion on request', believing 'on demand' held 'unnecessarily authoritarian overtones'. The Royal Commission of 1977 similarly defined abortion on demand as when 'the woman asserts a right to abortion regardless of the doctor's professional opinion' (Evatt 1977, v1: 156). For Leslie Cannold, the phrase 'on demand' failed to describe 'the complex and difficult decision-making process engaged in by a woman faced with an unwanted pregnancy' (2000: 61). In contrast, the Women's Abortion Action Coalition (WAAC) embraced the notion of 'demand' precisely because of its incongruity with a passive, maternal femininity (Albury 1979). The phrase 'on demand' frequently joins the notion of 'convenience abortion' to provide justification for retaining legal restrictions on women's access to abortion. Several politicians and journalists, for example, used the phrases repeatedly when expressing their opposition to the two bills discussed here (see, for example, Nader and Rood 2007; Shaw 2004).

While women who have abortions for no discernible or acceptable economic or social 'reason' were invisible amongst supporters of the two bills, they were hypervisible in the statements made by opponents, who repeatedly invoked the established fear of women's 'unfettered access' to abortion (Santoro, Senator; Australia 2006a: 123). Abortions, they repeatedly stated, were 'casual choices' related to lifestyle and convenience that signalled the commodification of children and parenthood in contemporary society. Australian women's access to RU486, it was feared, would turn 'the world's greatest vocation into a social convenience' (Heffernan, Senator; Australia 2006b: 44); it was a sign of 'our self-indulgent, convenient, modern, easy contemporary Australian lifestyle, [where] children are now seen in some sections as consumers and polluters and just plain hard work' (Vale, MP; Australia

2006d: 45). Some opponents implied that women had abortions solely to exercise a specifically female form of autonomy, even becoming pregnant just to do so:

> [T]hey do not need to be dictated to by anybody—that is their angle … [and opponents of abortion] are told, 'get out of the road. It's a woman's right to get pregnant. It's a woman's right to have an abortion. Don't you dare impose your will on my right to live my life the way I want to live it'. (Drum, MLC; Victoria 2008d: 3995)

Opponents argued that surgery and anaesthesia (in the case of the Commonwealth debate) and criminality (in the Victorian debate) placed necessary obstacles in between women and the abortions they desired. In the Victorian debate, opponents feared the decriminalisation of abortion would give women 'unfettered … open-slather access to abortion … [for] any and every reason' (Rich-Philips, MLC; Victoria 2008e: 4140). Abortion would be performed solely on the 'insistence of the mother', which would 'see women simply proceeding with an abortion as a matter of a process [and] that seems not just to be supportive at this point but to me almost borders on trying to be encouraging' (Atkinson, MLC; Victoria 2008c). Commonwealth parliamentarians were concerned that the availability of medical abortion would expand women's access to abortion and make the procedure more comfortable and straightforward, leading women to approach abortion with less hesitancy. One Liberal MP stated, 'I do believe that a woman having to see her doctor and go through a surgical procedure performed by a doctor gives her time to pause, reflect and change her mind' (Pyne, MP; Australia 2006c: 91); another claimed that the availability of RU486 would 'send a powerful message … that we as a community are becoming more indifferent to, or blasé about, abortion' (Robb, MP; Australia 2006d: 3). An opponent from the Labor Party employed similar rhetoric: '[s]ome have argued that RU486 … provides women with a choice that will make abortion easier for them and more readily available… [but] for me, "more" and "easier" does not necessarily mean better' (Hayes, MP; Australia 2006d: 158). Comments such as these show that many parliamentarians opposed the bills because they believed abortion should be difficult to obtain, stigmatised by the community, invasive, and uncomfortable; they therefore desired to obstruct women's access to abortion and, moreover, punish women who have abortions. This was a point made by Tanya Plibersek, who argued that the opponents strived to make abortion 'as difficult as possible to teach them a lesson … a punishment for having had sex with anything but procreation in mind' (Australia 2006c: 46–47).

With few exceptions, supporters did not counter suggestions that abortion should never be easy or convenient with the argument that abortion should be a comfortable, straightforward procedure women have ready access to; they argued that doctors would continue to play a major role in the procedure, and, moreover, that abortion can never be easy for women and no woman terminated a pregnancy simply for her convenience. Then Deputy Leader of the Federal Opposition, Jenny Macklin, stated, 'I do not know any woman who would find abortion an easy choice; it is always a difficult and emotional decision' (Australia 2006c: 52–53). Many parliamentarians based their support on the apparent fact that abortion was an extraordinarily difficult decision and traumatic procedure (Chapter 3). The idea that abortion is a difficult decision was seemingly a mandatory statement, made by the majority of supporters in both debates. Liberal MLC Wendy Lovell opined in the Victorian debate, for example, that 'I believe the decision to terminate a pregnancy is one that … women agonise over. The women who make that heart-wrenching decision deserve to be supported by legislation that provides them with the safeguards they deserve' (Victoria 2008c: 3910). This rationale implied that there should be no interference in women's abortion decisions because they were already 'punished enough by … their own conscience[s]' (Ley, MP; Australia 2006c).

Anti-abortion political views usually coincide with the belief that women are biologically programmed for mother-hood (Begun and Walls 2015). The opponents' insistence that women terminated their pregnancies for selfish reasons seems to contradict this trend, implying instead that all women are not selflessly maternal. Opponents countered this impli-cation, however, by proclaiming that women 'do not freely choose' (Kairouz, MLA; Victoria 2008a: 3334) abortion, but are coerced into abortion by abortionists, family members or partners. Alternately, women make the 'culturally conditioned' (Abbott cited in Noble 2005) choice to terminate their preg-nancies because Australia's 'convenient, instant, high-tech indulgent society' (Vale, MP; Australia 2006d: 45) tells 'young women that in some way parenting is not desirable and that it is demeaning to be a parent or a mother' (Petrovich, MLC; Victoria 2008e: 4123). For opponents, retaining legal restrictions on abortion would help re-orient women considering abortion in the right direction, re-installing children as happy objects. The idea that women have abortions against their true wishes or best interests is a salient feature of transnational abortion politics and allows opponents to argue for restrictions on abortion on the basis that they are actually helping women make the right choice (Siegal 2007); that they are protecting 'deeply conflicted and vulnerable' women from coercion by others (Merlino, MLA; Victoria 2008a: 3314): 'I believe that a woman does have the right to make her own choices, but unfortunately the pressure to have an abortion as a first option and the pressure that is applied to women often sees them making choices they regret' (Petrovich, MLC; Victoria 2008e: 4124).[6]

Whether parliamentarians depicted abortion as a decision that *was* never easy or convenient, or as a practice that should never be easy or convenient, the representation of abortion as a straightforward, convenient procedure that women should have the capacity to freely demand was either elided or deemed illegitimate. The arguments for and against the two bills were mutually reinforcing, hinging on and reinforcing the validity of a normative schema that presumes all pregnant women are oriented towards their foetuses as happy objects. While opponents wanted to enforce this norm through formal restrictions on women's choices, supporters believed no restrictions were necessary because women were always already aligned with the schema of maternal happiness. Both supporters and opponents attached penalties to aborting women's transgression from the maternal norm. For supporters, aborting women always suffer and punish themselves. For opponents, the criminalisation of abortion or a surgical procedure ensured that abortion was never easy or convenient. Parliamentarians unanimously characterised women who had abortions as vulnerable and in need of protection, whether through retaining (opponents) or decreasing (supporters) limitations on abortion. Both supporters and opponents argued, in very different ways, that women were forced to have abortions— by external circumstances beyond their control (supporters) or by cultural conditioning or coercion (opponents). The legitimate aborting woman invoked by supporters of the bills agonised over the 'heart-breaking' decision of abortion; the illegitimate aborting woman called upon by opponents held a deviant, self-interested desire that was a result of coercion and needed curtailment. The historically-sedimented binary between the 'good', suffering aborting woman and the 'bad', selfish aborting woman (Chapter 1) was thereby restated. This binary eclipsed the subject position of the unwillingly pregnant woman and the legitimacy of self-interested abortions: the idea that, for pregnant women, immediate non-pregnant bodies, childlessness or no more children may be happy objects achievable only through abortion appeared unspeakable.

AFFECT ALIENS

A women-centred abortion morality was present in the debates, articulated through themes such as enforced maternity and bodily integrity (for example, Allison, Senator;

Australia 2006c: 94; Plibersek, MP; Australia 2006c: 46–47).
In general, however, parliamentarians who supported the bills
rarely articulated a political or moral 'pro-choice' framework.
This avoidance was enabled by the common claim (which
showed a surprising unfamiliarity with abortion law) that 'the
battle over abortion and a woman's right to choose was fought
and won 20 years ago' (Gash, MP; Australia 2006d: 144).
Parliamentarians overwhelmingly represented their support
for the bills in terms of process: in the Commonwealth
debate, the means by which a pharmaceutical was assessed
for release in Australia; and, in Victoria, aligning the law with
clinical practice and community attitudes. When introducing
the bill she co-sponsored, National Party Senator Fiona Nash
claimed it 'is not about abortion ... We live in a society in
which termination is lawful ... This debate is not about being
pro-choice or pro-life' (Australia 2006a: 89). Similarly, the
then Leader of the Opposition stated in the Victorian debate:
'this is not a debate between choice and no choice ... [or]
about abortion or no abortion ... The choice for women is
available ... [this] is a debate about whether abortion should
be regulated predominantly under the Health Act or under
the Crimes Act' (Ballieu, MLC; Victoria 2008a: 3312). By
acknowledging that medical doctors performed abortions
for reasons in excess of the letter of the law, many supporters
argued that decriminalising abortion would ensure it was
regulated more effectively (El-Murr 2010).

In contrast, opponents of both bills presented themselves
as 'moral crusaders' and clearly articulated an anti-abortion
politics centred on belief in foetal life (Robb, MP; Australia

2006d: 3). In the Commonwealth debate, opponents argued that RU486 was not a therapeutic drug because, in the words of the Health Minister Tony Abbott, 'it does not improve life and it does not extend life; it stops babies from being born' (Australia 2006d: 114). As such, so the argument went, elected officials with accountability to the public should assess the approval of RU486's use in Australia, rather than the 'faceless bureaucrats' of the Therapeutic Goods Administration, who assessed all other forms of medication (Brandis, Senator; Australia 2006b: 24). Similarly, the majority of opponents of the Victorian bill argued that abortion was not a medical practice but a moral evil, and therefore must be completely prohibited or performed only when a woman's life was at risk.

Opponents argued that the two bills would result in legislative change much more radical than community attitudes towards abortion, connecting this extremism to 'the feminist sisterhood [which] has clouded sensible debate on the issue' (Panopoulos, MP; Australia 2006c: 55). True to the postfeminist sensibility outlined above, anti-abortion MPs frequently depicted feminism as an irrelevant and fanatical 'sectarian conflict' because of a presumed gender equality:

[T]he feminist struggle against patriarchal oppression in society has improved our society enormously. However, the excesses of identity politics, especially when it turns into zealotry, can be very nasty and irrational … [this bill] implements something very radical—a radicalism grounded in dogma. (Somyurek, MLC; Victoria 2008d: 4156)

The metonymic slide between the figures of the 'feminist', the 'selfish woman' and the 'aborting woman' configured abortion as an act women carry out to assert their individual power. Many opponents of the bills derided abortion as an exercise of 'female empowerment' with women choosing 'to have an abortion only because she sees it as her right' (Kairouz, MLA; Victoria 2008a: 3334). Tony Abbott deplored those women who regarded abortion as 'a badge of liberation from old oppressors', suggesting that only self-identified feminists terminate their pregnancies and they do so to gain more power in an already equal society (Australia 2006d: 114).

Even supporters of the bills characterised an approach that afforded women the capacity to choose abortion in all circumstances as 'extreme', arguing that the 'rational' and 'reasonable' position on abortion balanced consideration for foetal life with women's autonomy (Lindsay, MP; Australia 2006c: 96; Quick, MP; Australia 2006d: 22). A moderate approach was actually enshrined in the bill that the Victorian parliament debated, which limited a woman's choice to terminate her pregnancy to foetal viability, measured at twenty-four weeks' gestation. The Victorian Labor Government viewed the Victorian Law Reform Commission's (2008) recommendation of no threshold as too radical for debate. Very few parliamentarians called for abortion on a woman's request throughout her pregnancy. Women introduced both bills into parliament and, with few exceptions, voted *en masse* to support them. The bills were therefore a successful instance of female politicians uniting (against, predominantly, male politicians) to ensure greater reproductive freedom for women in the community.

There was, nevertheless, no solid reaffirmation of feminism's political legitimacy in the debates and, accompanying this, no firmly articulated, women-centred pro-choice position. This allowed opponents to reduce the argument for abortion to the abstract demand for 'women's choice', framing the debate as one between 'convenience or conviction' (Thompson, MLA; Victoria 2008a: 3365): 'the elevation of abortion choice as an incontestable right, like some golden calf [has been] presented in place of a more complete debate over the philosophy and value of life' (Santoro, Senator; Australia 2006a). The absence of feminist, women-centred arguments for abortion has also been noted in the British (Hadley 1997; Lee 2003: 86), American (Weitz 2010), and New Zealand (McCulloch 2013: 267) contexts.

In contrast to the disavowal or vilification of feminism in the debates, several parliamentarians (in a purportedly secular state) affirmed Catholicism's place in formal politics. This contrast played out in the Commonwealth debate when Green's Senator Kerry Nettle wore a t-shirt sponsored by the Young Women's Christian Association that read 'Mr Abbott: Keep your rosaries off my ovaries'. This t-shirt made an obvious gesture towards WLM's slogan and was a protest against the role Tony Abbott had played in inciting a rising anti-abortion sentiment in Australia's public and political domains (explored in Chapter 5), which he repeatedly explained and justified through reference to his Catholic faith (Abbott 2004). As the Minister for Health, Tony Abbott also held the veto over the importation of RU486 into Australia and was the most vociferous defender of retaining this entitlement. Nettle's action was ridiculed as 'unnecessary and unhelpful. It was offensive at worst and juvenile at best' (King, MP; Australia 2006d: 169) and 'a giggling, offensive insult to most Christians in general, and Catholics in particular … [that] bordered on the sectarian' (Neville, MP; Australia 2006d: 184). Coalition members frequently praised Abbott's work as Health Minister and legislators from both parties applauded his faithful adherence to religious conviction (for example, Burke, MP; Australia 2006d: 1; Beazley, MP; Australia 2006e: 38).

The discourse belittling Nettle's politics juxtaposed feminism with Catholicism. Politicians from both major parties and on both sides of the debate infantilised Nettle and, by implication, feminism, deriding her political position as immature and irrational—gendered terms associated with women and femininity—while bolstering the moral authority of Catholicism. They labelled Nettle's action as 'entirely inappropriate for someone who is an elected senator in the Australian parliament' (Albanese, MP; Australia 2006c: 94) and, in contrast, supported '[w]hatever Minister Abbott calls upon to inform his conscience' as 'his right' (Keenan, MP; Australia 2006c: 130). The binary contrasts between the infantile and mature, irrational and reasonable, that distinguished feminism from Catholicism mapped onto their relative alignment with the emotional script orienting women towards children as happy objects. While this emotional script is firmly embedded in Catholicism, feminism deviates. In the debates, the figures of 'the feminist', 'the aborting woman' and 'the selfish woman' were stuck together as affect aliens, cast as irrational, not because the rational other is without emotionality, but because their emotional sensibility was, to use Sara Ahmed's words, 'out of line with the affective community' (Ahmed 2004b: 41).

CONCLUSION

In the postfeminist context, emancipatory political projects such as feminism are cast as antiquated and irrelevant. The self-interested, autonomous, self-sufficient subject of choice is, however, fictitious; it utterly relies on labour that occurs within the family unit that, if not outsourced to feminised workers such as child carers and cleaners, is performed free of charge, usually by women, through the persistence of a selfless, other-directed, normative femininity (Brown 1995: 135–165). The equation of freedom with personal choice relies on and reproduces an autonomous subject that is fundamentally at odds with normative femininity.

The tension between autonomous choice and women's reproductive bodies is discursively resolved through the figure of the woman who has choices, yet whose orientation towards children as happy objects directs her choices towards motherhood. Happiness imprints normative femininity at the level of personal desire, ensuring the supply of reproductive labour in a manner that disguises the material and discursive constraints within which maternal desire is produced. The economy of maternal happiness is, in other words, a technology whereby motherhood has been re-naturalised through choice and thereby represented as an expression of personal freedom. Debates about abortion deploy and interpret what 'choice' means for pregnant women in a particularly intense way, and are subsequently a primary site where the current schema of normative femininity can be identified and interrogated.

There is a discernible trend in pro-choice politics that reinforces the view that questions pertaining to foetal life are the only moral issues involved in abortion. Taking the foetus as the subject of the abortion debate, maternal pro-choice politics argues that pregnant women are inevitably oriented towards their foetuses as happy objects, but must sometimes terminate their pregnancies to protect the welfare of those around them, particularly their potential children. The economy of familial happiness determines the grounds upon which certain women can be viewed as expressing their maternal desires, paradoxically, through abortion. Within this economy, only some women are believed to hold the resources to ensure their maternal happiness will correspond with their children's happiness; maternal happiness is linked to social virtue (selflessness) only when mothers are deemed capable of ensuring their children are (or will be) happy subjects. Representations of the 'happy child' construct the 'good mother' along axes of race, class, age and sexuality.

In this chapter I outlined and deployed normative accounts of female happiness to examine the anti-abortion sentiment that informs a strand in pro-choice politics I term 'maternal'. The activists and politicians that deploy this rhetoric support opening up women's access to abortion by depicting abortion as a decision that women agonise over—as a dramatic and difficult response to extraordinary circumstances that compromise a woman's ability to ensure the future happiness of her children. Within maternal pro-choice politics, abortion is not viewed as a rejection of motherhood, or as a legitimate practice pregnant women require to find happiness or fulfilment outside of motherhood; rather, a woman's decision to have an abortion is viewed as a temporary setback on her journey towards motherhood, and maternal happiness is continually restated through her choice of abortion.

Although Australia has some of the most liberal abortion laws worldwide, this is not because of widespread parliamentary or community support for principles such as self-determination or bodily integrity. Instead, the dominant argument in support of removing legal restrictions on women's choices presented pregnant women, including those who go on to have abortions, as oriented towards their children as happy objects. Restrictive laws were unnecessary, so this argument went, because women inevitably regulate their own abortion conduct. Recent law reform in Australia was therefore achieved through the disavowal, rather than recognition, of the subject position of the unwillingly pregnant women.

With normative pregnancy so deeply embedded in the promise of maternal happiness, abortion can only be viewed as a harmful choice, not only to foetuses, but also for the women who have them. If the foetus promises to bring women happiness, it becomes a grievable object when lost through abortion, and abortion carries with it the promise of grief. The next chapter considers the normative view that abortion harms women, turning attention to the grief that circulates alongside representations of the abortion experience. Grief, as we will see, accompanies happiness to regulate the conduct of women through the choice of abortion.

CHAPTER 3

THE GRIEF OF CHOICE

The child will be with me, in a negative sense, until I die. ('Debbie' in *The Age* cited in Cafarella 1992)

They feel the shadow of a baby following them. (Reist 2000: 44)

Once again, the issue [of abortion] has been kicked around the park like a football while … thousands of women … all over the country felt a quiet shudder of remembrance. A date. A moment frozen in time, rerun on a seemingly endless loop in the hope of a different outcome. A calculation of a birthday that never eventuated. The lonely grief of unspoken loss. (Hutchinson 2007)

Women are commonly expected to perpetually mourn the death of their unborn children after abortion. An emotion I term 'foetocentric grief' dominates accounts of abortion across varied, and indeed seemingly opposite, perspectives, such as those above from a woman speaking of her own abortion

('Debbie'), a prominent anti-abortion campaigner (Melinda Tankard Reist), and a well-known Australian pro-choice journalist (Tracee Hutchinson). The recurrence of foetocentric grief across multiple and diverse discursive sites is concerning because the emotion constructs pregnant women as already mothers to the autonomous 'children' within their wombs, a designation that produces abortion to be morally problematic and harmful to women. Foetocentric grief is a powerful means by which anti-abortion rhetoric has been disguised and its normative effects amplified, transmuted from politics into truths regarding what abortion entails and how women experience having an abortion.

Since the early 1980s, the transnational anti-abortion movement has increasingly shifted rhetorical focus away from protecting foetal life to feigning equal concern with the impact of abortion on women. Foetocentric grief emerged in US anti-abortion activism and has achieved the most legislative success in US states in the form of incremental restrictions on abortion, which claim to protect women from the harm of abortion (Siegel 2007). Scholars have traced the movement of 'women-centred' arguments against abortion to Australia (Cannold 2002), Canada (Saurette and Gordon 2016), New Zealand (McCulloch 2013: 123) and the UK (Lee 2003). This chapter begins by mapping the shift from a foetocentric to 'woman-centred' approach within anti-abortion politics, using the Australian context as a case study to examine a much larger trend. Increasingly from the mid-1980s, the anti-abortion movement could no longer gain political or public sympathy for its cause by arguing against choice and, instead, moved to make the choice of abortion appear punishing. By deploying foetocentric grief, the movement could also align with the emotional sensibility that shaped the normative orientation of 'the public' towards the women who had abortions—that of compassion. Instead of directing compassion towards the circumstances that forced women to have abortions, as it was in the dominant 'pro-choice' position to take shape at the end of the 1970s (Chapter 1), anti-abortionists directed compassion to the emotional lives of women after their abortions. After examining the emergence of foetocentric grief in the anti-abortion movement, this chapter considers the decidedly anti-abortion political effects of foetocentric grief before tracing the spreading emphasis on foetocentric grief outside of anti-abortion activism to broader cultural imaginings of what abortion is 'really like' for women.

Foetocentric grief has circulated with increased intensity since laws on abortion were liberalised at the turn of the 1970s. If we think of emotions as economic, as circulating between signs and objects and sticking to and generating particular bodies, the more an object is read through a particular emotion, in this case abortion through grief, the more the emotion is seen to be intrinsic to the object (Ahmed 2004a). Today, abortion has become virtually unmentionable in public discourse without some gesture towards grief or trauma. The counter-narratives of abortion proliferating in recent anti-stigma activism (Chapter 4) are a response to the powerful expectation that women perform grief upon their abortions and may signal a move away from the inevitability of foetocentric grief in time. At the moment, however, foetocentric grief is frequently called up in representations of abortion automatically, with no elaboration or explanation, so insulating the emotion from politics and the history of its production. This chapter makes this history, and the political forces giving it momentum, visible. The discourse of foetocentric grief merges disparate emotional and psychological states, including grief, trauma, sadness, regret and unhappiness. The slippage between different emotions works to construct abortion as loss and, specifically, the loss through death of an autonomous, material foetus. The merging of severe psychological conditions (trauma) with commonly experienced emotions (sadness) gives post-abortion grief the broadest reach possible while constructing the loss involved as profound and eternal.

Although the anti-abortion movement has achieved very little legislative success or popular support in countries such as Australia and the United Kingdom, the norms that animate this movement, specifically the positioning of pregnant women as already mothers to the autonomous children within their wombs, actually accord with broader ideologies regarding femininity and pregnancy. The similarity between the pregnancy norms circulating in public discourses and those of the anti-abortion movement explains why post-abortion grief has held significant appeal outside the anti-abortion movement. The norm of foetal motherhood has been consolidated alongside the proliferation of foetal imagery and ultrasound technologies, which have given visual form and cultural authority to the ideology of foetal autonomy (Lupton 2013: 33–51; Petchesky 1987). The development and increased use of *in vitro* fertilisation and surrogacy have further secured imaginings of the pregnant body as physically distinct from the foetus she carries (Lupton 2013: 24–27). Foetocentric grief has emerged in the same period as these technological advances. Indeed, as this chapter will explicate further, foetal motherhood and foetocentric grief are mutually reinforcing; both are naturalised through the other.

Because foetocentic grief emerges from normative accounts of pregnancy, it also pervades understandings of miscarriage. US scholar Linda Layne contends that an absence of feminist voices in accounts of the loss of wanted pregnancies has witnessed rhetoric supportive of anti-abortion politics pervade the field. Miscarriage is almost universally represented as the loss of an autonomous child. Layne argues that we should view foetuses as attaining personhood not in and of themselves but through their social relationships with others; women who have willing and wanted pregnancies may assume a maternal identity and begin imagining their world with their future child, bringing this world into material reality by, for example, creating a nursery. Their experiences upon miscarriage are, therefore, very different to the experiences of women who voluntarily terminate unwanted pregnancies (2003: 239–240). Historian Catharine Kevin (2011) and gender scholar Rebecca Stringer (2006) similarly find alternative models of miscarriage grief in Australian laws that frame pregnancy loss through assault or grievous bodily harm as a loss *to* the woman rather than the loss *of* an autonomous foetus, as in the Unborn Victims of Violence Act of 2004 (USA). There have been moves to introduce US-style legislation into Australia's most populous state, New South Wales; and in South Australia there was a proposal to extend the definition of stillbirth to cover the miscarriage of foetuses past twelve weeks of conception (Kevin 2012). Both proposed laws were emotively titled after the names parents had given to foetuses lost through violence (Zoe's Law in NSW) or miscarriage (Jayden's Law in SA), and forwarded under the premise that the current legislative framework does not recognise these lives and, because of this, the magnitude of the parents' (particularly mothers') grief. These legal moves indicate an increasing normalisation of foetocentric grief in accounts of pregnancy loss in Australia.

The focus on representations of abortion grief in this chapter forms part of a larger trajectory, where the multiple meanings of pregnancy and the foetus have been reduced to the model of foetal motherhood, a subject position that makes foetocentric grief the only intelligible emotion that women experience upon the cessation of pregnancy, whether through miscarriage or abortion.

CHANGING EMPHASES OF HARM: FROM THE FOETUS TO THE WOMAN

As noted in Chapter 1, in the 1970s there was a developing consensus in Australia and elsewhere (Hopkins, Reicher and Saleem 1996: 542) that the anti-abortion movement lacked, in journalist Claude Forell's words, 'compassion for the desperate' women who have abortions (1978: 8). In response to charges that it treated women who had abortions with callous disregard, RTL began to supplement its foetocentric activism with claims it was driven to protect women from abortion's harmful effects.

Abortion was associated with harm throughout the twentieth century, but until relatively recently, the harm ascribed was physical rather than psychological (Baird 2001: 198). Until abortion laws were liberalised, there was a cultural expectation that abortion harmed women physically, which compelled women who had abortions to attribute all subsequent reproductive health problems to their abortions, no matter how tenuous the connection (Baird 2001: 200–201). Barbara Baird labels such experiences forms of 'embodied deviance'—'the historically and culturally specific belief that deviant social behaviour … manifests in the materiality of the body' (Terry and Urla 1995: 2, cited in Baird 2001: 206). Although the image of the coat hanger remains a powerful symbol for pro-choice activists, historians have revisited the stereotype of the 'backyard butcher' to argue that their existed a vast network of skilled practitioners offering women abortion safely before laws were liberalised; most women had abortions safely, even before the laws were reformed and the provision of abortion was thoroughly medicalised (for example, Baird 1996). In the 1970s and 1980s, claims regarding abortion's physical consequences caused far greater media attention than its purported psychological effects (see, for example, Baker 1983; Connors 1976). Although complications from abortion have been extremely rare since the 1970s (Yusuf and Siedlecky 2002: 15), the popular belief that abortion causes infertility and several other forms of morbidity, including breast cancer, remains (Kirkman et al. 2010: 125), and the anti-abortion movement continues to make such claims (Ewing 2005: 15–18; Right to Life of Michigan 2017). The perceived harm of abortion has, however, been increasingly psychologised.

The increasing psychologisation of abortion was encouraged in laws that enabled abortion on the grounds of a pregnant woman's health or psychological welfare. The argument that abortion irrevocably traumatises women conflicted with the claim, as formalised in such laws, that abortion could be psychologically and emotionally beneficial for women (Leslie 2010). Ellie Lee notes that the increasing focus on the psychological consequences of abortion also formed part of a broader expansion of mental health categories and diagnoses to psychologise the entirety of human experience. The development of a 'syndrome society' during the twentieth century involved a redefinition of deviant behaviour from sinful to criminal and, finally, pathological (2003: 43–80). In keeping with this broader psychologisation of everyday life, there was an explosion of psychological research into abortion in the 1970s and 1980s (Lee 2003: 154–160). Although researchers overwhelmingly concluded that abortion holds no inevitable short or long-term psychological consequences for women, the psychological impact of abortion continues to be a subject of debate in more popular forums.

Within the general turn to psychology in legal and social discussions of abortion, and amidst the inefficacy of campaigns aimed at restricting women's lawful access to abortion, the transnational anti-abortion movement began championing for a 'new strategy to save babies' in the form of its pregnancy counselling centres (RTL 1979). In Melbourne, for example, the first of such centres, the Pregnancy Aid Centre (PAC), opened in 1980 next to the city's first abortion clinic, and regional centres were established in Victoria by 1983. PAC deliberately masqueraded as a neutral counselling centre to attract women considering abortion (RTL 1981b, 1983). In 1982, Melbourne's broadsheet newspaper, *The Age*, reported that fifty women visited the centre every week, attracted by advertisements in public transport and telephone directories that read: "Pregnant? Worried? We can help. Free Pregnancy Test at No Charge. Results in 30 mins. No appointment necessary' (Sullivan 1982). Obfuscating its connections with RTL, PAC gained government funding in 1981 (McGuire 1982; Yallop 1982) and was listed under emergency contact numbers inside the front cover of the telephone directory *White Pages* in 2001 (RTL 2001). Initially, the primary aim of the centre was to inform pregnant women that 'every abortion kills a baby'; but it also warned women of (fabricated) severe health risks (RTL 1982; Sullivan 1982).

Arguments against abortion on the basis of women's psychological wellbeing gained momentum with the establishment of organisations dedicated to 'women-centred' anti-abortion activism in the early 1980s, including Victims of Abortion and Women Exploited by Abortion (WEBA) (Lee 2003: 23; McCulloch 2013: 123).[1] In Australia, members of RTL established WEBA after the founder of the American organisation attended its 1983 convention (RTL 1983). WEBA (1986) aimed to end the 'conspiracy of silence … [regarding the] truth that abortion destroys a living human being … [and] traumatically affects the mind of the woman who allows her unborn baby to be destroyed'. Members claimed to have had abortions, calling on this personal experience to authorise their anti-abortion politics: they continually emphasised that '**we have been there**' (WEBA 1987–1988, bold in the original). WEBA spread its message of post-abortion harm through a twenty-four hour helpline, which offered women pre- and post-abortion counselling in order to help each aborting woman acknowledge that 'He or She [her "baby"] did exist and I have a right to grieve' (WEBA 1986). The organisation also provided schools and interested groups with public speakers and information pamphlets, and its members wrote regular letters to newspapers and appeared on the television and radio (WEBA 1988b; WHBA 1992). This outreach campaign reveals the primary goal of WEBA (1992): to prevent women from having abortions in order to, so it claimed, save 'the lives of those babies … [and prevent] real physical and psychological damage being done'. While Christian vocabulary and sentiment occasionally entered the pages of RTL newsletters—the organisation had a close affiliation with the Catholic Church and most of its members were Catholic—WEBA began as an explicitly non-denominational, Christian organisation. The organisation also held annual ecumenical services for 'the unborn' to 'assist' aborting women work through their losses.

Leslie Cannold argues that 'a key anti-choice, women-centred strategy is to replace the foetus with the guilt-ridden, self-hating, grief-stricken, victimised and finger-pointing "woman hurt by abortion" as the summarising image of what is wrong with legal abortion' (2002: 173). WEBA's newsletters cultivated this finger-pointing subject, forwarding the singular message that aborting women had, often unknowingly, killed their unborn children and would inevitably suffer eternal guilt and grief as a consequence. WEBA initially framed women who had abortions as exploited victims, driven to abortion 'by associates, by society's abortion mentality, [and] by abortion providers' (RTL 1984). In 1991, Women *Exploited* by Abortion became Women *Hurt* by Abortion under the premise that many women freely choose abortion, which must only compound their subsequent grief (1990b).

WEBA described itself in RTL newsletters as focused on saving 'the lives of the unborn' (RTL 1984), yet promoted itself in the media as distinct from RTL and concerned solely with helping women (West 1984). The Victorian Government conferred the status of a public benevolent institution on WEBA in 1988, making all financial contributions to the organisation tax-free (WEBA 1988d). In 1991, the rebranded WHBA was listed in the *White Pages* under Community Emergency and Help Services, which it promoted as acceptance amongst 'health workers ... [of] the devastating physical and psychological after-effects of abortion' (WHBA 1991).

In the mid-1980s, the American anti-abortion movement began to cluster the claims it was making regarding the emotional and psychological effects of abortion around the diagnosis of post-abortion syndrome (PAS). PAS gained prominence in Australia's anti-abortion community when WEBA and RTL jointly organised a conference on the condition in 1988. Dr Eric Seal, an anti-abortion psychiatrist at

St Vincent's (a Catholic) Hospital in Melbourne, defined PAS as a 'delayed or slow developing, prolonged and sometimes chronic grief-syndrome ... [causing] depression, aggression and personality change', compounded by the knowledge that the sufferer 'may have played a big part in the decision to abort the baby'. He claimed that all women who have abortions experience PAS, whether they acknowledge it or not (WEBA 1988a). Denial or repression of abortion trauma is a key symptom of PAS, and it is maintained that serious consequences can manifest several years, even decades, after the procedure. Such claims enable anti-abortionists to bypass findings of existing scientific research, which have generally focused on short-term experiences of abortion and overwhelmingly find no predictable or severe emotional response (Lee 2003: 29–31). Within the framework of PAS, the experiences of aborting women who do not suffer from PAS are attributed to a false consciousness and said to manifest in ways that women would not automatically associate with their abortions, such as a general anger towards the world.

Although celebrating RTL's President Margaret Tighe as the 'mother of the unborn' in its first newsletter, by the 1990s, WHBA (1995) claimed to be anti-abortion only because 'fewer abortions means fewer hurt women'. At the same time, RTL increasingly legitimated its politics through recourse to post-abortion harm. By the 1990s, slogans such as 'Help mother and baby' and 'Abortion: one dead; one wounded' appeared in RTL newsletters and protest banners alongside the more conventional 'abortion kills' (RTL 1993, 1994, 1995, 1999). Government funding and community sympathy for anti-abortion politics have increased the more organisations disguised their agenda of curtailing women's access to abortion. While RTL's foetocentric politics remain ingrained in its name, over time, WHBA's initial focus on saving foetal life became increasingly obscured behind its purported concern for aborting women. WHBA, however, only barely concealed its foetocentric agenda. Mother and child imagery pervaded its newsletter, which, for example, featured a da Vinci illustration of Madonna with child on its back cover; WHBA's educational video, 'The Other Victim', which it showed to university students and priests, and at RTL conferences, also betrayed WHBA's belief that the foetus was the primary victim of abortion (WHBA 1988c, 1990a, 1990b).

Today, women-centred arguments against abortion rarely if ever explicitly condemn abortion. Women's Forum Australia (WFA), formed in 2004 after an anti-abortion conference, epitomises this strategy. WFA's politics are best captured in *Giving Sorrow Words*, published in 2000 by one of its founding members, Melinda Tankard Reist, to widespread and favourable reviews in the print media (Baird 2013: 254). WFA also commissioned Selena Ewing's *Women and Abortion: An Evidence-Based Review* (2005) to present the case of foetocentric grief and trauma to parliamentarians. A 2006 senate inquiry into abortion quoted two doctors who commended the report as 'worthy of our attention' (Community Affairs Legislation Committee 2006), and it continues to be advertised on several anti-abortion websites (for example, Catholic Archdiocese of Melbourne 2016).

Reist and Ewing represented themselves as neutral and objective observers and researchers of the abortion experience. Although Reist claimed to advertise widely for participants and receive 250 responses, she only advertised in conservative Christian and anti-abortion publications, including WHBA's newsletter, and specifically for women 'who have experienced feelings of pain, loss and regret following their terminations' (WHBA 1997, 1998). *Giving Sorrow Words* was clearly an Australian counterpart to similar, international anti-abortion publications of testimonies of women harmed by abortion, including David Reardon's *Aborted Women: Silent No More* (1987), Nancy Michels' *Helping Women Recover from Abortion* (1988), and Melanie Symonds' *...And Still They Weep: Personal Stories of Abortion* (1996). Ewing's 'evidence-based review' of medical and psychological research drew heavily on the work of David Reardon, director of the American anti-abortion research organisation, the Elliot Institute, and the primary claims-maker of post-abortion syndrome (Ewing 2005: 23, 95). American sociologist Dallas Blanchard describes Reardon's work on abortion as '[a]n excellent example of pseudoscience used to purport support for preconceived conclusions. The author is an engineer with no training in the social sciences or social research' (1996: 120–121).

Reist presented *Giving Sorrow* as a forum for women 'conned out of their children' (2000: 11), whose 'bereaved, bereft, desolate, isolated' (1) experiences were ignored by the mainstream media, feminists and service-providers. In Reist's imagination, women were forced to have abortions with no warning of the procedure's devastating aftermath, a misguided 'view that a termination is really no big deal', and in a community that showed 'disdain for women suffering after-abortion trauma' (2000: 9–10). Ewing's report depicted a range of psychological and physical side effects of abortion, including trauma, depression, schizophrenia, PAS, self-harm, suicide, alcoholism and drug abuse (2005: 33).

Ewing and Reist called pregnant women 'mothers' and foetuses 'babies', merging the experiences of abortion, miscarriage, and stillbirth. 'Abortion', Ewing affirmed, 'is a perinatal loss, even when it is chosen' (2005: 33). Mimicking WHBA's therapy guidelines, Reist insisted that women who have abortions must acknowledge and commemorate their lost babies to help lessen their indelible grief:

> Many women hear babies crying in the night, calling for them. They feel the shadow of a baby following them. They have a need to … acknowledge the reality of the life that was inside them, and to farewell it … [through burying] a pair of booties or a teddy bear. (2000: 44)

Such commemorative rituals are common in miscarriage support groups, specifically in regards to the material objects pregnant women (and others) buy in preparation for their babies (Layne 2003: 103–144). It is highly unlikely that women who experience unwanted pregnancies they go on to terminate buy clothes or other items for future babies—a practice that helps materialise foetuses as babies. Reist's description is thus productive rather than descriptive. By linking abortion to the loss of wanted babies, gesturing towards burial sites and baby-like footprints and bodies, she, like Ewing, dissolves any division between embryos, foetuses and babies. Moreover, Reist and Ewing completely disregard a woman's subjective experience of pregnancy—whether she wants to be pregnant, remain pregnant, or be a mother—as well as the structural and interpersonal constraints that restrict pregnant women's choices.

'REAL CHOICE'

> [F]or those concerned with women's well-being and freedom, the negative impacts of abortion on significant numbers of women underscores [sic] the need for public policy, structural and cultural changes to enable women to make informed decisions without undue external pressures. (Selena Ewing, member of the Endeavour Forum 2005: 33)

Women-centred arguments against abortion attract support from individuals without extreme anti-abortion politics because, in line with Ewing's statement above, they work through, rather than explicitly aim to prohibit, women's choices. The movement's deployment of choice, however, shifts focus from autonomous choice to notions of 'informed choice' and the name of an anti-abortion organisation established in 2007, 'Real Choices'. Real Choices (2016) claims to be a 'professional education and training service', 'not a lobby or activist group. We have no religious or political affiliation'. Its purported neutrality authorises messages regarding the devastating impact of abortion on women; this constitutes the 'real information' it believes offers women 'real support [and] real choices'.

Reist originally advertised in forums such as WHBA's (1997) newsletter for women who felt they had been coerced into having an abortion, and represented abortion in *Giving Sorrow Words* as 'an act of obligation and obedience—pleasing others, [or a] maternal sacrifice for the greater good' (2000: 16). Reist's depiction of abortion as an act of maternal sacrifice is similar to maternal pro-choice politics (Chapter 2). Reist, however, asserted that aborting women were invariably coerced into their abortions, with coercion providing the antithesis of choice in the rhetoric of liberalism. Reist's focus on co-opting the language of 'choice' illustrates the symbolic importance this rhetoric held in discussions of abortion by the mid-1990s. Anti-abortionists found little success in countering the discourse of 'choice' with that of coercion and, instead, increasingly incorporated choice into is political program by focusing on claims regarding the emotional and psychological consequences of women's choices.

New policy goals accompanied the anti-abortion movement's rhetorical shift in focus from foetuses to women. Instead of advocating for re-criminalising abortion, and thus prohibiting women's choices, anti-abortion activists began concentrating on incrementally restricting abortion under the premise that such restrictions offer women 'informed' or 'real' choices. Laws of 'informed consent', for example, oblige doctors to warn women of debatable psychological and physical risks of abortion (Baird 2006a: 135–159). Ewing alluded to such laws when she invoked 'the negative impacts of abortion' to call for policy 'changes to enable women to make informed decisions without undue external pressures' (Ewing 2005: 33). Maria Caulfied, MP, deployed similar rhetoric when opposing the 2017 bill to decriminalise abortion in the UK, claiming that 'young and vulnerable women' needed to be protected from the 'risky procedure' and accusing the organised pro-choice movement of being 'firmly against helping women to make informed choices' (United Kingdom 2017).

Incremental restrictions have enjoyed particular legislative success in the USA. In July 2017, 35 US states required women to receive pre-abortion counselling, 29 of these states detailed the information that counsellors should provide to women, and 27 of them required that a fixed period of time, usually 24 hours, elapsed between counselling and the procedure. In 25 states, abortion practitioners had to inform women of the risks of abortion, including medically inaccurate information as to the effects on future fertility (4 states), breast cancer (5 states) and, most significantly for this study, its negative emotional consequences (6 states) (Guttmacher Institute 2017). In two states, scanning physicians must display the monitor so that women can see the ultrasound of their embryo or foetus and provide a verbal account of what can be seen; a further eleven require physicians to inform women of their right to view such images. These laws are justified on the pretext that women have the 'right to know' what their embryo/foetus looks like before proceeding with a termination. They presume that pregnant women are already mothers to their unborn children and attempt to coerce women into aligning with this view of pregnancy while also eliciting the concomitant emotion of foetocentric grief. Carol Sanger writes that 'Women's Right to Know Acts are concerned with maternal loss at seeing or imagining the death of one's child' (2017: 109); they require women to participate in a 'rite of full-term pregnancy' (122), and the foetal image is meant to 'foreshadow the impending loss by making the fetus as real a baby as technology now permits' (109). Such laws aim to bring 'women to their senses' and prevent abortion or, if this fails, invert 'the chronology of trauma by ensuring it precedes any abortion' (126), so punishing women for having abortions. Laws that require women to choose whether or not to bury or cremate their foetal remains (Sanger 2017: 85)—methods used for disposing of human remains and established mourning rituals—similarly attempt to align women who have had abortions with the role of mothers mourning their lost children.

In Australia, incremental restrictions have been introduced in three jurisdictions (and since rescinded in all but one) (Baird 2013: 254–255). In the most extreme example, the Osborne Act, active in the Australian Capital Territory from 1999 to 2002, forced doctors to show aborting women pictures of foetal development to ensure they knew what abortion 'really' entailed. The issue of abortion counselling has also been the subject of recurring political debate in Australia (Baird 2013), as it has been in the UK (Hoggart 2015) and Canada (Woodcock 2011).

When articulated as concern for women, Australian journalists have generally represented incremental restrictions as 'moderate', reasoned responses to the 'problem' of abortion (Baird 2013: 254–255). The claim that abortion decisions should be made with information regarding their consequences appears relatively unproblematic, but, in fact, constitutes a renewed form of gender paternalism. Laws of informed consent already govern medical practice, and abortion is one of few medical procedures that attracts additional provisions. The presumption that the state must protect women from making choices they will later regret positions women as vulnerable, weak, exploitable and potential victims (Siegel 2007). Such measures imply 'that a woman's judgment cannot be trusted' (Kirby 1998: 309) and assume that women passively 'consent' to abortions rather than actively desire them (Baird 2006a: 129–132). The presumption that women who consider abortion need counselling and state-issued information, while those continuing with a pregnancy do not, also reflects and restates the normative view that motherhood is the only unproblematic consequence of pregnancy.

As the legislative ramifications of foetocentric grief have been detailed and critiqued elsewhere (Baird 2013; Guthrie 2007; Siegel 2013; Suk 2010), the rest of this chapter will examine the political effects and normative influence of this emotion.

THE POLITICS OF GRIEF

The use of emotional and psychological experience to relay the truth of abortion is not a neutral act of description; it *does* something, holding the power to naturalise, in this instance, a profoundly political message. Personal testimonies of abortion, as Shoshana Felman and Dori Laub write of testimony more broadly, '*vow to tell*, to *promise* and *produce* one's own speech as material evidence for truth' (1992: 5). As I argued in the introduction to this book, recourse to an emotional state heightens the truth claim of testimony, for emotions are widely considered 'touchstones of personal reality', to use William Reddy's phrase (2001: 43); they are therefore productive of the 'truth' of the subject in so much as they are commonly believed to be automated reflexes that reveal a subject's deeply interiorised thoughts, personal history and aspirations for the future (Berlant, Nahafi and Serlin 2008).

If emotions are perceived to issue from the individual, and all women are believed to experience abortion similarly, as they so often are, then the subjects of abortion are assumed to share a fundamental essence. The essence perceived to unite the emotional experiences of women who have abortions is fundamentally maternal. Foetocentric grief firmly associates abortion with death and destruction while also organising the woman's pregnancy into a relationship between two autonomous subjects united by a natural and unbreakable mother-child bond. This is achieved through the singular attribution of abortion grief to the woman's (mother's) loss (killing) of her unborn child. As Reist explains the experience of abortion grief: 'A woman never forgets a pregnancy and the baby that might have been ... these were flesh and blood babies; for them, a baby died in abortion' (2000: 10).

The belief that abortion runs contrary to women's maternal natures has fueled anti-abortion activism since the

1970s (Chapter 1). It is hugely significant that depictions of foetocentric grief have increased the more women have been addressed as subjects of choice and capacity rather than bearers of a maternal destiny (Chapter 2). Foetocentric grief produces pregnant women as mothers, and foetuses as their babies, without an explicit foetal or pro-natal agenda. In fact, as we have seen, appealing to the consequences of abortion enables anti-abortion activists to deploy a central discourse of both pro-choice politics and conceptions of freedom in the contemporary era: that of choice.

Abortion carries no predictable acute or prolonged emotional or mental health consequences for women (Lee 2003: 154–169; Major et al. 2009). As the scholars of miscarriage grief cited above have shown us, it is also problematic to presume that women who do grieve are experiencing the loss of their autonomous foetuses. Grief does not necessarily derive from the death of a loved one, but also from the loss of an ideal or belief (Freud 1957). Thus, if experienced, grief following abortion could relate, for example, to a woman's fantasies pertaining to her pregnancy. Such fantasies would involve an imagined future (as a mother or co-parent with a loved one, for example) and could include the possibility, but by no means inevitability, that the woman envisioned the foetus as separate to herself. Grief could result from internalised ideologies pertaining to pregnancy and motherhood: incorporating the ideal of foetal motherhood into one's experience of pregnancy could, for example, be productive of grief. Instead of opening up the abortion experience to multiple and diverse emotions, the anti-abortion movement disavows the voices of the women who do not incessantly grieve their abortions, as well as the multifarious voices of the women who do grieve. Abortion grief is singularly organised around foetal death, framed as the death of the woman's child; thus only one script, one explanation is provided for the experience. Instead of 'giving sorrow words', then, Reist and anti-abortionists like her give sorrow *so few words.*

The abortion grief most commonly represented in antichoice publications is a pathological, melancholic grief. Reist's claim that aborting women 'feel the shadow of a baby following them' (2000: 44) closely mirrors Freud's description of melancholia as when 'the shadow of the object fell upon the ego' (1957: 249). The foetus, thus transposed, becomes a constant, absent presence in the woman's life, constantly judging her for making the wrong decision. The caustic, self-berating, melancholic relationship between the aborting woman (mother) and her lost foetus (child) produces abortion as a momentous and unforgettable experience that forever damages the woman's sense of self—this is the basis of Reist's (2002) claim that 'although a baby is forever, so is an abortion'.

The melancholic's inability to let go of the past, its recurrent intrusion into everyday life, is similar to Freudian definitions of trauma. While melancholia can result from everyday losses, however, trauma usually results from 'an event outside the range of expected human experience' (Prager 2008: 409). Abortion is an everyday rather than extraordinary event, experienced by approximately one in three women. Articulating abortion through trauma, best captured in post-abortion syndrome, which is modeled on post-traumatic stress disorder, is thereby performative rather than descriptive; it produces abortion to be a non-normative, violent and intrusive event that is life-threatening, involving a 'crisis of death' (Caruth 1996: 6). In descriptions of abortion grief, the 'death event' involved in abortion obviously gestures towards foetal death (Lee 2003: 27). Foetal death also, significantly, signals another death—that of aborting women's motherhood and the mother-child bond.

Through its description as traumatic, abortion is produced as fracturing 'the self by breaking the ongoing narrative, severing the connections among remembered past, lived present and anticipated future' (Brison 1999: 40). Motherhood is thus naturalised as the dwelling place, the sense of self and anticipated future, that abortion ruptures. This is why, according to anti-abortion logic, women powerfully desire to have children after their abortions, through violent means such as kidnapping if necessary; they desperately aim to feel, in Reist's words, like 'life-giver[s]' rather than 'baby killer[s]' (2000: 41). Only motherhood can orient women away from their traumatised, post-abortion psyches. The description of abortion as inherently grievable and traumatic generates a circular logic. Abortion is taken to be inherently traumatic because aborting women are mothers to their aborted foetuses and the perceived inevitability of abortion grief and trauma then produces aborting women as mothers.

As a mode of subject regulation, foetocentric grief does not appear to have affected the number of women having abortions, which has remained relatively consistent since the liberalisation of abortion law (Sage and Chan 2005); women's experiences of abortion also remain unaffected—

as mentioned, they are not characterised by extreme grief. Foetocentric grief, instead, reconciles contradictory modes of femininity: on one hand, the postfeminist discourse of women's freedom, as actualised through 'choice'; and, on the other, heavily circumscribed norms of gender that fixate on motherhood as a woman's anchoring point (Chapter 2). The primary function of foetocentric grief is thus restorative. In foetocentric grief, as Valerie Hartouni writes of PAS, 'motherhood is reiterated as a woman's "true" desire and interest as well as innate need' (1997: 43). If we think, alongside Judith Butler (1990), of expressions of gender as producing, rather than emanating from, gendered subjects, the citation of foetocentric grief restores aborting women to cultural viability. Motherhood becomes a pregnant woman's choice even when, paradoxically, her choice was abortion.

The project of delegitimising (or, for that matter, legitimising) abortion through recourse to each woman's emotional state is a way of individualising and de-politicising abortion, helping to delineate reproduction and parenting as decisions free from social or economic influence.[2] This fits into a broader context of individualisation, where women are deemed capable of controlling their fertility through contraception and responsible for doing so until they have gathered the economic and social resources deemed critical to mother effectively (Chapter 2). With pregnancy and motherhood reinscribed as a woman's autonomous, yet responsible, 'choice', abortion is believed to result from a series of bad or irresponsible choices. From this perspective, foetocentric grief can be viewed as a warning: if you get pregnant unintentionally and have an abortion, indelible grief will follow. The emotion also works as a penance, or punishment, not only for, in Dr Seal's words, playing 'a big part in the decision to abort the baby' (WEBA 1988a), but also for failing to act responsibly. The 'grieving aborting woman' could thus be considered a contemporary reiteration of the 'fallen woman' (Reekie 1997), allotted a life of misery as a consequence of her sexual and moral misconduct.

The presumption that abortion grief is, firstly, inevitable and, secondly, the consequence of a woman ending the life of her unborn child, narrows the possibilities for thinking about abortion to support the politics and goals of anti-abortionists. Abortion manifests as an act that kills an autonomous being rather than, for example, the cessation of an unwanted pregnancy; and aborting women are framed as inevitably and always mothers rather than women who, it could easily be imagined, say 'no' to motherhood on at least one occasion. If contained within the movement, the anti-abortion implications of foetocentric grief would be more transparent. As we have seen, however, organisations dedicated to the promotion of abortion grief and trauma often disguise their anti-abortion agenda; moreover, foetocentric grief has come to dominate narratives of the abortion experience more generally and, perhaps most surprisingly, those informing some iterations of pro-choice activism.

MATERNAL PRO-CHOICE GRIEF

Foetocentric grief accompanies maternal happiness as a primary emotion structuring the maternal pro-choice position detailed in Chapter 2. Accompanying the reification of foetuses as 'happy objects' for pregnant women, and bolstering the view that foetal life is the only moral issue at stake in abortion politics, maternal pro-choice advocacy proposes that foetocentric grief is not only an inevitable response to abortion, but, often, the only ethical response.

In the epilogue to Kathleen McDonnell's *Not an Easy Choice* (1984), Ellen Herman summarises one of the book's central messages as 'Abortion brings with it the dual themes of exercising freedom and experiencing pain' (ii). For McDonnell, 'pain' was the price women paid for the 'freedom' of abortion. The celebrity feminist Naomi Wolf, famous internationally after the publication of her best-selling *The Beauty Myth* in 1991, caused significant debate amongst academics and the broader feminist community when she published a piece in *The New Republic* in 1995 claiming, not so much that grief inevitably flowed from abortion, but that it was the ethical duty of women to grieve their abortions. Wolfe reiterated the by then familiar claim that pro-choice activists have relinquished 'the moral frame around the issue of abortion' and continue to cling 'to a rhetoric about abortion' forged through a 'series of self-delusions, fibs, and evasions'. The pro-choice movement, she continued, failed to recognise that abortion was an intrinsically selfish and sinful act that destroys autonomous human life. Although Wolfe continued to support abortion, she imagined a world with:

real gender equality ... in which every young American woman knows about and understands her natural desire as a treasure to cherish ... [and where] we would probably use a very different language about what would be—then—the rare and doubtless traumatic event of abortion. That language would probably call upon respect and responsibility, grief and mourning ... [and] describe the unborn and the never-to-be-born with the honest words of life. And in that world, passionate feminists might well hold candlelight vigils at abortion clinics ... commemorating and saying goodbye to the dead.

Wolf's description of abortion bears several similarities to representations of post-abortion syndrome: it invokes a naturalised maternal desire and the figure of 'the unborn', dwells on abortion grief and trauma and designates commemoration and remembrance as the only means to atone for the sin of abortion.

Leslie Cannold published *The Abortion Myth* (1998) shortly after Wolf's opinion piece. In this book, Cannold implied that a woman's emotions as she approaches, experiences and remembers her abortion determine the legitimacy, or otherwise, of her decision (Chapter 2). She juxtaposed the decision made 'thoughtfully, sorrowfully and with respect for the sacredness of pregnancy and with love for their could-be child' (1998: 127–128) with the abortion decision that 'was just plain wrong' because it 'did not reflect a woman's "feelings" and "love" for her could-be child' (1998: xiv). In contrast to anti-abortionists, Cannold supposed that women 'kill through care' when having abortions (1998: i) rather than out of ignorance of self-interest. Bertha Alvarez Manninen has recently drawn on Cannold's work to propose a 'prochoice grieving ritual ... [that] should acknowledge that fetal death is of some consequence ... [and] the destruction of fetal life is so very unlike the destruction of any other part of a woman's body' (2013: 675). Although Manninen depicts the foetus as 'part of a woman's body', she also reiterates the presumption that abortion inevitably involves grief and that this grief issues from the loss of a foetus. Manninen's suggestion that a woman would experience the loss of a body part, say an arm or an eye, less severely than the cessation of an unwanted pregnancy only makes sense in a logic underpinned by belief in the essential otherness of the foetus as the woman's child, or potential child, and the maternal bond she shares with that future child. Erased in Manninen's politics is the subject position of the unwillingly pregnant woman, for whom abortion could be considered a welcome and beneficial choice.

We can see, then, a discernable shift in strands of anti- and pro-choice activism towards a focus on women's emotional and psychological experiences of abortion and a belief in the inevitability of foetocentric grief. Foetocentric grief has also pervaded representations of abortion in the media more generally (Lee 2003: 223; Purcell et al. 2014: 1145–1146). This chapter turns to consider the increasing circulation of foeto-centric grief in a selection of Australian newspapers, focusing first on how activists have increasingly deployed foetocentric grief to communicate their politics in this medium before turning to representations of the abortion experience more generally.[3]

THE POLITICS OF GRIEF

Australian newspapers rarely mentioned women's personal experiences of abortion in the 1970s and 1980s; women's experiences did not feature prominently in abortion politics, as they do today, and newspaper coverage focused on significant events (such as law reform or government inquiries into abortion) and the views of activists, church officials and other public figures.

Significantly, the first detailed reference to the experience following abortion coincided with the inaugural meeting of Women Exploited by Abortion (WEBA) in 1984. The newspaper article recounted 'Helen's' story of three coerced abortions, a resultant incompetent cervix leading to miscarriages, her ongoing trauma and guilt, her conversion to Catholicism, and her search for forgiveness and healing through Right to Life's Action Problem Pregnancy Centre (West 1984).[4] The accompanying commentary cited Germaine Greer's assertion that abortion counsellors inappropriately shielded women from feeling guilty about their abortions by failing to tell them that 'the bones of the foetus must be broken for a 12-week termination, [and] that later it is dismembered and the skull crushed'. Greer opined that this absence of information appropriately protected women from grieving their terminations, although her focus on abortions performed after the first twelve weeks of pregnancy, which are relatively infrequent, worked to secure a connection between abortion and (baby-like) foetal death.

By the early 1990s, Greer's abortion politics underwent a subtle shift when she claimed that all women grieved their abortions. In an opinion piece published in Australia's largest broadsheet newspaper, *The Sydney Morning Herald*, Greer (1992) characterised abortion as a 'painful ... sad and onerous duty' that women undertook 'with grief and humiliation' in a society that offered them little support in their mothering role. Why, Greer asked, was abortion 'presented to them [women] as a privilege ... [when it is] the last in a long line of non-choices?' While drawing attention to the structural limitations that are hidden under the rhetoric of choice, such as the labour involved in parenting, Greer's universalisation of abortion grief affirmed its inevitability. It is little wonder, therefore, that Melinda Tankard Reist quoted from Greer at length in *Giving Sorrow Words* (2000: 23–25).

Wolfe's 1995 article provided an occasion for reflection and debate on the experience of abortion in the Australian media. Australian pro-choice commentators strongly refuted Wolf's depiction of abortion as ethically and morally suspect (Kissane 1995). They generally did so, however, not by celebrating the benefits of abortion for women; rather, they claimed that, contrary to Wolf's assertion that women *should* grieve abortions, abortion already and invariably causes, in Leslie Cannold's (1995) words, 'a woman great grief and pain'.

The revisiting of the abortion issue by celebrity feminists Germaine Greer and Naomi Wolfe along with the publication of Cannold's *The Abortion Myth* determined that, by the late 1990s, the mutually enriching narratives of maternalism

(Chapter 2) and foetocentric grief had come to dominate the public articulation of pro-choice politics. Thus, when opponents of a bill (broadly definable as 'pro-choice') brought in the Western Australian Parliament trivialised women's reasons for terminating their pregnancies in 1998, well-known Australian journalist Virginia Trioli (1998) wrote of an acquaintance who 'works in a women's health clinic' and swears that women consistently break 'into wrenching sobs' after their abortions. In response to the Federal Minister of Health's admonishment of 'convenience abortions' in 2004 (Chapter 5), a woman wrote a letter to the editor of *The Age* adamant that, contrary to popular accounts of abortion, 'I didn't take the easy way out … It broke my heart, and I grieve to this day, but I know I made the right choice for me' (Monagle 2004). In the lead up to the Victorian bill to decriminalise abortion in 2008, two prominent political figures revealed their abortion experiences through gesturing towards grief and trauma (Nader 2008; Nader and Cooke 2007). Journalist Melinda Houston (2008) used these stories to argue that the Australian community should treat the women who have abortions with compassion:

> admitting that terminating a pregnancy is traumatic isn't the same as admitting abortion is wrong. It's simply acknowledging the fact that it's an awful decision to have to make, and one in which women need support.

Some pro-choice advocates have publically contested reports that abortion is an inevitably traumatic event that causes ongoing grief (Vick 2002). Then Democrats Senator Lyn

Allison (2008), for example, commented in 2008 that an abortion she had years previously had solved, rather than agitated, her emotional problem. Grief itself and the work it does in the context of abortion—specifically how it links swiftly, incontestably, to the loss through 'death' of the material foetus—is, however, rarely if ever interrogated.

Foetocentric grief formed a bridge between pro-choice and anti-abortion positions. The publication of *Giving Sorrow Words* in 2000 gave momentum to the media circulation of women-centered, anti-abortion arguments. Melbourne's top-selling newspaper, the tabloid *Herald Sun,* did not mention Reist's anti-abortion credentials and accepted her claims unreservedly, deepening their rhetorical force through reiteration:

> Abortion is sold to women as … a chance to … be mistress over one's destiny. Well that's the party line, the one that evolved with 1960s feminism. If women have the right to choose, however, they also have the right to know the full implications of that choice. Which is where Melinda Tankard Reist steps in. (Cresswill-Myatt 2000)

In the 2000s, women-centred arguments against abortion became the dominant way anti-abortionists publicly opposed moves to reduce legal restrictions on abortion in Australia and elsewhere (Lee 2003: 22–23; Saurette and Gordon 2013: 172). Thus in 2006 when moves were under way to make the medical abortifacient RU486 available to Australian women, anti-abortion activists expressed concern, not for foetal life, but for women being subjected to '[t]he sight of foetal tissue and body parts' being expelled from her body (Birnbauer 2006). Such claims shored up autonomous foetal personhood, obscuring the fact that tissue expelled in medical abortion is usually embryonic (similar to menstruation which, needless to say, is unlikely to shock women) and never baby-like (De Costa 2007: 8). Later that year, the executive officer of the Respect Life Office at the Catholic Archdiocese of Melbourne opposed moves to decriminalise abortion in Victoria because of the 'tsunami of grief' such a measure would unleash: '[w]e should be working to ensure that the law protects vulnerable women and children from the harm of abortion. There is no need to remove abortion from the Crimes Act. Women deserve better than abortion' (Riordan 2006). Similarly, Charles Francis QC (2007)—founding member of the anti-abortion, anti-feminist organisation The Endeavour Forum—wrote in 2007 that the '[p]hysical and mental harm done to women by abortionists should be a real concern of our MPs'.

From the 1980s, as the anti-abortion movement made a strategic shift from foetal to women-centred arguments against abortion, anti- and pro-choice advocates converged to represent ongoing grief and trauma as the inevitable consequence of abortion. Abortion grief and trauma also came to dominate accounts (many of them first-hand) with no explicit political agenda: purported neutrality that amplified their claim to describe what abortion is 'really like' for women.

THE EVIDENCE OF EXPERIENCE

In August 1992 a story published in *The Age* entitled 'The Heartache of Abortion' began: 'Debbie wants to talk about what few women dare mention … [the] decision that shattered her life'. Debbie, a mother of four, lamented that 'the pain of ending a life of an unborn child is rarely discussed … [that] child will be with me, in a negative sense, until I die. There will always be a fifth child' (Cafarella 1992). Anna King Murdoch's abortion story similarly emphasised the haunting presence of her aborted 'child'. In response to plans to market RU486 in Australia in 1994, King (1994) wrote that immediately after her termination she imagined the

> delicate form with arms and legs … I had lost that day … That discovery of a secret, instinctual knowledge was probably the most profound of my life. The truth was that the loss was incalculable and unforgettable. And forever.

Unlike Debbie, Murdoch did not regret her abortion. Echoing Debbie's account, however, she relayed 'the truth' of abortion through women's maternal instinct and the apparent fact that she had 'lost' her baby, replete with 'delicate … arms and legs'.

Unabated grief also dominated 'Allison's' recollection, published alongside rumours that the federal government would cut government funding for the procedure in 1996:

> I felt that it was … [s]acrificing one life for another … [and] said my goodbyes [to the foetus] the night before …

Two or three years down the track I was aware that I was still thinking about it every single day, and as I was getting older it wasn't getting any better.

Another woman's account accompanied this one and told a very different story: '[i]t is an emotional time, you have a bit of a cry, but I've never looked back. I didn't see it as killing my baby because I didn't see that I had a baby'. Expert testimony, however, bolstered the force of Allison's narrative. Along with anti-choice spokespeople, Professor David Healy, chairperson of the Department of Obstetrics and Gynecology at Monash University, maintained that there are 'aspects of regret in all women. *Abortion for any woman is a tragedy*, nobody denies that' (Curtis 1996, emphasis added).

In May 2002, the main character of the popular Australian drama series *The Secret Life of Us*—Dr Alex Christensen, played by well-known actress Claudia Karvan—had an abortion in what *The Age* described as a television first. The show's narrator and Alex's flatmate, Evan, noted after the abortion 'a look in Alex's face I hadn't seen before—a sadness that hadn't been there yesterday'. Alex did not, however, suffer severe emotional or psychological distress following the procedure. *The Age*'s coverage was largely positive, but the weight of negative affect attached to abortion saw the reporting journalist use seemingly mandatory words such as 'agonising' and 'bleak' to describe the episode (Tarica 2002). Some letters to the editor celebrated the episode's relatively straightforward depiction of abortion, including one woman who noted its similarity to her own experience, free of hassle and pain

(Allen 2002). Many others admonished it for failing to 'show a broken Dr Alex' (Capello 2002; Regan 2002). In a lengthy opinion piece, Reist (2002) asked: 'Will she cry "I just want to hold my baby" over and over again?'

Ginger Eksleman's (2005) personal account of abortion would have delighted Reist. After lamenting her former ignorance as a feminist gender studies' student eager to have an abortion 'as a rite of passage', Eksleman became painfully aware that it was 'my baby that I killed':

> After the abortion I did not return to or continue the life I
> had before … I realised … I had been misinformed … The
> 'unbiased' information and language, supposedly feminist,
> did not make me feel empowered. It denied my truth.

Eksleman's self-presentation as a pleasure-seeking, abortion-hungry feminist before her abortion, a caricature lifted from anti-abortion publications (for example, Reist 2000: 9), alongside her implicit championing of laws of informed consent, suggests she had at least some communication with anti-abortion organisations such as Women's Forum Australia. Nevertheless, *The Age* published her story in addition to several letters to the editor congratulating Eksleman for sharing her 'powerful and truthful insight into abortion' (McCudden 2004):

> Usually those we hear from are the ones who sail through
> the experience and simply pick up their lives where they
> left off before the interruption of an unwanted pregnancy.

But these women are the exception. Abortion is a life-changing event. (Smith 2004)

The experiences of women who have relatively trouble-free abortions do appear in the media. A week after Ekselman's piece, Cyndi Tebbel (2004) wrote of her 'fast and painless' abortion, the supportive staff at the clinic and asserted that, '[a]t the end, I experienced nothing more than relief. And I have no regrets'. Stories like Tebbel's, however, feature in short letters to the editor or as part of larger articles, which also report a negative experience to perform media balance. As Barbara Baird notes, 'representations of the suffering aborting woman are abundant' (2001: 197), and stories of women who suffered terribly after their abortions have received the most newspaper coverage over the last thirty-year period. The distribution of public space to particular emotions of abortion is political, and the politics of foetocentric grief are decidedly anti-abortion.

The stickiness of grief to abortion can be seen in the editorials *The Age* and the *Herald Sun* published in support of the 2006 Commonwealth Bill to open the way to the availability of the abortifacient RU486 in Australia. The *Herald Sun* (2006) wrote that '[t]he personal experiences shared by MPs in recent weeks have shown the emotional scarring that can accompany an abortion'. *The Age* (2006b) reflected that '[t]he issue of abortion inevitably raises passions and can be a traumatic experience for women'. These statements show the slippage between abortion, trauma and grief, where the mention of abortion automatically evoked negative affect. Although the editorials suggested that abortion *could* be a negative experience, implying that it *may not be* in some cases, the constant reiteration of negative affect alongside abortion eclipsed the element of uncertainty residing in 'can'.

The salience of foetocentric grief in representations of abortion does not automatically translate into each woman's experience of abortion. A counter-discourse, considered in the conclusion to this book, emphasising women's relief after abortion has also emerged. The development of this counter-narrative reflects the discursive normalisation of foetocentric grief, which provides women with a forceful narrative script they are impelled to cite; one that allows them to recuperate their abortions within the frames of intelligibility constituting a normative female subject. In cases where women do not feel so powerfully affected by their abortions, they too may be incited to explain or justify their lack of 'proper' affect. The narrative of foetocentric grief is the 'embodied deviance' Barbara Baird (2001) describes, transported from the physical to the emotional and psychological realms. The narrative of foetocentric grief attributes any subsequent negative psychological or emotional feelings women experience to their abortions. As such, the expected psychological and emotional harm of abortion is elastic and far-reaching.

Foetocentric grief serves as a warning to women experiencing unwanted pregnancies that they will suffer if they deviate from the reproductive happiness path by terminating their pregnancies. When deployed in relation to abortion, grief works on the reverse side of happiness: if, as I argued in Chapter 2, foetuses are always, inevitably positioned as 'happy objects' for pregnant women, they become grievable objects when lost through abortion (or, indeed, miscarriage, a form of loss that has similarly been reduced to foetal death). Happiness and grief form an economy of choice marked by the presence or absence of a child/foetus; this economy reifies a normative pregnant body, which is represented as 'having' (a properly oriented maternal desire and a pregnancy that will result in a child and motherhood), a 'having' that is reinforced through images of the aborting woman as 'lacking' the qualities (self-lessness) or aspirations (motherhood) required to ensure her happiness. I conclude this chapter by briefly considering how maternal happiness juxtaposes with abortion grief to form an emotional economy of abortion. To do so, I return to the parliamentary debates of the mid-2000s (Chapter 2), which considered whether women should have access to medical abortion (Commonwealth) and whether abortion should be decriminalised (Victoria).

THE EMOTIONAL ECONOMY OF ABORTION

> [Abortion] is the most traumatic procedure that anybody would want to have, and I know there are long-term mental and physical risks, so, rightly, a woman would not choose to have an abortion just because her pregnancy was unwanted. (Jeannette Powell, Member for Shepparton, Victoria 2008a: 3349–3350).

The grief and trauma of abortion was a prominent theme in the Commonwealth and Victorian debates of 2006 and 2008.

Supporters of the bills cited this emotional script to argue that women should have greater access to abortion because, regardless of the legislative context, women will attempt to avoid abortion because of its devastating effects. Jeannette Powell, a Victorian MLA from the conservative National Party, for example, expressed her support for liberal abortion laws by arguing that, given that abortion was 'the most traumatic procedure' and carried 'long-term mental and physical risks', no woman would 'choose to have an abortion just because her pregnancy was unwanted'. First trimester abortions are safer than continuing with a pregnancy and childbirth (Raymond and Grimes 2012) and, as noted, abortion does not inevitably carry any risks to a woman's mental health. Furthermore, most women do indeed terminate pregnancies that are unwanted (as opposed to 'unplanned' or 'unintended'). Gestures towards grief and trauma in Powell's statement worked to occlude and elide this probability.

Opponents of the two bills invoked a narrative of harm to bolster the argument that the state must protect women from abortion, claiming 'there is abundant evidence that abortions can cause psychological damage, depression and even suicide' (Damian Kavanagh, MLC; Victoria 2008d: 4097). Opponents in the Commonwealth debate further proposed that the state must protect women from medical abortion, which 'researchers suggest ... is more psychologically traumatic than the surgical procedure' (Julian McGauran, Senator; Australia 2006a: 143) because (and remember: medical abortion generally looks and feels much like heavy menstruation) of the 'consequences of delivering a dead embryo at home' (David Tollner, MP; Australia 2006d: 139).

In stark contrast to depictions of abortion, parliamentarians uniformly presented pregnancy and parenthood as the 'greatest joy in life' (Hugh Delahunty, MLA; Victoria 2008a: 3345). References to the delights of pregnancy and parenthood seemed to compensate for some members' support of the two bills. One MLA affirmed that '[m]otherhood has brought me the greatest joy of my life, and as the mum of a beautiful three-year-old son I know how precious and valuable human life really is' (Mary Wooldridge; Victoria 2008a: 3307). Opponents conjured up an image of children as 'precious gifts of life' to communicate the humanity of the foetus and the inherent, often sacred, bond between women and their children that exists through pregnancy and beyond (Gary Blackwood, MLA; Victoria 2008a: 3348). The constant reiteration of the themes of motherhood and the maternal-child bond demonstrates the centrality of women's identities as mothers to the debates. The dual processes of exaggerating the negative effects of abortion and silencing those relating to pregnancy, childbirth and mothering reifies both the normative happiness of motherhood and the grief of abortion. One female MLA supported decriminalising abortion in Victoria by explicitly contrasting these positive and negative emotions: '[f]or those, including myself, who have experienced the pure joy of giving birth to a child ... the ending of a pregnancy for whatever reason and under whatever circumstances would be the cause of great anguish' (Helen Shardey, MLA; Victoria 2008a: 3318).

The attribution of happiness and unhappiness to objects does far more than simply describe particular feeling states: it involves a judgement about whether or not that object is good or harmful for us (Solomon 2003). The Benthamite ethic of maximising pleasure and minimising pain has become a commonsense mantra on how to live the 'good life' (Ahmed 2010b: 4–5). Of all 'emotion words', it is happiness, Sara Ahmed writes, that is most closely tied to ethics, because 'for some, the good life is the happy life. Or the virtuous person is the happy person. Or the best society is the happiest society' (2010b: 205). Thus within the logic of happiness '[y]ou can attack anything by saying that it is the cause of unhappiness' (203). Put simply, the representation of motherhood as happy confirms that motherhood is good for women and, likewise, the presumption that abortion is unhappy generates abortion as being bad for women: maternal happiness and abortion grief converge to produce aborting women as maternal subjects.

The emotional economy of grievable abortions and joyful motherhood gains strength through supporting discourses, such as the designation of women without children as 'childless'. When compared to the alternative designation 'childfree', the term childless presumes that being without a child is loss and incompleteness, and that wholeness involves having children. Childless is an adjective usually attached to women rather than men; thus the designation carries with it particularly gendered assumptions pertaining to completeness (Gillespie 2003). The designation 'childfree', in contrast, acknowledges the restraints on time and money that come with parenthood, and allows space for re-imagining mother-hood as loss (of former independence, for example). Tellingly, regret or loss upon motherhood are virtually unspeakable feelings (Donath 2015).

The articulation of 'childless' women as eternally bereft, much like the women who have abortions in anti-abortion propaganda, is evinced powerfully in narratives of 'baby hunger'. In a prominent Australian example of this transna-tional narrative, in 2000, Germaine Greer (2000) wrote of her two abortions and her stubborn unawareness as a young woman that holding a child in her arms would be 'the happiest experience of my life'. 'Though I have no child of my own', Greer lamented, 'I still have pregnancy dreams … I'm [still] waiting'. Several well-known Australian women approaching middle age took up the theme of maternal longing, with author Sophie Cunningham's 2002 opinion piece the most cited example:

> My longing for a child in my early thirties was intense beyond imagining—I would gasp in pain, or cry whenever I saw a baby … That, for me, was a form of longing that felt driven by chemistry. I did not feel I could choose to long, or not long, for a child.

Just as the woman who grieves her abortion commands greater public attention than the woman with no regrets, the woman who yearns for a child she may never have is the dominant figure of the woman who ends her childbearing years with no children. The depiction of a biological, and thus universal and ahistorical, desire for a child powers both narratives. Cunningham's depiction of the pain and anguish at failing to achieve the norm—motherhood—demonstrates how emotions attach us to the fantasy of the 'good life' (Berlant 2007): the fantasy of motherhood draws women to motherhood, *making culture feel like chemistry*. The emotional economy of abortion, which contains promises of maternal happiness and abortion grief, promotes a similar affective attachment to normative femininity.

CONCLUSION

In the mid-1980s, the anti-abortion movement increasingly concealed its aim to protect foetal life behind purported concern for the women who have abortions. Since then, foetocentric grief has moved outside the anti-abortion movement to dominate public discussions of abortion, precluding other potential interpretations of the experience. Foetocentric grief hosts normative assumptions that powerfully secure anti-abortion arguments pertaining to the harm of abortion—as an act that destroys autonomous life and leaves women perpetually mourning their unborn children.

The repeated articulation of abortion as a grief-inducing experience has, over time, congealed to discursively produce abortion as an experience that naturally elicits grief. By citing foetocentic grief, aborting women are restored to the norm of foetal motherhood. The incitement to intelligibility explains why we constantly see women's maternal desire and instinct invoked in narratives of abortion; and the repeated relegation of women's investment in motherhood to desire erases its production as such, as well as the labour involved in maintaining its stability. Foetal motherhood and foetocentic grief are each naturalised through the other. The historicisation of foetocentric grief presented here is a means of opening up a subject position that rationalises the social policing of pregnancy, including through the widespread censure of abortion.

Grief works alongside happiness to convey the good and bad of pregnancy choices. The emotional economy of abortion choice in contemporary Australia is structured as a relationship between presence and absence, whereby having a child is normative, promising women happiness, and deviations from this course are marked by loss, grief, regret and longing. This emotional economy issues from and secures a naturalised reading of maternal desire and generates pregnant women as already mothers and other women as either mothers, mothers in waiting, or as longing for a child they will never have. As long as this narrative is the sole descriptor of pregnancy, abortion will stand against nature, order, the ethical, the happy and the right, and for the unnatural, disruptive, disorderly and traumatic. Anti-abortionists describe abortion as an 'unspeakable loss'. I have suggested here, however, that loss dominates the cultural landscape of abortion, and it is the losses brought by motherhood—i.e. the loss of a life outside of motherhood—that are, in actual fact, unspeakable.

The emotional economy of abortion choice rests on a particular view of pregnancy and pregnant subjectivity and contains promises of fulfillment or devastation, producing a maternal identity for women through the choice of abortion. Women cannot escape the fantasy of maternal happiness that so narrowly circumscribes the acceptable parameters of their (other-centred) identities and (maternal-focused) aspirations. The way abortion—a choice not to mother (in at least one instance)—is incorporated within the normative frame shows how remarkably flexible and powerful the ideology of maternal happiness is: it survived WLM's radical attack on biological determinism and the increasing normalisation of the abortion choice (Chapter 1), and has reinvented itself through neoliberalism's celebration of choice (Chapter 2). Motherhood now, apparently, becomes a woman's choice even when her choice is abortion. The emotions of maternal happiness and abortion grief do not emanate from women's experiences of abortion; rather, they allow for the discursive rehabilitation of a fact— the significant number of women who have abortions—with an ideal or ideology—the naturalisation of motherhood and maternal desire. In this way the ideology of maternal desire can retain cultural authority despite the heterogeneity of women's lives and desires.

In Chapter 4 I add shame to the emotional economy of abortion sketched thus far, which will help explain why grief and maternal happiness continue to dominate representations of abortion despite studies that consistently show that women's experiences of abortion are diverse, multifarious and more likely to be marked by positive emotions, particularly relief, than negative ones. Shame, or the fear of shaming, deters women from speaking about their abortions in public forums, meaning that abortion is commonly represented by people (often men) who have not actually had abortions. Thus, ideas about how the generic subject 'women' would *or should* experience abortion predominate, paving the way for stereotypes, norms and ideologies of femininity to power narratives of abortion.

CHAPTER 4

SHAMEFUL CHOICES

The 1 in 3 Campaign is a grassroots movement to start a new conversation about abortion—telling our stories, on our own terms. Together, we can end the stigma and shame women are made to feel about abortion. (1 in 3 Campaign 2016)

Abortion stigma is rooted in narrow, gender-specific archetypes that inform cultural meanings of pregnancy termination, including archetypal constructs of the 'feminine', of procreative female sexuality, and of women's innate desire to be a mother ... Abortion can signal multiple transgressions, including participating in sex without a desire for procreation, an unwillingness to become a mother, and/or a lack of maternal-fetal bonding (Cockrill and Nack 2013: 974–975)

Over the last decade, abortion stigma has become a dominant trend in abortion activism and research (Purcell 2015). Anti-stigma abortion activism emerged in the USA and is, in part, a response to the nation's increasingly restrictive legislative context. Within web forums and Twitter activism, the anti-stigma movement has grown transnationally, moving into countries such as Ireland (Johnston 2015), where abortion remains heavily criminalised, as well as into countries, including Australia (Fishwick 2015) and Canada (Prasad 2015), that enjoy some of the most liberal abortion laws worldwide. The transnational scope of anti-stigma activism is partially due to its recognition that the law has a limited hold over the regulation of abortion. Abortion stigma helps produce and rationalise restrictive abortion laws, and, in countries where abortion is legal, leads to a lack of government commitment to ensuring adequate abortion facilities and discourages medical professionals from training and working in the area of abortion provision (Harris et al. 2011; Martin et al. 2014; Ripper 2001). Stigma also encourages women to conceal their abortions from others and thereby view their experiences as individual deviations from the norm and, potentially, a sign of their individual culpability for becoming pregnant and having an abortion (Astbury Ward et al. 2012; Cockrill and Nack 2013; Rocca et al. 2015; Shellenberg et al. 2011). Anti-stigma abortion activism and scholarship aspires to normalise abortion. The activist web forum '1 in 3', for example, is titled after the proportion of women who are predicted to have abortions in their lifetime, drawing attention to the frequency of abortion and the shared nature of the experience.

Anti-stigma activism and scholarship holds resonance with the radical abortion politics of the Women's Liberation Movement (WLM; Chapter 1). Within this movement, activists argued that the patriarchal conflation of women with motherhood, and women's sexuality with reproduction, compelled women to view abortions as shameful, guilty secrets they had to hide from other people (WAAC 1975a: 18). In order to 'overcome the terrible stigma attached to abortion', they believed it was 'necessary for women to get up in the streets and state they have had abortions and that they believe that it is every woman's right to decide' (WAAC 1974a). More recent campaigns, including *#ShoutYourAbortion* and the 1 in 3 Campaign, similarly focus on 'consciousness raising' (although this term is no longer used) through individual and public storytelling. Like the WLM, contemporary researchers locate abortion stigma in historically and contextually contingent 'archetypal constructs of the "feminine"' (Cockrill and Nack 2013: 974). According to Kumar, Hessini and Mitchell's influential formation, abortion stigma is 'a negative attribute ascribed to women who seek to terminate a pregnancy that marks them, internally or externally, as inferior to ideals of womanhood' (2009: 626).

Abortion shame is, in part, an internalisation of abortion stigma and, as we shall see, is also a consequence of norms of femininity that change over time and context. This chapter examines the regulative effects of abortion shame and historicises, and thereby de-naturalises, the emotion. Shame marks an individual as having failed against social mores and as personally responsible for this failure. Individualising the responsibility for abortion, and for becoming pregnant unintentionally, is a necessary precondition for abortion shame. When abortion laws were liberalised at the turn of the 1970s, abortion was widely considered to be a source for shame because of the normative expectation that single women would remain celibate and married women would want children. Abortion was a sign of failure against these normative expectations. As pre-marital sex has become normative, the norm eliciting abortion shame has changed to the expectation that both married and unmarried women should regulate their fertility through contraception to ensure that all children conceived go on to be born.

After mapping the norms that underpin abortion shame, this chapter moves to consider how different modalities of shame attach to reproductive bodies along axes of race, age and class. In doing so, I turn attention away from shame, a deeply internalised feeling of failure against social expectations and norms, to shaming, an action or gesture intended to produce the feeling of shame in its objects. By bringing the discussion from shame to shaming, the book shifts attention away from considering how aborting women are represented as individual gendered subjects to their representation as members of a community—this theme is continued in Chapter 5. Different modalities of shaming attach to pregnant women depending on how the community measures the value of their potential children. Whereas some women are shamed for abortion, others are shamed for having too many children.

Even when women can legally choose and readily access abortion, women who make this choice are represented as 'failures' or 'losers' and the dual processes of abortion shame and shaming incite them to feel this way. Shame and shaming seek to punish women who have abortions, governing their conduct through the choice of abortion and constructing a hierarchy of reproductive choices, and choice-makers, in the process. The chapter begins with a brief overview of shame and its enmeshment with representations and experiences of abortion.

ABORTION SHAME

Although pro-choice activists have long recognised that shame and shaming diminish women's authority in decisions over their pregnancies, these emotional registers remain under-researched. Shame registers one's deep failure as a social being and is, therefore, simultaneously deeply personal and intensely social. In shame, a subject experiences disconnect between how they perceive themselves and their ideal other— the image of the self the subject wants to be, strives towards, and measures the self against (Manion 2003; Williams 1993). For the psychologist Silvan Tomkins, shame is 'felt as an inner torment, a sickness of the soul' (1995: 133), and Elspeth Probyn similarly writes that '[s]hame goes to the heart of who we think we are. … [it] reveals with precision our values, hopes, and aspirations' (2005: x). As a negative evaluation of the self by the self, a subject is at once the subject and object of shame. Sara Ahmed writes that:

> shame requires an identification with the other who, as witness, returns the subject to itself … My failure before this other hence is profoundly a failure of myself to myself.

In shame, I expose to myself that I am a failure through the gaze of an ideal other. (2004b: 106)

The ideal other is a subject position formed in relation to the social norms that bind communities together. For this reason, shame, whilst deeply felt and interiorised, is also 'the premier social emotion' (Scheff 2003: 239), measuring the degree to which we 'belong', or are marginalised, from our communities. Thus social anthropologist Maree Pardy asserts that shame is 'an emotion of belonging *par excellence* … that at its heart is about generating and maintaining social bonds' (2009: 196).

Shame can also be viewed, in Sara Ahmed's words, 'as *the affective cost of not following the scripts of normative existence*' (2004b: 107). While signalling an individual's transgression from the shared norms, values or ideals that hold communities together, shame also induces 'a strong attachment to the rejecting other, that very attachment that made the person vulnerable to shame in the first place' (Pardy 2009: 204). Subjects of shame can reintegrate into the ideals or norms they fail against, for shame indicates an attachment to the social ideals they have failed to emulate (Ahmed 2004b: 107). All non-normative bodies—as measured against the invisible white, heterosexual, middle-class, male (etc.) standard—pass through shame. Girls pass through shame to adulthood, and the failure to become normatively feminine (through, for example, being pregnant and wanting an abortion) offers a further occasion for shame (Halberstam 2005: 226). Women are 'perpetually attuned' to shame not only because the female body is non-normative, but because women's bodies are normatively read through the sites of corporeality, sexuality and sex, which are all particularly prone to shaming (Bartky 1990: 96; Freud 1961: 133).

An individual's sense of shame is very different to public acts of shaming, which Elspeth Probyn likens to 'a football or even a grenade lobbed at an opposing camp' (2005: 79). Although shaming aims to produce shame in its objects, who are considered to have failed the community or nation, it does not inevitably lead to shame, which relates to one's perception of oneself (as a failure). Shame shares many similarities with guilt, and guilt is therefore included in the ensuing examination. Both emotions reflect a subject's sense of failure according to social expectations, norms or values. When compared to guilt, however, shame is the more 'intense and aversive experience', leading subjects to conceal its causes more frequently and feel a greater sense of isolation and inferiority (Tangney et al. 1996: 1265). Shame is articulated less freely than guilt, for while shame reflects a subject's self, guilt speaks to the subject's actions (Nathanson 1987: 4). The source of abortion guilt would, in other words, be the woman's abortion, which could signal an aberration to the self. In shame, the woman holds herself responsible, with the deviancy of abortion reflecting a flawed, inadequate, immoral or pathological self.

Shame is, then, a feminine emotion that registers an individual's sense of failure as a social being, sticking to non-normative bodies, and, with particular force, to sex and the female body. We can see in this definition alone why abortion is a site particularly prone to shame and shaming. Because shame involves a sense of personal failure, individualising responsibility for unwanted pregnancies is critical to sustaining abortion shame and shaming. The individualisation of blame for unwanted and unplanned pregnancies has remained consistent since the liberalisation of abortion law at the turn of the 1970s, yet, as we shall see, the norm eliciting this self-blame has changed from the ideal of pre-marital chastity to the expectation that women can and should use contraceptives to control their fertility.

SHAME, IMMORALITY, IRRESPONSIBILITY

> Guilt about abortion has been, and in most societies continues to be, deliberately induced as part of a traditional system of social control. In such circumstances it is superfluous to ask whether [abortion] patients experience guilt—it is axiomatic that they will. (Illsley and Hall 1976: 85)

Guilt was the first emotion scholars highlighted when examining the emotional and psychological consequences of abortion for women. In a review of psychological literature on abortion in 1976, Illsley and Hall (from the backgrounds of medical sociology and medicine respectively) concluded that abortion guilt was 'deliberately induced' in nearly every society and, as a consequence, women inevitably felt guilty about their abortions. Like other researchers in the era (for example, Rosen and Martindale 1980: 103), Illsley and Hall argued that abortion guilt was a key mode of social control, used especially to regulate women's sexual conduct to uphold the idea that legitimate sex for women occurred within marriage for the purpose of procreation (1976: 84).

The normative trajectory of women's lives progressed from premarital chastity to marital maternity, with each stage carrying distinct modalities of abortion guilt and shame: premarital sex in one instance and a married woman's refusal of maternity in the other. This pattern, evinced through the Anglophone West (see, for example, Conditt 1990: 33), held true in the Australian context. A study conducted in 1975 of women who had abortions in Melbourne's first legal abortion clinic found that while single women felt guilty about getting pregnant, married women felt guilty about their abortions. The source of guilt for single women was, then, the pregnancy—or, more accurately, the sex leading to pregnancy—while for married women it was not wanting a child. Contrary to the common perception that abortion guilt was inevitable, however, the study also found that only a third of the thirty-two women interviewed experienced guilt (Wainer 1975; West 1984); this finding suggests that, although there was a powerful expectation for women to feel guilt and shame about their abortions, many women did not in fact internalise these emotions, a disjunction between expectation and experience that I consider further below. Reflecting on this data in the 2000s, the researcher Jo Wainer, a prominent activist who had opened the clinic with her husband Bertram Wainer, noted that in the 1970s, 'being pregnant without a wedding ring was considered deviant by many' and unmarried pregnant women were commonly viewed as immoral and even sinful (2008: 33). This was high-lighted in the Women's Electoral Lobby's (1975) submission to the Royal Commission on Human Relationships, which noted that 'Single girls are taught that premarital sex is wrong'. For the unmarried woman, pregnancy was an acute source of shaming and a discrete abortion was one means of reducing or escaping this form of social ostracism (Wainer 1975: 13). As a woman recounting her abortion years later remembered, 'I felt I was a bad girl to have become pregnant before I was married' (cited in Kissane 1998: 4). Married women, in contrast, were expected to want children, meaning that those who had abortions were, as one woman reported to the Royal Commission of 1977, 'made to feel frightfully ashamed of not wanting to be pregnant or have a child' (Evatt 1977, v1: 116).

The idea that married women had abortions simply because they did not want to have children was virtually unspeakable in public discussions of abortion, which generally stereotyped women who had abortions as single (Evatt 1977, v1: 122–130; Gregory 2005: 310). Statistics collected on abortion in Australia suggest that this stereotype had limited purchase: unmarried (not necessarily 'single') women accounted for only 58 to 65 per cent of women having abortions in the 1970s, a figure that remained relatively steady until the end of the millennium (Yusuf and Siedlecky 2002). Although poor, married mothers could justify having abortions for the welfare of their existing children (Chapter 1), this could be seen as a displacement of shame to poverty rather than freedom from shame altogether.

The increasing availability of abortion after the law reforms at the turn of the 1970s constituted one of several socio-cultural shifts of the era that changed attitudes towards unmarried mothers and sexual morality. Other shifts included greater access to the contraceptive pill, the introduction of income support for single mothers, government-funded family planning services, and the closure of maternity homes (Reekie 1998; Swain and Howe 1995). Researchers examining the psychology of abortion in the 1970s were aware that the traditional gender order was in a state of flux and this would affect how women experienced abortion. A dominant strand in the literature argued that women who had abortions internalised traditional views pertaining to women's sexuality despite their own sexual transgressions. Researchers argued that unmarried women who had a high level of internalised 'sex guilt' did not use contraception (which involves sexual competence and know-how) or used it ineffectively leading to unwanted pregnancies and, often, abortions (see for example, Gerrard 1977; Harrison 1973). Based on research with women who had abortions in Michigan, Raye Rosen and Lois Martindale forwarded the opposing view that women who had abortions generally tended to have a 'feminist orientation, including acceptance of one's own sexual activity, and manifest concern with one's own rights' (1980: 107). As a consequence, they generally accepted their abortions on an emotional level and felt little if any guilt. These studies, although offering widely different interpretations of the cause of abortion guilt, nevertheless shared concern with guilt as the primary emotion associated with abortion and connected abortion guilt to normative expectations pertaining to women's sexuality that were in an intense period of change at the time of publication. Researchers did not, however, foresee the nascent strength of a norm that has since come to replace the sanction on non-procreative sex for women: that of a woman's responsibility to use contraceptives in order to prevent unwanted pregnancies.

The imperative to control one's reproductive body transformed during the twentieth century from a wish to a decidedly gendered social obligation. Carol Smart (1992) traces the early history of modern contraceptive devices in the UK to the nineteenth century, where medical, legal and scientific discourses combined to cast women's sexuality as unruly and in need of discipline and control. Today, such modes of discipline and control are thoroughly normalised through the collective fantasy of what Lealle Ruhl (2002) terms a 'willed pregnancy'. Articulated in concepts such as 'planned parenthood' and 'birth control', this fantasy presents pregnancy as the consequence of a rational and deliberate choice. Under the regime of contraceptive responsibility, a woman should not get pregnant unless she wants a child and, as I will detail below, she can guarantee its financial and emotional wellbeing. Pregnancies are framed as preventable and such prevention is seen to reflect responsible, and successful, womanhood (Lowe 2016: 50). In the domain of contraception, therefore, the concept of 'choice' for women is configured as a choice in contraceptive method rather than whether or not to use contraception (Granzow 2007).

There are several causal factors behind the increasing norm of contraceptive use for women. In the 1970s, for example, laws restricted the advertising of contraceptive devices in Australia and elsewhere, and doctors or chemists would routinely refuse to prescribe the contraceptive pill to unmarried women (Evatt 1977, v1: 47–51; McLaren and McLaren 1997: 19; Smyth 2000: 108–109; 58–60). Since then, there has been a proliferation in the type of contraceptives available for women (there have been, tellingly, no parallel development in contraceptives for men), and contraceptive devices have become more affordable and widely available. Contraceptive use was also normalised alongside the public visibility and availability of abortion. Since laws on abortion were liberalised at the turn of the 1970s, a major strand of pro-choice activism has called for the decriminalisation of abortion precisely by representing the procedure as a necessary 'last resort' (ALRA 1972b) to the more desirable method of preventing the birth of unwanted children: contraception (Chapter 1). The leading slogan of the Abortion Law Reform Association (ALRA) was 'Abortion—a right; Contraception—a responsibility'; within strands of pro-choice activism, abortion was commonly framed as a sign of cultural backwardness, with the assumption that the demand for abortion would decrease when contraceptive use increased (ALRA 1974a; Women's Electoral Lobby 1975). Women's liberationists cautioned against the 'propaganda about responsible contraception', arguing this 'takes its toll; a[n unwanted] pregnancy is visible proof of personal failure', leading women who had abortions to feel shame, guilt or at least 'embarrassed about needing an abortion' (Albury 1979: 23).

The aspiration that contraception will eventually eradicate the need for most abortions has remained fixed in strands of pro-choice rhetoric, such as that communicated through the slogan that abortion should be 'safe, legal and rare' (Weitz 2010). This slogan was popularised by the Clintons in the 1990s and gained international traction, so that, for example, it became Tony Abbott's official position on abortion in the Australian election campaign of 2013 (Cannold 2013). Abbott became Prime Minister after this election; as Minister of Health from 2003 to 2006, he was outspokenly anti-abortion (Chapter 5). The mantra that abortion should be 'safe, legal and rare' allows politicians to oppose restricting women's access to abortion while also aligning with the view that abortion is undesirable, reaffirming the well-established view that abortion is a 'necessary evil' rather than a social good (Chapter 1). The mantra powerfully reiterates two unstated, interlocking norms of women's responsibility: first, to discipline their reproductive bodies through the successful use of contraceptives so that, second, they can assume maternal responsibility for all the embryos they conceive.

By reciting a separation between contraception and abortion, pro-choice activists helped provide the historical conditions that produced a distinction that was neither natural nor inevitable (Lowe 2016: 48–49). Barbara Brookes argues that the Offences against the Person Act 1861 (UK), which criminalised abortion in Britain and formed the basis of Australian law, was out of touch with popular views regarding when life began and the related widespread practice of taking an abortifacient to 'bring on' menstruation (1988: 14). At the beginning of the twentieth century, abortion and contraception remained 'fused in the popular mind in the single category of birth control' (2). Early birth control advocates drew a material and moral distinction between abortion and contraception; in 1929, for example, editors of Margaret Sanger's *Birth Control Review* named 'The Abolition of Abortion and Infanticide' as one of ten reasons for birth control (cited in Imber 1979: 825). During the interwar years, the medical profession joined the birth control movement to warn women of the 'wrongful- ness' and 'danger' of abortion (Brookes 1988: 72). The split between abortion and contraception was adopted as an inter- national norm in the official report of the United Nations (2014) International Conference on Population and Develop- ment in 1994, which stated that 'in no case should abortion be promoted as a method of family planning'. The historically produced separation of contraception from abortion focuses research into the development of new contraceptive technol- ogies on preventing fertilisation—anything else, as Beverly Winikoff writes, 'might be accused of being abortion'. As a consequence, technologies that require relatively rigid modes of self-regulation, such as the contraceptive pill, which women must take at approximately the same time every day, remain privileged over those that, as Winikoff continues, 'could exact- ly match what women say they want: something very effective, very safe, inexpensive and reversible, with minimal require- ments to use' (2014: 28).

In order for abortions to become rare, the vast majority of conceived pregnancies must go on to produce babies. While in debates over abortion, policymakers assume some respon- sibility for ensuring this—by often contradictory measures, such as putting condom vending machines in high schools or promoting abstinence—ultimately, each individual woman who engages in heterosexual sex is held responsible for preventing unwanted pregnancies. Academic studies of contraceptive use generally focus on female subjects and often have the explicit aim to, as a study published early in 2014 stated, improve the 'consistency of use and ease of access to effective birth control to prevent unintended pregnancies' (Dixon et al. 2014: 341). A study from the early 2000s found that 95 per cent of Australian women who were likely to be fertile and have sex with men used some form of contraception (Richters et al. 2003). Women use contraceptives for a range of reasons, not only to prevent unwanted pregnancies. The high number of women who use contraceptives nevertheless suggests there is an expectation from others, and a self-expectation, to do so. As the rising efficiency and availability of contraceptives has increased women's ability to control whether they become pregnant, women have become normatively obliged to effectively and efficiently use contraceptives; thus constraint (in the form of a cultural obligation to use contraceptives) has accompanied the increasing freedom from reproductive norms of sexuality. Yet the disciplinary regime accompanying the proliferation of contraceptive devices is often left uninterrogated, disguised in part because the proliferation and use of contraceptives is one development of the twentieth century most associated with women's freedom in the West (Phillips 2009).

The norm of contraceptive responsibility obfuscates the fallibility of contraceptive methods, the side effects of contraceptives, and the discomfort some women feel when taking them (Mills and Barclay 2006). Healthcare professionals often fail to disclose the full range of side effects to women; Pam Lowe suggests this is to help ensure women 'make the "right" or "rational" decisions' by using rather than forgoing contraceptives (Lowe 2016: 60). The norm of contraceptive responsibility also takes contraception and its use outside the realm of social relationships and power. Intimate sexual relationships between men and women take place within a web of gendered power relationships that can make it difficult, for example, for women to negotiate safe sex practices with male partners. The stringent use of contraceptives is also somewhat dissonant with broader ideologies of sex as being unrestrained and spontaneous (Boyle 1997: 82–101). When the gendered responsibility for contraceptive use is overlaid onto this, we can see that the control women are expected to exercise over their reproductive potential in heterosexual relationships is not applied to men at the same level. The expectation that women must protect themselves against unwanted pregnancy means that women's sexuality has remained fused with reproduction and maternity, a fusion enabled by the simultaneous erasure of reproduction and the privileging of pleasure in male sexual bodies.

There is no law or other form of coercive power inducing women to take contraceptives or, in countries where women can access abortion lawfully, to continue their pregnancies to term if contraceptives fail. How, then, is the responsible pregnant body—the woman who controls her reproductive potential to ensure that all the embryos she conceives go on to be born—policed? One mechanism is the historically produced hierarchy between contraception and abortion, which views abortion as qualitatively distinct from contraception and as, ultimately, wrong (Brookes 1988: 2). The wrongness of abortion, and rightness of contraception, ultimately rests on the norm of foetal motherhood (Berlant 1997: 99); this norm works alongside that of the 'willed pregnancy' to produce an encompassing reproductive schema, where all pregnancies conceived go on to produce babies, and pregnant women and their foetuses are automatically assigned the identities of mother and child. Within this schema, contraceptive use signals proper responsibility for the self, and abortion manifests as a failure of individual responsibility. The ideal female sexual and reproductive body is controlled and contained; opposed to the excessive, unrestrained reproductive and sexual body of the aborting woman (Baird 1998b: 8). This contrast shows continuity between the imperative to use contraception and the idea that women should refrain from sexual activity altogether if they do not want children: sexual restraint is no longer considered abstinence, but good contraceptive behaviour.

It is 'extremely common' for women who have had abortions to feel that they have failed in their responsibility to use contraceptives effectively (Kirkman et al. 2010: 126; Ryan et al. 1994: 136). This sense of individual failure is a precondition for abortion shame and shaming, which require abortion to be positioned as blameworthy and this blame to be thoroughly de-contextualised and individualised. Aborting women are shamed for being irresponsible in many ways. The popular pro-choice slogans that abortion should be 'safe, legal and rare' and 'Abortion—a right; Contraception—a responsibility' are technologies of shaming; as are the widespread beliefs that improved sex education programs and greater access to contraceptives could and should prevent most unwanted pregnancies (and thus abortions). Following the Abortion Law Reform Association's lead, politicians from the 1970s onward have generally supported liberal access to abortion alongside the promotion of sex education programs and greater access to contraceptives to ensure that, to return to the slogan, abortion should be safe, legal and, also, rare (for example, Fiona Nash, Senator; Australia 2006a: 1089; Jenny Macklin, MP; Australia 2006c: 53).

The assumption that effective contraceptive use should eliminate the need for abortion underwrites much public health research into abortion—one typical study, for example, cites statistics on abortion as proof that '[t]here remains a need for continuing emphasis on better contraceptive use' (Yusuf and Siedlecky 2002: 15). Similarly, state health policies frequently view abortion as 'a resolvable problem with the healthcare provision of contraception' (Beynon-Jones 2013: 105). Women who have abortions are also designated as failures through contraceptive counselling, a routine component of the abortion procedure (Ryan, Ripper and Buttfield 1994: 193). Recent standards for Scottish abortion services, for example, explicitly require that 60 per cent of women leave abortion clinics with 'one of the more effective methods of contraception' (Beynon-Jones 2013: 105). Although perhaps not intended this way, this practice could easily be read as a reprimand for irresponsible conduct and incitement to ensure that women act responsibly in the future. Accompanying the stereotype that aborting women are single is the persistent belief that they are young and sexually inexperienced, which further encourages women who have abortions to feel foolishly culpable for their pregnancies. As examples of this frequently reiterated generalisation, journalists and parliamentarians spanning the last forty years have labelled aborting women: 'appallingly irresponsible' (Race Mathews, MP; Australia 1973: 1981); 'young and blithely unaware of the facts on contraception' (Stephens 1987a); and the 'young and foolish [people] who make very stupid mistakes' (Helen Shardey, MLA; Victoria 2008a: 3318). Today, the idea that aborting women have failed in their responsibility to use contraceptives successfully provides strangers with a platform from which to judge and blame them. When Greens MLC Coleen Hartland, for example, told her story of abortion to the media in the lead up to the decriminalisation of abortion in Victoria in 2008, saying she terminated her pregnancy because she was unable to financially support a child at the time, a letter to the editor in Melbourne's broadsheet newspaper *The Age* read: 'I wonder if she had heard of contraception, or maybe she was too poor' (Davis 2008).

While the ideal of a chosen pregnancy is a major source of abortion shame and shaming, the negative judgement women internalise in shame relates not to a woman's culpability for the unwanted pregnancy *per se*, but to her blameworthiness for getting pregnant unintentionally *and then* having an abortion. Approximately 40 per cent of pregnancies worldwide, including in Australia and the USA, are 'unplanned'

(Baird 2006a: 143; Finer and Zolna 2014; Singh et al. 2010). The experiences of women with unplanned pregnancies resulting in birth are not, however, surveyed for guilt and shame, in sharp contrast to the preoccupation 'with "guilt" as an unavoidable consequence of abortion' in medical literature (Ryan, Ripper and Buttfield 1994: 30–32). A huge body of scientific literature has amassed on the 'psychological sequelae' of abortion (Lee 2003: 152). In contrast, the experiences of women who continue unplanned pregnancies to term are not constructed as a 'problem' that requires investigation to the same degree. Thus the shame generated by a sense of failure to use contraceptives effectively is frequently activated only when a woman chooses abortion. This is because abortion symbolises a further failure—of not being maternal, or of being selfish.

FAILED MOTHERS

I examined the stereotype of the 'selfish aborting woman' in Chapter 2, where I argued that the narrative that abortion is an incredibly difficult decision that women make in the best interests of their potential children allows individuals to rehabilitate abortion to the norm of maternal selflessness for pregnant women. Here I take up this argument by looking at how women internalise this narrative when speaking about their own abortions, and I suggest this can be read as a means of responding to, abating or managing the guilt and shame that accompany the 'selfish aborting woman' stereotype.

In their review of nineteen papers that examined women's abortion experiences from eight countries, published between 1996 and 2008, Maggie Kirkman et al. found that 'decisions to terminate a pregnancy were often influenced by the desire to be a good parent ... [aborting women's] own needs coincide with those of the potential child' (2009: 377). Kirkman et al.'s subsequent research further supported this conclusion. Based on interviews with sixty women presenting at the Pregnancy Advisory Service at the Royal Women's Hospital (Melbourne) in 2007–2008, Kirkman et al. asserted that for many women, abortion was 'a solution if you are not ready for motherhood' (2010: 124). The researchers drew on the work of philosopher Carol Gilligan to argue that, for women, abortion decisions presented a 'problem of care and responsibility in relationships' (124). They reported that aborting women were often preoccupied with countering the perceived image of themselves as, in the women's own words, 'cruel', 'heartless', 'cold', 'cold-hearted', 'detached' or 'disconnected', positioning themselves instead 'as having warm feelings and being aware that they ought, as women, to sacrifice their own needs for others' (124–126).

Social scientific research constructs the problem it seeks to investigate, making it impossible to fully disentangle researchers' questions, objectives and findings from the experiences they report and analyse (Reekie 1998: 166–167). Kirkman et al.'s study is located in a field of abortion scholarship focused on women's reasons for abortion, a field that bolsters a more general incitement for women to justify their abortions to others, with such justifications determining the broader social acceptance and cultural endorsement of each woman's choice. Kirkman et al.'s research is also influenced by maternal pro-choice politics, which supports abortion by disavowing the possibility of a 'selfish abortion', claiming instead that women terminate pregnancies because of their maternal responsibility towards future children (Chapter 2). Drawing on scholars such as Leslie Cannold and Carol Gilligan, Kirkman et al. 'build a picture of women … with a badly-timed pregnancy, for whom abortion is identified as a difficult solution to a complex problem' (2010: 128). Kirkman et al. designate unwanted pregnancies as 'badly-timed' pregnancies and reinforce the narrative that abortion is inevitably an incredibly difficult and complex decision for women; these rhetorical gestures perpetuate the norm of motherhood for pregnant women, which works to re-position abortion as deviant and, consequently, a site for shame and shaming.

Kirkman et al.'s research also suggests that women who have abortions internalise a sense of failure against the norm of female selflessness—this is evidenced in the women's concern to frame their abortions as difficult decisions undertaken for the best interests of their potential children. The depiction of abortion as selfless is a response, I would suggest, to the default position that abortion is a selfish decision. In its attachment to selfishness (a sign of a woman's failure against the other-centred norm) abortion is a trigger for shame. Shame registers an aborting woman's self-evaluation as (at least possibly, or easily perceived by others as) selfish, irresponsible and reckless, and the narrative of a difficult abortion undertaken because of a woman's responsibility towards her potential child helps counteract this. The narrative that abortion is, in Kirkman et al.'s words, 'a difficult solution to a complex problem' is performative, working in a similar rehabilitative fashion as grief (Chapter 3); by reciting it, women can restore their identities to normative expectations and ideologies, particularly those pertaining to motherhood. Abortion shame can be seen, to redeploy Ahmed's phrase, as the 'affective cost' of failing according to the related norms of the willed pregnancy and motherhood for pregnant women. Yet through shame, women can also '"*show*" *that … [their] failure to measure up to a social ideal is temporary*' (2004b: 107). In this way, shame can be pejorative *and* restorative. Aborting women register their failure through shame, and this acknowledgment, and subsequent attempts at rehabilitation through identification with the selfless (maternal) ideal, re-aligns them with the values and norms they have failed against.

Concealment is another method women employ to manage abortion shame and shaming. Shame is a deeply internalised emotion and the dynamic of shame is to render its sources 'unspeakable'. One of the most measurable aspects of abortion shame is therefore the high proportion of women who routinely conceal their abortions from other people. Most women anticipate that, if disclosed, their abortions would incite negative judgement from others and, through fear of shaming and an internalised feeling of shame, engage in a practice of selective disclosure, generally concealing their abortions from friends and family members (Astbury-Ward et al. 2012). This secrecy encourages women to view their abortions as isolated, lonely and abnormal events (Astbury-Ward et al. 2012; Kumar et al. 2009; Major and Gramzow

1999). Aborting women's voices are also frequently absent in public debate about abortion. Abortion secrecy helps secure the norms that the practice of abortion threatens to reveal as tenuous and frequently transgressed. For example, abortion silence obscured the high proportion of women who had sex before marriage while this was considered morally deviant; 'shotgun marriages' or seclusion followed by adoption of the child were further tools of concealment (Swain and Howe 1995: 47–52, 141–142). Today, abortion silence disguises the fact that not all pregnant women want to be mothers, and women do not simply 'choose' to become pregnant when they want to be mothers.

The silence that abortion shame engenders prevents women from citing and, moreover, reciting the discourses surrounding abortion; this process of recitation enables norms of gender to open up to instability and a '*de*constructing possibility' (Butler 1993: 10). Women who have abortions may enact this process of repetition, recitation and displacement within their personal reflections and memories. The anti-stigma movement aims to 'break the silence' and has encouraged more women to do so in public forums, particularly those found online (Sanger 2017: 226–228); nevertheless, abortion, including the personal experience of abortion, is generally represented by people who have not had abortions themselves, which affords significant space for stereotypes of women and presumptions about how they would *and should* experience abortions to drive socio-cultural representations. Secrecy also, in Carol Sanger's words, 'distorts the quality of lawmaking by omitting from public consideration whatever information would emerge if abortion were not a discrediting closeted matter' (2017: 68). Representations of abortion, and laws pertaining to abortion, then (re)solidify and regulate norms of femininity (Sheldon 1993).

There is a cyclical and self-perpetuating relationship linking normativity, shame and secrecy that is difficult to fracture. The shame that saturates abortion encourages secrecy, which then helps sustain norms—the willed pregnancy and foetal motherhood—that are, in fact, frequently transgressed. Abortion is thereby rendered exceptional rather than routine. The shame-silence-exceptionality-shame cycle produces another, where normative femininity and discourses of abortion (including its emotional registers) are mutually perpetuating. Maternal femininity elicits the narrative of a difficult abortion followed by grief and shame, and these emotions are then taken as proof of the naturalness of maternal femininity. These self-perpetuating cycles help explain why the same emotions are repeatedly attached to abortion across multiple discursive sites; concealment and secrecy, effects of the non-normativity of abortion, make such emotions resilient to displacement and change.

Abortion is a routine component of women's reproductive lives. The frequency with which women conceal their abortions from others, however, indicates that they often internalise the experience as an abnormal and deviant one that others would not readily accept. Abortion is commonly perceived to result from a series of bad choices: the contraceptive and sexual choices leading to unwanted pregnancy, then the selfish choice of abortion. With a woman's need for abortion so individualised, the abortion decision, and the abortion procedure, are abstracted from any social or economic context. Shame does not merely compel aborting women to view their abortions as bad, therefore, but to view themselves negatively—specifically as potentially selfish, irresponsible failures—which acts as a form of self-punishment. Shame, therefore, works in tandem with happiness and grief to regulate a responsible, maternal ideal for women through their choices and despite their abortions. Shame polices the boundaries of normative femininity, inciting aborting women to regulate their own conduct by remaining silent about their transgressions from the norm. Maternal femininity is thereby sustained despite the high numbers of women who have abortions.

I have so far argued that over the last forty years the norms that aborting women are measured against, and sometimes measure themselves against, have changed from those of premarital chastity and marital maternity to the ideal of contraceptive responsibility and the 'willed pregnancy'. Within the regime of contraceptive responsibility, each woman is incited to use contraception effectively to ensure that all babies conceived go on to be born. Thus, while a woman's unwanted or unplanned pregnancy provides the conditions for shame, individualising the responsibility for pregnancy, shame is not necessarily triggered unless she decides to terminate her pregnancy. There is a further component of this formation I mentioned in passing but did not examine in full. Namely, the norm of the responsible female subject uses contraception until she has gathered the necessary financial, social and educational resources to mother effectively. As a consequence, some pregnancies are marked as irresponsible and problematic regardless of whether they lead to birth or abortion. The distribution of pregnancy shaming depends on how a woman's pregnancy aligns with her allotted reproductive responsibilities to the broader community.

A NATION'S SHAME

> [E]very abortion is a tragedy, and up to 100,000 abortions a year is this generation's legacy of unutterable shame. (Tony Abbott, Australian Minister for Health, 2004–2007, Australia 2006d: 114–115)

Politicians and other influential public commentators frequently depict abortion as a nation's shame, a sentiment commonly communicated through the discourse that there are 'too many' abortions. In the words of Tony Abbott in his role as the Australian Minister for Health, abortion is the 'unutterable shame' of a generation. With this pronouncement, Abbott reiterated several common anti-abortion assumptions. The idea that a generation is responsible for the nation's abortion rate, for example, depends on a fantasy that there were far fewer abortions before women's access to the procedure was legally sanctioned. I leave discussion of this, and the politics behind discussing abortion in terms of the nation or the nation's abortion rate, for Chapter 5. The rest of this chapter focuses on the 'too many abortions' discourse as a technology of shaming that targets specific bodies for failing the nation.

Barbara Baird has written that the proclamation that there are 'too many abortions' inscribes 'the body of *each* pregnant woman who has an abortion, or who wants one, with unacceptable excess. For if it is not her, then who is it who contributes to there being "too many"?' (1998b: 9) The 'too many' discourse is a technology of shaming that targets all women who have abortions; yet shaming for reproductive failure more generally is distributed according to a class- and race-based logic, revealing that it is the abortions of a particular demographic that are constructed as the real problem for the social body. White, middle-class, post-teen women are shamed for having too few children (and too many abortions); conversely, women who fall outside this norm are frequently shamed for having too many children.

The virtues that successfully controlling one's reproductive body are said to display—sexual restraint and responsibility—have historically been associated with white, post-teen, middle-class women. For instance, in Australia, the Royal Commission on Human Relationships of 1977 presumed that such women were likely to use contraceptives effectively, grouping migrant women, Indigenous women, and teenagers as individuals with 'special contraceptive needs' (Evatt 1977, v1: 104). Since the 1970s, the figure of the 'teen mother' has been an especially maligned 'excessively reproductive body' (Tyler 2008). She is commonly assumed to be sexually immature and irresponsible; she is also a classed body, associated, increasingly with the advance of neoliberal modes of governance, with welfare dependency (Chapter 2). Since the liberalisation of abortion laws, proposed solutions to the national 'shame' of teenage abortion and motherhood recommend moral education, involving instruction in sexual restraint or contraceptive use (Beaumont 2004; Dunn 2004; Dunn et al. 2004; Fitzgerald 1976; Stark 2008; Stephens 1986; Toy 2000; Westmore 1976).

Initiatives aimed at preventing teenage pregnancy are premised on the assumption that pregnant teenagers are failures regardless of whether they have abortions or become mothers. To return to the rhetoric Tony Abbott used to construct abortion as a social problem: '[i]f half the effort were put into discouraging teenage promiscuity as into preventing teenage speeding, there might be fewer abortions, fewer traumatised young women and fewer dysfunctional families' (cited in Shaw 2004: 1). In this statement, Abbott seemed to designate all (female) teen sexual behaviour as 'promiscuous', sidestepping contraception in favour of chastity, a feature typical of conservative, anti-abortion talk. If these women's irresponsible sexual escapades did not result in abortion and traumatised women (Chapter 3), he presumed they would lead to teenage motherhood, which he matter-of-factly framed as 'dysfunctional'. By attaching abortion to teenage bodies, Abbott further associated abortion with immaturity and recklessness.

While Abbott designated teen pregnancy as a site for shaming whether it led to abortion or motherhood, those who are not opposed to abortion in all instances often construct abortion as the less shaming alternative. This was the implication of the speech one MP gave in support of decriminalising abortion in Victoria, which invoked the image of 'impoverished women living on our high-rise public housing estates … in a number of cases very young women, in their early 20s—who have had two, and in some cases three, children' (Wynn, MLA; Victoria 2008a: 3339). Politicians and the wider community are far more accepting of abortion amongst women on welfare payments, teenage or otherwise, than women who are not (Chapter 2). Motherhood is an acute source of social shaming for women on welfare, particularly teen women, whom politicians and the media deem as unable to support their children emotionally or financially.

Associated with low levels of education (a sign of middle-class respectability) and welfare dependency, teen mothers are figured in the national imagination as, to deploy Imogen Tyler's phrasing, 'hypervisible "[f]ilthy whites" … A whiteness contaminated with poverty' (2008a: 25). Accompanying the excessive reproductive bodies of 'filthy whites' are those of non-white women. Women who are marked by their race are routinely denigrated for being unfit mothers and for having 'too many' children (Flavin 2008; Jones 2013; Roberts 1997). For example, Project Prevention, established in the USA and moving to the UK in 2010, pays users of alcohol or drugs to accept long acting reversible contraceptives (LARCs) or, in the USA only, sterilisation (Lowe 2016: 56–57). The figure of the 'pregnant drug user' or 'crack mum' is saturated with connotations of race and class (Roberts 1997: 156–157). In a further example, in 2006 the Australian government amended the policy commonly termed the 'Baby Bonus' so that Aboriginal women living in remote Indigenous communities of the Northern Territory and all (Indigenous and non-Indigenous) women under the age of eighteen would receive the maternity payment in instalments rather than as a lump sum. The government claimed that this policy amendment would curb the irresponsible reproductive behaviour of these sections of the community (Cutcher and Milroy 2010).

The Howard Government introduced the Baby Bonus as an attempt to boost Australia's population in response to the country's declining fertility rate (Kevin 2009). Thus by placing limitations on this payment for teen and some Aboriginal women, the Government was explicitly absenting them from the more general incentive placed on women to have more children. The declining fertility rate was also articulated alongside the suggestion that Muslim women were having too many children; as Shakira Hussein notes, '[d]emographic rivalry has become a prominent theme in global discussions about Muslims and Islam' and Muslim women are frequently represented as 'repulsive breeders of the enemy horde' (Hussein 2016: 123). The former Liberal MP, Danna Vale, notoriously drew abortion politics into fears pertaining to the comparative birth rates of Muslim and non-Muslim women in 2006, when she predicted that Australia would soon be a Muslim nation because 'we are almost aborting ourselves out of existence' (cited in Maiden 2006). Responding to critics who noted her exclusion of Muslims from the category 'Australian', she soon clarified the statement, further emphasising the distinction she was drawing between the under-fertility of 'mainstream' Australians and the excessive fertility of Muslims: her comment, she clarified, 'was aimed at mainstream Australia, not members of the Australian Muslim community ... It is non-Muslim Australians who are not having enough children'

(Vale 2006). At the 2003 Population Summit in Adelaide, convened as a response to the declining fertility rate, Malcolm Turnbull (2003), another Liberal MP (and Prime Minister from October 2015), compared low fertility rates in Western nations to excessively reproductive third world nations, particularly 'Moslem [sic] countries'. He warned that '[a]t the peak of our technological achievement the Western World appears to have lost the will to reproduce itself', adding that low fertility rates present the 'gravest threat to Western society'. Turnbull thereby transplanted onto the international arena the historically-cemented, localised fear that, in Vale's words, 'mainstream Australians'—non-Muslim, non-Indigenous, and presumably white—were not having enough children, positing the excessively fecund bodies of 'third world' women as threatening Western civilisation itself.

National worrying over the excessive fertility of 'filthy whites' and racially-marked women is a response to the declining fertility of middle-class, white, educated women. Such women, in Imogen Tyler's words, are 'continually chastised for "putting career over motherhood" and "leaving it too late" to have children' (2008: 30). Because the excessively reproductive body—non-white, welfare dependent, or teenage—is shamed for having too many children, the 'too many abortions' discourse implicitly targets and circumscribes the under-fertile bodies of middle-class, post-teen, white women. This uneven distribution of shaming for reproductive failure is symptomatic of a crisis in whiteness.

Because the ideal of a willed pregnancy references, as it produces, a white body, reproductive choice, whether it be abortion or other forms of contraception, is associated with the very bodies the nation wants to reproduce (Phillips 2009). Subsequently, one of the discourses used to communicate women's supposed freedom in the West contains the seeds of its own undoing. The ideal of a 'willed pregnancy' is presented as a decidedly secular and Western discourse associated with modernity, education, and women's freedom. Its normalisation alongside declining fertility rates in the West has driven a fear that the 'wrong women'—religious, atavistic, uneducated, and oppressed, confined to the private sphere and to a life of perpetual reproduction—are having too many children (Dogra 2011). When taken as part of the schema of 'stratified reproduction' (Roberts 1997), the idea that abortion is a nation's shame reads like an admission that white sociocultural dominance is waning, converting this fear into the individual pathology (and excess) of aborting women. To apply Sara Ahmed's formulation of national shame to this example, white aborting women fail to reproduce the nation's offspring and are thus 'shaming by proxy: they do not approximate the form of the good citizen' (Ahmed 2004b: 108).

CONCLUSION

Women who have abortions enter into a web of abortion shame and shaming. Shame is an index of one's sense of belonging to a community and success as a social being, and an abortion signals a woman's failure to belong in several ways. Measures of belonging and success are firmly tied to sociohistorical context, ensuring that the precise norms aborting women fail against change over time. The shift from the ideals of pre-marital chastity and marital maternity to that of contraceptive responsibility has altered the landscape of abortion shame over the past fifty years. Historical variability in the triggers for abortion shame suggests that abortion, in itself, is not a source for shame. The persistence of abortion shame since the period of liberalisation also indicates, however, that abortion has remained antithetical to norms of appropriate and responsible female conduct through this era.

Abortion shame and shaming regulate conduct without resort to external regulative forces, such as the law, in a way that powerfully naturalises (by individualising and de-politicising) normative values, practices and beliefs. Although shame works outside of the law, shame and shaming are intensified in jurisdictions that criminalise abortion and designate the women who have abortions as criminals. The law codifies normative morality, thus criminalisation acts as an intensified mode of shaming (Cook 2014). The designation of women who have abortions as outsiders has, however, survived the decriminalisation of abortion because of the continued attachment of women's sexuality to reproduction, the maternal identity of pregnant women and the multiple vectors that work to ascribe the value of women's reproductive choices differentially along axes such as age, race and class. With shame converting the non-normativity of abortion into a sense of personal failure, aborting women materialise as failed selves.

Although I have suggested in this chapter that shame can be measured through women's secrecy, in the absence of other empirical indicators for shame it is worth considering whether shame, in fact, belongs to the realm of experience or representation. Shame certainly works alongside abortion grief and maternal happiness to discursively realign aborting women with social ideals and expectations, particularly those pertaining to motherhood and women's sexuality. Norms pertaining to contraception and pregnancy may produce an expectation that women will experience guilt and shame upon abortion, but women could very well internalise alternative ideals and expectations when making their experiences meaningful. We can say with certainty that women are shamed for having abortions through various means, but whether or not women commonly internalise this shaming as shame is more difficult to gauge.

Silence is a management strategy women employ to minimise the shaming that accompanies abortion. Women can also manage shaming by narrating their abortions through reciting the emotional economy I have outlined in this book—that of a difficult decision undertaken for the welfare of those around them, particularly their potential children, with negative consequences, including grief, shame and guilt. The incitement to remain silent about abortion dissuades women from displacing the narrative that so powerfully delineates how women should experience abortion. Shame, or protection against shaming, fuels the perpetuating relationship, where normative femininity powers and is consolidated and confirmed through discourse on abortion. With normative, maternal femininity regulated through the choice of abortion, this choice is (re)produced as a source of shame and shaming. And so the cycle endures, and abortion continues to be framed as a consequence of individual irresponsibility and as a non-normative, exceptional choice for pregnant women to make.

This chapter moved us from considering abortion in terms of broader norms and ideologies pertaining to gender and gendered subjectivities to considering the role discourses of abortion play in the formation of nations and national identities. I examined the relationship between abortion and national identity here by considering shaming as a socio-political tool that marks some reproductive bodies as belonging to, and others as excluded from, the nation. Chapter 5 turns to examine the nationalist register of abortion discourse in more detail, considering how control over reproduction is key to attempts to manage the size and constitution of a nation's population.

CHAPTER 5

THE NATION'S CHOICE?

A certain imam from the Lakemba mosque actually says Australia is going to be a Muslim nation in 50 years' time … I didn't believe him at the time. But when you look at the birth rates … we are aborting ourselves almost out of existence by 100,000 abortions every year. You multiply that by 50 years—that's 5 million potential Australians we won't have here. (Vale, Federal Member for Hughes cited in Maiden 2006)

Third World immigrant births will be an outright majority of all babies born in Britain by the year 2030 … Britain faces immanent colonisation via the womb. (British National Party 2016)

Reproduction is critical to the project of nation building, for the number and 'type' of people born—or, in the case of abortion, not born—bears directly on the size and constitution of the body politic. Thus, the comparative rate of birth and abortion between citizens that are designated to be 'desirable' and 'non-desirable' are a repeated source of concern for nationalists. In a webpage calling for funds to support its campaign, the British National Party (BNP) compares 'Third World' with 'indigenous British babies' to warn of 'colonisation via the womb'. The webpage features an image of a white baby with blue eyes embedded into the British flag with the slogan 'endangered species alert'. This type of rhetoric is a classic reversal, where Britain, whose position as a first world country was gained through its violently expansionist empire, is perceived to be under threat from the invasion of those it colonised. Sharing the racialised logic of 'stratified reproduction' (Roberts 1997), a former Australian MP, Danna Vale, compared 'Australian' with 'Muslim' births to warn that 'we [Australians] are aborting ourselves almost out of existence'. In both these examples, mutually constitutive categories of people—the 'Muslim' and 'Third World immigrant'—are excluded from, and posed as threats to, the nation; women are also prescribed a very particular role in ensuring the survival, or destruction, of the body politic: breeders of the nation or its others. The gendered role of motherhood is thereby mapped onto nationalist aspirations for the future, a future articulated in racist and racialised tones.

This book has, until this point, been concerned with examining the cultural politics of abortion in terms of ideologies and norms of gender, race and class. We have seen how ideas of maternal happiness and reproductive shame attach to bodies differentially according to stereotypes of the 'good mother', a stereotype that is continually affirmed through her pathological others to be white and in possession of the social and economic resources deemed integral to her capacity to mother effectively, without state support. Stereotypes of the 'good mother' determine the cultural acceptability of pregnant women's reproductive choices, whether they are abortion or motherhood. In the previous chapter, I argued that stereotypes of the 'good mother' differentiate the women who are commonly supposed to have 'too many' children from those who are considered to have too few (and 'too many' abortions). This chapter continues examining abortion in terms of broader national schemas of reproduction, taking as its conceptual focus national debates about the abortion rate, which are often carried through the commonsense dictum that there are 'too many abortions'. The idea that the nation's abortion rate should be reduced is frequently cited as, in pro-choice, former president Barack Obama's words, 'common ground' that unites anti- and pro-choice forces in a singular aim (cited in Freedman and Weitz 2012: 39). While Chapter 4 examined the statement that there are 'too many abortions' as a technology of shaming, here I focus on the cultural politics of fear that animates the discussion of abortion in terms of numbers and the nation's abortion rate. In doing so, I consider how, within the cultural terrain of abortion, the foetus is not only represented as a pregnant woman's 'baby', but also a citizen of the nation.

The work of Australian abortion scholar Barbara Baird offers us a way of thinking about how debate about abortion aids the process of nation building. Baird argues that nationalist debates over abortion represent an attempt to discipline white women's reproductive bodies to reproduce the white nation.

Debating the 'problem' of abortion is an attempt to, in Baird's words, 'make like reproduce like'; it is also 'a displacement activity where anxious white nationalists can performatively reinstate white power' (2006b: 214). By expressing anxiety over abortion and a wish to act in order to reduce the abortion rate, individuals transform women's reproductive bodies into objects to be worried about and managed, and themselves into agents who have the power to enact such forms of management. This is of course a fantasy of control for, ultimately, it is each pregnant woman who decides whether or not to have an abortion.[1]

This chapter builds on the connection Baird identifies between anxiety over the abortion rate and white nationalism. It begins by considering the role reproduction plays in racialised nation building before outlining how anxiety and fear generate the figure of the 'foetus-citizen'. The chapter then brings this theoretical framework to bear on the specific context of Australia, examining two periods of moral panic pertaining to abortion—the 1970s and mid-2000s. After showing the existence of these two parallel moral panics, the chapter moves to examine their underlying causes. In times of national crisis, I will argue, the aborting woman can become a conduit for fears relating to more than the practice of abortion. The fear circulating around her relates to a fundamentally unmanageable anxiety that the white hetero-family is under threat and will not remain the dominant form of social organisation into the future. The white aborting woman relays historically-sedimented fears of white vulnerability; this vulnerability is inextricable from the promotion of the white hetero-family as a national ideal and the will to secure the series of gendered and racial privileges this ideal helps sustain.

REPRODUCING THE WHITE NATION

In order to examine the politics of abortion as a mode of racialised nation-building it is necessary to establish a connection between race, reproduction and nation. The following section does this in two stages: the first examines the connection between race and nation, and the second between reproduction and the race-nation bind.

'The nation' is a socio-historical construct forged through a continual process of demarcating who belongs, and who is excluded from, the body politic (Hage 1998). Such technologies of inclusion and exclusion take many forms, ranging from the formal designation of which people should be afforded the legal rights and protections of citizens to the informal norms that construct a national character through manufacturing shared values, traditions, histories and futures. Informal and formal modes of exclusion work together: so, for example, the denial of the writ of *habeas corpus* to asylum seekers in countries that have regimes of mandatory detention is rationalised through stereotypes of the 'bogus Asylum Seeker', 'terrorist' or 'queue jumper', which depict such people as undeserving of citizenship rights and as potentially injurious to the nation (Bashford and Strange 2002; Tyler 2013: 75–103).

The concepts of race and nation were forged contemporaneously; both are constitutive of one another, with race forming the fictive unity around which notions of national belonging are communicated. National ideas of belonging in Australia (Hage 1998), Canada (Simpson 2016), New Zealand (Spoonley 2015), the UK (Gilroy 1991; Lonergan 2012) and the USA (Bailey and Zita 2007; Martinot 2007) are formed through what Ghassan Hage (1998) terms a 'White nation fantasy'. This is 'a fantasy of a nation governed by White people, a fantasy of White supremacy', where 'the nation as a space is structured around White culture' (18), and white people are routinely positioned, and position themselves, as rightfully dominating demographically and controlling national space through, for example, their disproportionate representation in cultural mediums, parliaments and judicial systems. Race was initially conceived of in biological terms. From the late twentieth century onward, whiteness has come to operate more generally as a form of cultural capital communicated through an 'Anglo-ness'—this is no longer a biological property (although white skin is certainly an important marker of whiteness), but a 'democratic-tolerant-freedom-of-speech' essence (Hage 1998: 123). Cultural racism operates through the designation of some communities as pathological or dysfunctional (Balibar 1991; Gilroy 1993). Within nationalist logic, such communities need to be excluded from the nation, either literally (through controls on migration, for example) or through assimilationist policies (such as 'Burqa Bans') aimed to make 'them' more like the national 'we'.

Race is attached to reproduction because it is commonly supposed to be an 'essence' that is carried from one generation to the next (Weinbaum 2004: 8). This perceived essence is biological, carried through markers such as skin colour, and also forms the cultural values (including religious) and patterns of behaviour that are said to pass from one generation to the next. In the US context, for example, Steven Martinot (2007) argues that criminality is commonly perceived to be a form of learnt behaviour transmitted inter-generationally within African American communities. In this way, African Americans are blamed for their own social marginalisation and broader structural inequities are made invisible. Black mothers are particular objects of blame.

The biological process of reproduction is gendered feminine (Chapter 4), and women are also seen to bear primary responsibility for raising children and the inter-generational transmission of cultural values and social mores this entails (Anthias and Yuval-Davis 1989; Lentin 2004; Lonergan 2012: 36–37). Because the nation is conceived of as a 'reproducible racial formation' (Phillips 2009: 608), women's reproductive labour is a national resource harnessed in the project of making, and remaking, racialised, national communities, so that, as Martinot writes of the US context, '[t]he birth of American whiteness and national identity converge across and through the race-marked bodies of women' (2007: 92). Women's reproductive labour is managed through several interlocking means. In the early to mid-twentieth century in Australia, the USA and Canada, for example, state officials routinely took Indigenous children away from their families for the purpose of assimilation (Fournier and Crey 1997; Jacobs 2009); Indigenous women—along with Latina and African American women in the US context—were also subject to practices such as coerced contraception, unsafe forms of contraception and forced sterilisation into the 1970s (Moreton-Robinson 2000: 171; Roberts 1997; Stote 2012). In her landmark text *Killing the Black Body,* Dorothy Roberts (1997) identifies institution-alised processes in the USA in the 1980s and 1990s where black pregnant women who tested positive for recreational drugs where given the options of abortion or jail (181); black women who entered the criminal justice system through detected drug use were also given the options of an extended jail sentence or Norplant (176), a long-acting reversible contraceptive (LARC) that was taken off the market in 2002 due to serious side effects, including blindness and brain tumours (Watkins 2010). After being trialled on black and poor white women in the USA, Depo Provera, another LARC, was banned in the country in the late 1970s because of its side effects, which included cancer and sterility; nevertheless, health professionals continued to prescribe the contraceptive to black and poor white women in the UK (in the 1980s) and Indigenous women in Australia (in the 1970s), who were unaware of these dangers (Daylight and Johnstone 1986: 64; Jones 2013). The drug, re-introduced in the USA in the 1990s, continues to be used disproportionately amongst Indigenous and African Ameri-cans (Volscho 2011). Recent changes to welfare in the UK and USA cap welfare payments, replacing systems based on the number of dependent children, similarly attempting to limit the reproductive potential of 'deviant' populations or at least punish those perceived to have 'too many' children (Jensen and Tyler 2015; Lonergan 2012: 32–33).

The state control of abortion, as actualised through the law, is another means of managing women's reproductive potential for the purpose of nation building. China notoriously subjects pregnant women to forced abortions in order to meet its population targets (Scharping 2013), and abortion law was liberalised in most of India in 1971 as a strategy to curb population growth (Hirve 2004: 114). Within the Anglophone West, restrictions on abortion have historically been rationalised as a means of accelerating the birth rate amongst those designated as 'national breeders'. Concern about the future of the white population—spurred by lowering birthrates and an increase in non-Anglo immigration—was one reason abortion was criminalised in nineteenth century America (Beisal and Kay 2004). In Australia during the first half of the twentieth century, two royal commissions investigating the nation's future demography conceptualised abortion as a 'loss to the nation' (cited in Mackinnon 2000: 114) and admonished (white) Australian women for having abortions and thereby 'refusing their duty to the nation' (Mackinnon 2000: 112). In Britain, parliamentarians hoped that medical doctors would use their powers under the Abortion Act 1967 to encourage 'desirable' women to continue with their pregnancies (Lonergan 2012: 32–33). These disparate examples show that women are perceived to jeopardise the nation by having *or not having* abortions depending on where they live and how their bodies are read through schemas of nationalist maternity.

Ideas and ideologies of nationalist maternity are rationalised through cultural imaginings of the 'good mother'; throughout the Anglophone West, this figure is constructed as white and middle-class through the constant circulation of images of neglectful or pathological other [m]others, including black 'Welfare Queens' (Feder 2007: 72) or mothers of 'crack babies' in the USA (Roberts 1997) and the 'chav mum' in the UK (Tyler 2008). In Australia (Conor 2016), Canada (Kline 1992; Salmon 2011) and the USA (Jacobs 2009), Indigenous mothers have been exemplars of pathologised maternity. While the rationalising discourse of eugenics transformed into one of 'dysfunctional communities' through the twentieth century, schemas of normative and deviant motherhood remain enmeshed in the colonial project.

National debates about belonging are written onto and carried through the reproductive bodies of women; women's reproductive bodies are thereby a target of measures aimed to control the population by encouraging certain women to have babies and dissuading or preventing the fertility of others. Discussions of abortion in terms of the nation or the population—for example, in terms of the population's abortion rate—are therefore inherently 'biopolitical', a Foucauldian term used to designate 'that domain of life where power has taken control' (Foucault 2008; Mbembé 2003: 12). In such debates, the foetus is constructed as a future citizen of the nation. In the next section I look at foetal citizenship and its enmeshment with national love, fear and anxiety—the organising emotions of this chapter.

FOETAL BIOPOLITICS

Nationalist visions of the 'good life' involve a nostalgic longing for what never was: a nation populated by happy, white, nuclear families (Hage 1998: 40–42, 74–76). When the nation fails to deliver the 'good life' it has promised, one's invest-ment in the nation is often intensified and displaced onto the future, which is posited as the place where one's love for the nation will be reciprocated (Ahmed 2004b: 130). The figure of the white child—and foetus—holds a prime position in the social imaginary because it contains the promise that the 'good life' will materialise in the future (Ahmed 2004b: 130). The white foetus can be considered a 'happy object' (Ahmed 2010b) that binds communities together through orienta-tion towards a shared vision of the future. To return to BNP's crude imagining of white babies as an 'endangered species', the advertisement aspires to appeal to a white audience by juxta-posing the ideal image of a white or 'indigenous'-populated Britain of 2030 with its immigrant-infested alternative. In this way, the foetus/child contains a 'cluster of promises' (Berlant 2007) that displace anxieties about, as Lauren Berlant asserts, 'whose subjectivity, whose forms of intimacy and interests, whose bodies and identifications, whose heroic narratives—will direct ... [the nation's] future' (Berlant 1997: 6).

The foetus-citizen is thereby a figure generated not only by national love, but by the fear and anxiety that accompany one's affective attachment to the nation. Here I use fear to denote an 'affective politics' that shapes the political contours of the nation rather than personal experience (although it may induce and be generated by this). The emotion of fear repels the 'us' of the nation away from those perceived to threaten the values and fantasies it hopes to preserve (Ahmed 2004b: 8, 64); fear of racialised outsiders is a, perhaps *the*, key mech-anism through which the 'we' of a nation is constructed as a singular entity (Martinot 2007: 96). Fear is an emotion closely related to anxiety, with both linked to a feeling of potential loss or injury. Anxiety, however, engenders a more pervasive sense of insecurity and vulnerability because it has no fixed object; and as Ahmed writes, '[t]he more we don't know what or who it is we fear *the more the world becomes fearsome*' (Ahmed 2004b: 69).

Ahmed locates her work on the cultural politics of fear within Ulrich Beck's thesis that national identity in late modernity is forged through a solidarity based on insecurity and shared risk rather than need (Ahmed 2004b: 72; Beck 1992: 49); in Ghassan Hage's (2003) formulation, 'worrying' has become the primary means of expressing one's attachment to the nation. A key aspect of the late modern state of generalised 'social insecurity' (Wacquant 2009) is the production of the national abject figure of the 'bogus asylum seeker' or 'queue jumper' and the associated figure of the 'ethnic' or 'third-world-looking' migrant, both of which are cast as threats to the nation (Hage 1998; Tyler 2013). They threaten the integrity of the nation's borders by arriving in the country without a visa, or threaten the nation's resources in terms of the strain on welfare or health services they are widely taken to represent. The 'migrant crisis' that began in 2015—and the porous national borders it makes visible—is both a symptom and further exacerbation of globalisation, a phenomenon that has challenged the integrity of nations as sovereign states, resulting in attempts to re-secure national borders and reify an ideal of national homogeneity that never existed (Brown 2010). Brexit, the election of Donald Trump, and the rise of nationalist parties in Europe and Australia are (in part) symptoms of broader attempts at 're-nationalisation' (Luibhéid 2004).

The management of reproduction is another mode of re-nationalisation; this is co-articulated alongside controls on migration through the figures of the 'pregnant asylum seeker' or the 'ethnic migrant woman', who are frequently depicted as national abjects (Huang 2008; Lentin 2004; Lonergan 2012; Luibhéid 2004). Just as threats to national sovereignty have justified the re-securing of national borders, there has been, in Imogen Tyler's words, 'the securitisation of reproduction ... a gendered effect of the crisis ... [whereby] the nation-state is imagined as under threat from the reproductive force of foreigners' (2013: 111). While (non-white) 'foreigners' are frequently deemed to be excessively reproductive, white women are often chastised for their low fertility rates. In nationalist panics over the abortion rate, as we will see, abortion is read as both a sign and symptom of this crisis.

The management of migration and reproduction exist alongside a further biopolitical technology—that of dis-avowal. In the British context, disavowal refers to 'colonial aphasia'—the 'occlusion of knowledge ... disremembering, a difficulty speaking' (Stoler 2011: 125) or finding the vocabulary to talk about the violent and exploitative British Empire upon which Britain built its global economic and geopolitical position. This disavowal is achieved through a transformative logic, which, through the body of the invading, post-colonial citizen-migrant, recasts Britain, in Paul Gilroy's words, as 'the primary victim, rather than principle beneficiary, of its colonial dominance' (Gilroy 2003: 32; Hall 1999: 7). In settler colonies, disavowal refers to the systemic forgetting that white belonging to the nation is grounded on the theft of Indigenous lands as well as the ongoing Indigenous sovereignty over those lands (Birch 2002; Wolfe 1994).

The technologies of disavowal, exclusion and reproduction are entangled and mutually reinforced in the creation and re-creation of racialised nations. The co-articulation of these technologies is evinced in the epigraphs to this chapter. Danna Vale, MP, disavowed Indigenous claims to sovereignty by claiming for herself, and white Australians more generally, the role of 'national domesticator', controlling who belongs to the nation and the nature of their participation in national life (Hage 1998). She excluded Muslims from full belonging to the body politic by contrasting them to the 'we' of the nation. Finally, she called upon non-Muslim (white) women to reproduce the nation. The web page of the British Nationalist Party similarly disavowed the violence of empire, casting 'indigenous' Britons as the victims of 'third world immigrants', who are positioned as colonisers, a colonisation operationalised 'through the womb'. With women reduced to their reproductive organs, the BNP summoned 'indigenous' British women to reproduce and so liberate the nation from its invaders.

Disavowal (of colonisation and/or indigenous sovereignty), exclusion (of certain bodies from the nation) and reproduction (of white, middle-class women) are intersecting technologies for managing national anxiety. Nations are anxious by their very constitution, for they are never 'made', but are in a constant process of 'remaking', a process that, in exposing the vulnerability of national sovereignty, never ends.

Because anxiety has no fixed object, management involves converting the nation's generalised, foundational anxiety into specific objects of fear. This conversion enables a fantasy of containment to be sustained, where the nation manages or expels feared objects from the body politic, so preserving the object or ideal that is perceived to be under threat (Ahmed 2004b: 67). Some figures of fear transform over time. In Australia, for instance, the fear of the 'Yellow Peril' that caught the white nationalist imagination through much of the twentieth century transformed into the figure of the 'Muslim' at the turn of the millennium (Hage 1998). Some objects of fear reappear. In the late nineteenth and into the first half of the twentieth century, a transnational discourse likening abortion to 'race suicide' circulated in Australia, Canada, New Zealand, and the USA, including in government reports into the population, which produced the figure of the 'white aborting woman' as a threat to the nation (Beisel and Kay 2004; Mackinnon 2000; McCulloch 2013; McLaren and McLaren 1997).

The white aborting woman is constituted as a threat to the nation because, if national love is framed as a relationship of reciprocity, where the nation promises its citizens 'the good life' in exchange for their labour (Ahmed 2004b: 34, 124), for white women, the service specifically required is their reproductive labour. Disobeying this indenture, aborting women will not carry their pregnancies to term, even for the nation. The figure of the white aborting woman thereby becomes a conduit, where the anxiety that whiteness will not be reproduced into the future is displaced onto a material object. This displacement identifies a legitimate source for fearing a non-white future while offering the potential that the threat can be contained and the white nation preserved. This process occurs through a preoccupation with the abortion rate. Taking the case study of Australia, the rest of this chapter shows that concern with the abortion rate has arisen in times of intense worrying about the future racial demography of the nation, an anxiety that makes the entangled biopolitical technologies of disavowal, exclusion and reproduction acutely visible. In this way, I demonstrate the nationalist and racialised investments driving the politics of abortion, and forge connections between the politics of abortion and other nationalist politics, including those over immigration.

THE BIRTH OF A POLITICAL PROBLEM—THE 1970S

In countries that liberalised abortion laws at the turn of the 1970s, the ensuing decade witnessed a series of parliamentary debates and government reports that attempted to manage or come to terms with the new status quo (Chapter 1). I focus here on how three Australian measures—two parliamentary bills and a royal commission—constructed abortion as an issue of national concern, mapping an increasing preoccupation with the abortion rate as a potential threat to the nation.

During the debate on the Medical Practice Clarification Bill (commonly termed the McKenzie-Lamb Bill) of 1973, which sought to decriminalise first trimester abortions in the Australian Capital Territory, parliamentarians generally cited abortion figures to argue that the law must properly regulate a medical procedure that was so common (Tony Lamb, MP; Australia 1973: 1969). Although many parliamentarians called for a reduction in abortion numbers (David McKenzie, MP; Australia 1973: 1967), this was not a prominent theme in the debate. This private member's bill did not pass the lower house, but led eventually to the establishment of the Royal Commission on Human Relationships, which reported in 1977. The Royal Commission was established largely because parliamentarians felt they needed accurate data on abortion to meaningfully debate the issue. The Commission estimated that 60,000 abortions were performed in Australia annually (Evatt 1977, v1: 58).

The figure of 60,000 was repeatedly cited during debate on the Lusher Motion of 1979, at which time the abortion rate had become a fixture of concern for parliamentarians, regardless of party membership or their views on abortion. The majority of parliamentarians who supported the bill, which sought to cut government funding for abortion, voiced their 'deep concern' with Australia's abortion rate, particularly when compared to its birthrate. They argued that the cessation of government funding for the procedure would reduce abortion numbers. Stephen Lusher framed his motion in these terms (Australia 1979a: 964), and a proposed amendment added the explicit sentiment that: 'this House expresses its deep concern that for every three live births in Australia there is one abortion' (Ross McLean, MP; Australia 1979a: 967). Emotive and alarmist language accompanied judgement about the abortion rate; it was declared, for example, to be 'alarming' and a cause for disgust, evincing an 'abortion syndrome' and 'the steady growth in the abortion mentality amongst ... [Australian] citizens' (John FitzPatrick, MP; Australia 1979a: 986; Ian MacPhee, MP; Australia 1979a: 999; Ross McLean, MP; Australia 1979a: 969; Les McMahon, MP; Australia 1979a: 1004). In addition to targeting government funding for abortions, supporters framed the debate as an indictment against state laws, particularly those in the most populous states of New South Wales and Victoria, which had, they claimed, 'open[ed] the gateway to enable abortion on demand', allowing for 'mass slaughter' and 'open slather' on abortions (Kevin Cairns, MP; Australia 1979b: 1099; David Connolly, MP; Australia 1979b: 1111). Many opponents of the bill expressed similar concern with the abortion rate, but believed the motion would not affect it (for example, Barry Simon, MP; Australia 1979b: 972). One member stated that, 'I abhor abortion ... and I would do all that I could to prevent it' (Barry Jones, MP; Australia 1979b: 1107). Another, while opposing the motion, nevertheless commended it for serving 'to remind and perhaps in some cases awaken the Australian population to the grave and continuing problem of the number of abortions in this country' (James Porter, MP; Australia 1979b: 1122).

Margaret Tighe, the longstanding President of Right to Life Australia, communicated the organisation's support of the Lusher Motion by declaring abortion to be a 'national tragedy of great magnitude' (*The Sun* 1979). The phrase 'national tragedy' would come to prominence in national debate on abortion when the Federal Health Minister, Tony Abbott, repeated the phrase twenty-five years afterward. His comments heralded a period of intensified public and political focus on abortion on a scale not witnessed since the Lusher Motion.

A NATION'S TRAGEDY—THE 2000s

Tony Abbott, a conservative Catholic with an anti-abortion agenda, was appointed as the Minister of Health in 2003 during the third term of the Howard Government (he was the Prime Minister of Australia from 2013–2015). In one of his first speeches in the position of Health Minister he attracted widespread media attention when he asked 'Why isn't the fact that 100,000 women choose to end their pregnancies regarded as a national tragedy' (Abbott 2004)? Abbott's speech followed a period of agitation for legal clarity surrounding abortion in Western Australia (1998), the Australian Capital Territory (1998) and Tasmania (2001). This agitation resulted in laws that confirmed and tightened medical control over the procedure through provisions such as informed consent and led eventually (after a brief period of tightened controls on abortion in the territory) to the ACT becoming the first jurisdiction in Australia to decriminalise abortion in 2002 (Baird 2006a). Abbott's intervention into abortion politics pushed the issue, which is largely a matter of state law, onto the Commonwealth political agenda. His speech incited fervent debate on the abortion rate, with a chorus of politicians and journalists echoing his concerns (Shaw 2004; Shanahan 2004). *The Age* journalist Amanda Dunn (2004) captured what was represented to be a developing consensus: '[b]oth sides of the abortion debate agree that the number of terminations in

Australia is too high. So what can be done?' Not surprisingly, prominent anti-abortion politicians and organisations eagerly retained public focus on abortion, with Nationals Senator Barnaby Joyce (who is currently the leader of the conservative Country Party and Deputy Prime Minister of Australia), for instance, speaking on 'The tragedy of abortion in Australia' at the 2005 Right to Life Conference (*Herald Sun* 2005).

The conservative abortion politic that emerged in the wake of Abbott's speech culminated in a Private Members Bill to remove the veto Tony Abbott enjoyed as Health Minister over the release of the abortifacient RU486 to the Therapeutic Goods Administration for approval for use in Australia and the Victorian bill to decriminalise abortion (Chapter 2). The fear that Australia had 'too many abortions' permeated the two debates, moving across political affiliations and parliamentarians' views on abortion. Nearly all speakers in both debates referenced abortion numbers, with those who supported liberal abortion laws arguing they would not have any impact on the abortion rate, and opponents claiming that, if successful, the bills would see the abortion rate increase. Discussion of abortion in terms of the numbers performed and the implicit assumption that the abortion rate needed to be reduced were taken to be truths that bridged the otherwise divergent views of supporters and opponents of the two bills. So, for example, one Victorian MP from the Liberal Party, who opposed decriminalising abortion, confidently asserted that 'all members of this house and of our communities would agree that too many abortions are being performed' (Ryan Smith, MLA; Victoria 2008a: 3362). A Labor MP who supported the bill similarly urged parliamentarians to 'put aside our polarised views on this issue and commit to working together to reduce the rate of abortion' (Jenny Mikakos, MLC; Victoria 2008c: 3941). Supporters and opponents used similar language to condemn Australia's abortion rate. Then Prime Minister John Howard, who opposed the Commonwealth bill, declared that 'the Australian community is unhappy' with the current abortion rate (Australia 2006e: 133). Coalition members who supported the bill similarly stated that they were 'appalled' and 'deeply troubled' by the number of abortions performed in Australia (for example, Judith Adams, Senator; Australia 2006a: 116); these numbers were purported to constitute 'a national disgrace' (Sussan Ley, MP; Australia 2006c: 87) and a 'terrible tragedy' (Michael Keenan, MP; Australia 2006d: 129). Supporters from the Federal Opposition endorsed this sentiment, condemning the abortion rate as 'unacceptable and simply astounding' (Steve Gibbons, MP; Australia 2006d: 153).

The intense circulation of the discourse that Australia had 'too many abortions' in 1979 and the mid-2000s represented moral panics pertaining to the abortion rate, producing the aborting woman as a figure who threatened the nation. The panics were in no means confined to these years. Rather, in 1979, the Lusher Motion led to an intensification of the public debate on abortion occurring through the 1970s. The moral panic of the mid-2000s culminated in the Commonwealth debate in 2004, but the 'too many abortions' discourse re-emerged with veracity in the debates to decriminalise abortion in Victoria in 2008. These two panics occurred despite the notorious inaccuracy of abortion statistics and the distinct probability that abortion rates have remained relatively stable since laws were liberalised (Chan and Sage 2005).

In his classic definition, Stan Cohen defines moral panic as when a 'condition, episode, person or group of persons ... become[s] defined as a threat to societal values' (1972: 1). The declaration of a threat legitimates government action aimed at preventing or containing that which is apparently threatening, thereby securing these social norms or values (in the present case white reproduction) as social goods worth protecting (Ahmed 2004b: 64). Statistics occupy a central role in precipitating moral crises (Hall et al. 1978: 9). By turning abortion into a number, the tens of thousands of women who have abortions annually, and the diverse and heterogeneous contexts in which their need or want for abortion arises, are regularised and made quantifiable, ripe for management and control. Enumerating abortion turns it into a 'problem' of government while de-politicising this process by transforming political problems and aspirations into objective, technical measurements (Rose 1991: 647). This process is intensified when numbers are taken to represent 'too many', which Ghassan Hage identifies as a 'nationalist practice concerned with one's relation to territory', organising an imaginary relationship between those who manage national space and the objects of management (1998: 32).

The very processes of enumeration and declaring something as constituting 'too many' suggest that moral panics over abortion relate to broader national anxieties pertaining to which bodies should populate the nation. As we will see, the characteristics of these ideal citizens are revealed through the articulation of abortion numbers alongside other fears, including those surrounding divorce, homosexuality and immigration. Such chains of association reveal a pivotal logic relating to the stability of the white nuclear family into the future—fantasies held together in part by the figures of the white mother and her foetus/child.

POPULATE OR PERISH

The 'moral domino theory', which circulated widely during the 1970s, shows that concern over the abortion rate was implicated in anxieties much broader than the number of abortions being performed. Drawing on Cold War rhetoric, this theory proposed that liberal abortion laws would 'open the floodgates' (Hawkin 1973) and ensure that the nation's moral and social fabric was 'eroded from within' (Tom McVeigh, MP; Australia 1979b: 1109). Anti-abortion activists and politicians have maintained that abortion threatened 'the very foundations of our society' since the movement's beginnings (for example, *The Age* 1973), and concern that abortion would cause 'the erosion of the values that have held our society together for so long' continued into the debates of the 2000s (Jan Kronberg, MLC; Victoria 2008d: 4000). The belief that abortion leads to, or is representative of, the demise of the moral and social order is a transnational phenomenon, and as with so much abortion rhetoric, is led by, and reaches its ultimate expression in, the US context, where the prevalence of abortion signals proof of the degenerate and deviant modern world that (neo)conservatives conjure in their aspiration to reinstall a nostalgic vision of the past (Chapter 1).

The use of the metaphor of 'the flood' to describe abortion deepens its implication in perceptions of national crisis. Politicians, journalists and other prominent social commentators—usually, but not always, with an anti-abortion agenda—have expressed concern that abortion law reform opened the floodgates to general moral and social degeneracy since at least the 1970s (Bernie Finn, MLC; Victoria 2008e: 4086; Hawkin 1973; String 2001). The historically-sedimented fear that undesirable others are flooding Australia relates to the nation's perceived vulnerability as an island, culturally identified with yet physically distanced from Britain, and with an immense and ultimately indefensible border. A flood connotes an explosive breech of border, which poses a serious and irrevocable threat to the Australian people and the nation's natural resources (Ahmed 2004b: 76; MacCallum 2002). When people or practices are likened to floods threatening Australia's security, asylum seekers, for example, present an external threat. Conversely, abortion threatens to erode the white nation from within.

When placed as an issue of national concern, abortion comes to symbolise, implicitly or otherwise, a threat to the white nuclear family, its attendant privileges, and the racialised national future it represents; yet the more precise values that abortion is perceived to threaten depend on the socio-historical context in which abortion panics arise. The 1970s witnessed significant socio-cultural and legal changes in the Western world in response to the various movements that collectively formed the New Left. The Women's Liberation Movement (WLM), the Civil Rights Movement, Indigenous activists, and gay liberationists destabilised white, heterosexual men's privilege to stand as the uncontested norm in relation to a series of others (Berlant 1997). In Australia, the rise of the New Left met with the election of the reformist Labor Government led by Gough Whitlam in 1972. The liberalisation of abortion law in several Australian jurisdictions thereby coincided with a raft of significant legislation that loosened the legal regulation of white hegemony and the nuclear family. Chief amongst these changes were the recognition of Indigenous citizenship (1967), the official abolishment of the White Australia Policy (1973), welfare payments to single mothers (1973), no-fault divorce (1975), anti-discrimination and equal opportunities legislation, and the decriminalisation of homosexuality in many jurisdictions (Jupp 2002: 19–36; Swain and Howe 1995: 196–208).

A nostalgic longing for the gender certainties that existed, at least in law, before abortion laws were liberalised fuelled the abortion politics of many members of the House of Representatives (which was composed solely of white men in the two debates on abortion in 1973 and 1979). This nostalgia was conveyed in expressions such as 'society today is ugly' (Barry Simon, MP; Australia 1979a: 972), or '[w]hat has happened to this country' (John Fitzpatrick, MP; Australia 1979a: 985), as well as lamentation for '[t]he good old fashioned values upon which we have based our whole civilisation, our whole existence' (Mick Cotter, MP; Australia 1979b: 1111). Several parliamentarians singled out marriage and the family as the social institutions that abortion particularly threatened:

> [T]he demand for abortion on request is part of the manifestation of the change of values occurring in our society … one which raises a serious threat to the continued existence of the basis of our society—the family … The trend of which I speak is evident in such matters as [the] call for the legalisation of homosexual acts, [and] for the making easier of divorce. (Doug Anthony, MP; Australia 1973: 1982)

The association of women who had abortions with homosexuals and divorcees in this statement intensified the perceived threat they posed to the (family) values holding the Australian community together.

In the 1970s, cracks in the perceived hegemony of values pertaining to sex and the family were met with a demographic crisis spurred by lowering fertility rates in most Western countries and an emerging global consensus that non-Western countries were over-populated, with over-population endangering Western hegemony as well as the world's natural resources (Ziegler 2013). The intense concern over the population, and the perceived economic and ecological crises this was perceived to engender, was reflected in the popularity of the 1968 international bestseller *The Population Bomb*, written by US professor Paul Ehrlich and his (unaccredited) wife Anne. In 1976, Australia's birthrate fell below replacement level and it continued to fall

(Australian Bureau of Statistics 2012). The concurrent flow of asylum seekers into Australia fleeing Timor and the Vietnam War brought a further demographic challenge; this was the first humanitarian intake of asylum seekers into Australia since the cessation of the White Australia Policy shortly beforehand and rekindled the historic fear that Australia was vulnerable to an 'Asian invasion'; this fear became a major political issue in the 1977 federal election (Jupp 2002: 183). Lowering birthrates, concerns about the global population, and a flow of asylum seekers into Australia were demographic shifts that help explain why, unlike in the McKenzie-Lamb Bill of 1973, the abortion rate was a prominent theme in debates over the Lusher Motion of 1979.

Within this context, abortion was frequently debated in terms of the loss of future citizens. Parliamentarians sometimes explicitly referred to aborted foetuses as future Australians. Australia's future prime minister, Paul Keating, who opposed the Lusher Motion, nevertheless pronounced that '[a]bortion threatens the nation through the destruction of its children' (Australia 1979b: 1098). The anti-abortion movement has referred to aborted foetuses as Australians since it was established (*The Age* 1970; Francis 2002); this is a nationalist, anti-abortion rhetoric that continues to circulate internationally through statements such as 'Abortion is 27 Percent of Deaths in England, Wales' (Collier 2012) and 'Abortion is the number one killer of black lives in the United States' (TooManyAborted 2017). The foetus further manifests as a citizen through the common practice of viewing the abortion rate alongside the nation's birthrate, which presumes uniformity in the object of measurement. One *Herald* poll in 1978, for example, asked readers, 'Australia's abortion rate is at least 50,000 a year compared with 226,000 births. Do you think abortion should be continued?' (*The Herald* 1978).

One MP opposed the Lusher Motion because 'Australia has a need for population' (James Bradfield, MP; Australia 1979b: 1094); another drew on a transnational pro-natal discourse (Condit 1990: 62) that opposed abortion through evoking fears of a financial crisis brought as a consequence of an ageing population:

> [These] are children that Australia cannot afford to lose. … the transfer of thousands of the present generation into the incinerator … [will lead to] a situation whereby an increasing number of older people will need to be supported by a dwindling number of working aged people. (Bruce Goodluck, MP; Australia 1979b: 1088)

In the most widely reported speech of the day, the Minister for Health, Ralph Hunt, warned that:

> [T]oday we are heading rapidly for a zero growth rate … In the long term, the consequences of the loss of this human potential and potential consumer demand will be reflected in fewer employment opportunities in this country unless we are prepared to engage in a massive immigration program to try to fill this great land of ours. (Australia 1979b: 1077)

Hunt went on to claim that abortion threatened the employment opportunities of young women by enabling and encouraging married women to remain in the workplace. The capitalist ethos running through his speech, which identified Australians as workers and consumers, was therefore clearly gendered: men should engage in paid employment; young women should work (presumably in low skilled jobs) until married, then reproduce more consumers and producers.

Hunt contrasted Australia's need for population with 'developing countries, where over-population is a real problem' (Australia 1979b: 1076). This contrast resonated with a survey reported in the Royal Commission on Human Relationships of 1977, which found that Australians supported fewer restrictions on abortion in developing countries such as India than in Australia (Evatt 1977, v3: 214). Concern regarding the survival of Australian life into the future, rather than foetal life in general, thus appears to have motivated Hunt and many Australians' opposition to abortion.

Liberal MP David Connolly placed Australia's zero population growth in the international context, communicating his support for the Lusher Motion by stating that:

> No country with the manifest resources of Australia can indulge itself in a de facto policy of zero population growth and expect to have the luxury of deciding indefinitely its own destiny in a world where the availability of space and resources will play an even greater part in deciding the affairs of nations. Perhaps it is a truism, but

Australia as we know it must populate or perish. (Australia 1979b: 1111)

Connolly framed abortion funding, and by inference liberal laws on abortion, as a 'de facto policy of zero population growth', undermining Australia's success in the competition for world resources. Connolly's invocation of an empty land—like the 'great land' evoked in Hunt's speech—ripe with natural resources and in need of a healthy (white) population is a classic iteration of the fantasy of *terra nullius,* which legitimated Australia's settler-colonial project and, as he reiterated, carried the imperative for the nation to 'populate or perish' (Walker 1999: 154–155; Wolfe 1994: 93–95). Hunt spelt out the alternative to white reproduction: massive immigration.

A POPULATION CRISIS

Australia's fertility rate continued to fall from 1976, reaching an all-time low in 2001 (Australian Bureau of Statistics 2012). Nascent apprehension regarding Australia's ageing population in the Lusher Motion had, correspondingly, reached the level of critical, national concern at the turn of the millennium, culminating in 'Population Summits' held in Melbourne and Adelaide in 2002 and 2003 respectively (Vizard et al. 2003; National Population Summit 2004). After attending the Melbourne summit, Christopher Pearson (2002)—weekly columnist for the conservative broadsheet newspaper, *The Australian,* advisor to the Liberal Party, and personal friend of Tony Abbott—criticised the Howard Government's failure to develop a population policy. He applauded himself for representing 'a small minority who identified the fertility rate, rather than immigration, as the crux of the matter', and deplored 'the 100,000 abortions now carried out each year in Australia and the cumulative loss of well over a million citizens since the 1970s'.

Intensified focus on birth and abortion rates came amidst widespread fear regarding the alternative solution to Australia's population concerns: immigration. The racial politics of the Howard Government (1996–2007) are well documented, manifesting acutely in a renewed preoccupation with the menacing figure of the 'boatperson' in Australia's media (Betts 2001). The Government represented Australia as besieged by threats, both internal (aborting women, Indigenous people, and 'third-world-looking' people) and external (asylum seekers) (Altman and Hinkson 2007; Hage 2003). The crisis stemmed from the fragility of white socio-cultural dominance in Australia and was, more specifically, a crisis in white male authority. Panics over national security are gendered, involving masculine protection of a feminised land, deemed vulnerable to penetration by outside forces (Brown 2010: 130). Thus the heightening of global security in the wake of September 11 corresponded with an intensified, masculine and militaristic nationalism (Hunt and Rygiel 2006). In Australia, this was joined by a popular and political narrative, growing since the early 1990s, of a masculinity crisis propagating the idea that, as the leader of the nationalist One Nation Party claimed in 1996, 'the most downtrodden person in this country is the white Anglo-Saxon male … [T]he balance has gone too far' and now (white) men—and especially boys—no longer 'know what to do' (cited in Hage 1998: 182). Several inter-related phenomena fuelled the perceived crisis, including: the increased public visibility of single parent and queer families (with the concomitant concern that boys were growing up with no permanent, heterosexual 'father figure'); girls' outper-formance of boys in all levels of education; men's experiences with the family court and the coinciding growth of the 'men's movement'; and the heightened participation of non-white men in Australia's socio-political domain (Bode 2006; Murrie 1998).

With white women's motherhood a point at which gender and racial orders are reproduced, it is no accident that the purported crisis in white masculinity was met with several policies that encouraged (married) women to have children and stay at home to raise them. Then Prime Minister John Howard and treasurer Peter Costello introduced the Baby Bonus (a fixed sum payable to women upon the birth of a child) in 2002 with the battle cries of, respectively, 'come on, come on, your nation needs you' and 'one for your husband, one for your wife and one for the country' (Shaw and Farouque 2004). Such explicit pro-natalism had, by that time, become increasingly common (Kevin 2009); the concomitant re-pathologisation of a series of 'other [m]others', and particularly Muslim (Hussein 2016) and Indigenous mothers (Cutcher and Milroy 2010), reveals it was targeted mainly at white women.

With (white) women very clearly called upon to choose the nation by reproducing, those who terminated their pregnan-cies were positioned as threatening the social good of white reproduction. Abortion was likened to momentous events of national mortality. Anti-abortionists compared the lives taken in abortion to the most venerated Australian martyrs— soldiers killed in war (Cameron 2004). Tony Abbott referred to Australia's 'abortion epidemic' (Grattan and Wroe 2004). An editorial in Melbourne's tabloid the *Herald Sun* (2006) worried about Australia's 'abortion toll'.

Danna Vale's exhortation that Australia risked becoming a Muslim nation because 'we are aborting ourselves out of existence' reiterated the metonymic association between abortion and non-white immigration. Tellingly, the government's response to Vale's remarks recapitulated rather than challenged the underlying logic that Australia is and should remain a predominantly white country as well as the appropriateness of discussing abortion in terms of Australia's future ethno-racial demography. Immigration Minister, Senator Amanda Vanstone, reassured the public that '[i]n the next 50 years Australia will remain what it is today—a predominantly English-speaking, multicultural and diverse country' (Frenkel 2006). National Party member De-Anne Kelly claimed that Vale's facts 'were alarmist and simply wrong' (Australia 2006c: 74). Shadow Minister Laurie Ferguson similarly reassured the public that 'the Islamic intake of population to this country is actually declining' (Australia 2006d: 190).

Vale's speech in the Commonwealth debate over RU486 was steeped in nostalgic longing, with the white nuclear family occupying centre stage. Vale took the prevalence of abortion amongst women in 2006 as testament to the fading good life that existed when 'children were valued' and abortion prohibited by law (Australia 2006d: 45). At the time, abortion was repeatedly linked to the general erosion of the patriarchal nuclear family, and not merely by those articulating an anti-abortion agenda. In response to Abbott's speech of 2004, the Governor General declared that he would like to see Australia's abortion rate reduced to zero, reasoning that:

> We've got a million kids now living with a single parent, mostly women, and most of them through no fault of their own are probably doing it very hard ... I think boys, in many cases, now are growing up without access to a male role model ... [and] are going to grow up with a big problem of how to be men, how to treat others, and so on. (cited in Hudson 2004)

Ostensibly, Australia's abortion rate has nothing to do with single parenting and male role models for children; if, however, abortion numbers are viewed as a site where more general anxieties pertaining to the patriarchal nuclear family are expressed, this slippage is perfectly intelligible. The Governor General, a role that is meant to be non-partisan and essentially apolitical, prefaced his comments about abortion with the statement that 'I don't want to get into the rights and wrongs of it, or the political debate'. This comment is suggestive of how the sentiment that Australia had 'too many abortions' worked as a mode of common sense, an illusory abstraction from politics that disguised, and amplified, its intensely regulative nature.

Tony Abbott (2004) similarly framed the abortion rate in terms of the security of the nuclear family. In his notorious speech labelling abortion a 'national tragedy', he suggested that a focus on abortion should succeed government policies that had: 'backed the Catholic bishops' challenge to lesbian *in vitro* fertilisation, singled out stay-at-home mums for extra financial assistance … [and] sought to allow Catholic schools to offer scholarships to male teachers'. In this way, Abbott fixed the aborting woman alongside the lesbian (and, less explicitly, the working) mother as a threat to the family, an institution secured by stay-at-home mothers and male teachers as paternal role models for children in Catholic schools. Abbott introduced his concern with abortion by asking:

> Why isn't the fact that 100,000 women choose to end their pregnancies regarded as a national tragedy approaching the scale (say) of Aboriginal life expectancy being 20 years less than that of the general community? … When it comes to lobbying local politicians, there seems to be far more interest in the treatment of boat people, which is not morally black and white, than in the question of abortion which is … The sense that things aren't right and that every person has a duty to make a difference is at the heart of the Christian calling and helps to explain the relative strength and solidarity of countries like ours.

Because Christianity is a primary signifier of whiteness in Australia (Stratton 2011: 7–9), Abbott's suggestion that Christianity bound Australia together in 'strength and solidarity' restated white governmental belonging. While conceding that the gross discrepancy between Aboriginal and non-Aboriginal life expectancy in Australia constituted a 'national tragedy', Abbott displaced the tragedy of Indigenous life expectancy with focus on the life of foetuses. Mental health experts repeatedly link systems of detention to self-harm and suicide (for example, Robjant et al. 2009); thus Abbott's character-isation of abortion as a 'morally black and white' issue, in contrast to the detention of asylum seekers, implied that the life of foetuses was more valuable than that of asylum seekers.

During both moral panics, journalists, politicians and members of the broader public designated Australia's abortion rate as a problem that belonged to 'us' and as something that had 'got out of hand' but could be brought under control (Grattan and Wroe 2004). In the debates of the mid-2000s, for example, legislators exclaimed that '[a]s a society, *we* must do more', and '*we* should be trying to do everything possible to reduce the number of abortions in this state' (Gordon Rich-Philips, MLC; Victoria 2008e: 4149, emphasis added). By framing abortion as a social problem that 'we' *should* judge and *can* manage, politicians and the broader community constructed a fantasy of control over the procedure. The act of debating abortion transforms pregnant women considering abortion into objects under the control of the people who worry about, evaluate and manage them (Baird 2006b).

Opponents of abortion have enacted this fantasy at the level of the law, hoping to prohibit abortion, limit the means of obtaining it, eliminate government funding for the proce-dure, or, in recent times, introduce incremental restrictions on abortion, such as pre-abortion counselling (Baird 2006a:

139–140). For those looking to curtail the abortion rate through the law, the fantasy of control over abortion relies on another: that no abortions, or at least dramatically fewer, occurred before laws were liberalised. This was the undercurrent of Tony Abbott's assertion in the Commonwealth debate that: '[t]here would not be anyone under fifty in this country who has not come up close and personal against this issue' (Australia 2006d: 114–115). Abbott's absurd suggestion that abortion has only been an issue people have faced since laws liberalised women's access to the procedure constructed an imagined past, used to amplify the troubled present, where the prevalence of abortion is regarded as both symptom and cause. In contrast, those who support liberal abortion laws imagine that improved sex education programs and reliable contraception, and contraceptors, would prevent the need for the majority of abortions arising (Chapter 4). Both fantasies displace pregnant women as the people who determine how many abortions are performed in Australia. The idea that the nation—be it Australia or anywhere else—has too many abortions turns the nation into the subject of abortion, obfuscating the fact that it is individual women who have abortions, and that abortion has always (Riddle 1999) and will always be a component of women's reproductive lives, regardless of laws regulating the practice.

CONCLUSION

The encouragement of white reproduction stands alongside disavowal (of Indigenous sovereignty) and exclusion (of certain immigrants) as technologies that aspire to manage the anxiety of white belonging to the nation. In certain periods, this constitutional anxiety focuses on manageable objects of fear as a means of attempting to restore or preserve that perceived to be lost or under threat. In Australia, the aborting woman emerged in 1979 and the mid-2000s as an acutely feared object. During these years, unease pertaining to the perceived vulnerability of Australia's borders to intruding others converged with anxieties regarding Australia's fertility rate, the stability of the nuclear family, and the gender order as a whole. As a figure implicated in and threatening to all these demographic trends and socio-cultural structures and values, the aborting woman became a site of projection where individuals could 'performatively reinstate' (Baird 2006b: 214) authority over the practice of abortion, restoring women's identities to the family and white women's bodies to the nation.

The fear circulating around and producing the figure of the aborting woman is a consequence of a history of maternal citizenship for white women and is intensified by her metonymic association with other figures posed as threats to the security of the white nation fantasy and its key institution, 'the family'. In 1970s Australia, these figures included the homosexual and divorcee, and in the 2000s, the figures of the lesbian mother, the Muslim, and the asylum seeker. Like these figures, aborting women threaten the fantasy of what the nation's future should be, a fantasy that involves nostalgic longing for a fabricated past composed of happy, white, hetero-families. The fantasy future conglomerating these objects through fear would have no abortions, at least amongst white women (Baird 2006a), and tight controls on migration. In this imaginary future, white women would choose the nation rather than abortion, aligning with the nation in orientation towards their future children as happy objects.

CONCLUSION: A VIABLE ABORTION

When the choice of abortion is depicted visually, the woman considering the choice is usually seated alone, looking wistfully into the distance in deep contemplation and with a sense of foreboding. She is portrayed as being deep within her emotional world, with the weight of the choice, which is fully hers to make, pressing upon her. The colours are muted or dark. Such sombre imagery is not benign or reflective of how 'women' (as though they are a homogenous group) approach or experience abortion; rather, it conveys an emotional economy of abortion that is reinforced across various discursive sites and is intensely political.

The last fifty years have witnessed radical shifts in the cultural meanings of abortion and the structures and norms of gender they rely on and reinforce. The emotions that are routinely attached to abortion emerged in response to this period of change. Although the Women's Liberation Movement (WLM) offered a critique of the cultural politics of abortion guilt and shame, descriptions of the experience of abortion in the 1970s focused on the physical rather than the emotional, and particularly the morbidity and mortality of illegal abortion. WLM framed abortion as an issue of self-determination and bodily integrity and in relation to a critique of reproductive sexuality and compulsory motherhood, and these concepts have remained fixed in the cultural imagery of abortion. WLM's radical abortion politics were, however, largely disavowed in the normative account of abortion choice to take shape over the course of the decade.

Attention to the emotional experience of abortion became an increasingly prevalent strand of anti-abortion activism from the mid-1980s onward, and enabled anti-abortionists to assume a compassionate stance towards the women who had abortions. A politics of abortion based on compassion formed a synergy between strands of anti- and pro-choice activism, transforming the people who feel compassion—activists, parliamentarians or 'the public'—into the subjects of debate, and the women who have abortions into objects to be discussed and debated by others. Within such a politics, aborting women appear as victims, either of the circumstances that led them to abortion or to the emotional and psychological effects of abortion. As victims, they are presented as vulnerable and in need of protection, whether this protection comes in the form of liberal abortion laws and sympathetic doctors, or alternatively, laws designed to prevent women from making the potentially injurious choice of abortion. Women's vulnerability and victim-status is entrenched in dominant iterations of abortion politics; this reinforces women's status as dependents (on the state, for example, for their protection) and, in Reva Siegel's words, 'violate[s] the dignity of women who are fully competent to make decisions' (2008: 1796).

While appeal to the emotional experience of abortion enabled anti-abortionists to defend their politics against accusations of antipathy towards women who had abortions, pro-choice activists turned to emotional experience to counter the stereotype of the 'selfish aborting woman', who has continued to surface in arguments for retaining restrictions on women's access to abortion. The narrative of a difficult choice followed by grief and regret enables pro-choice activists to argue that removing restrictions on abortion would not drive pregnant women into abortion clinics. According to this rhetoric, abortion is a profoundly unpleasant and damaging procedure that no woman would choose to have unless she saw no viable alternative. This argument supposes that women invariably monitor their own abortion conduct, meaning that the law or individual doctors do not need to act as gatekeepers of abortion, and restrictive laws are redundant and unnecessarily punitive. Although serving differing political purposes, we can see that strands of anti- and pro-choice activism converged to represent abortion as an emotionally harrowing experience.

There was further confluence in the norm of femininity that powered this emotional script of abortion. In the 1970s, three distinct images of aborting women aligned with differing interpretations of choice: the 'desperate woman' forced to have a termination because her life circumstances prevented her from mothering the child effectively; the 'independent woman' who sought a life outside of motherhood; and the 'anti-mother', who killed instead of nurtured her child. Although these discursive figures continue to exist, the figure of the woman who makes the heartbreaking decision to have an abortion, and suffers indelible grief and guilt as a consequence, has also emerged. Within the WLM and anti-abortion movement of the 1970s, aborting women appeared as 'affect aliens', oriented away from the normative affective script of maternal happiness (Ahmed 2010a), with women's independence from motherhood conceived of in either positive or negative terms depending on the movement. The grief-stricken aborting woman is, in contrast, oriented in the right direction. Dominant strands of anti- and pro-choice rhetoric are articulated through the prism of maternal femininity, so that there is no escape for pregnant women: motherhood becomes a pregnant woman's choice even when they choose to have abortions.

The meanings available to women as they approach, experience and remember their abortions have become heavily circumscribed, and this operates through the rhetoric of choice, rather than through appeals to explicitly restrict women's choices. The concept of choice is now normalised in the context of abortion. There is broad support for women's choice, albeit in varying degrees and often only in specific instances, and it is difficult to argue that pregnant women should be forced to continue their pregnancies to term. Cultural representations of abortion, however, work to elide the fact that some pregnant women do not want to mother the foetuses they are carrying. This elision works to recuperate the high incidences of abortion with maternity femininity and the concomitant norms of the willed pregnancy and foetal motherhood, which together designate pregnant women as already mothers to autonomous foetuses, and require women to control their reproductive potential until they have gathered the necessary economic and social resources to mother effectively. These normative schemas produce a powerful expectation that all pregnancies conceived go on to produce babies; against this expectation, abortion figures as a failure of each woman's personal responsibility. With the cause of abortion so individualised, the procedure and the people who have it are removed from their political, economic, social and cultural contexts.

The depoliticisation of abortion is achieved through the rhetoric of choice; and the emotions that have become attached to abortion are a primary means by which intensely social meanings about abortion are made to appear natural, enabling assumptions about abortion to circulate as truths. Emotions hold the power to naturalise profoundly political messages about abortion. The norms of the willed pregnancy and foetal motherhood determine the emotions that are sayable (grief, shame, guilt, maternal happiness) and virtually unsayable (happiness, gratitude, hope) in the context of abortion. This is why we hear the same emotions continually articulated alongside abortion. The continued repetition of these emotions over time and across various discursive sites removes the emotional economy of abortion from the conditions of its production. Uniform representations of gendered emotional experiences are also one means by which gender is naturalised and made to appear unamenable to social or cultural change. This is because emotions are commonly viewed to reflect a subject's inner life, so the belief that women experience abortion similarly transforms the subject of abortion—woman—into a pre-cultural entity.

The emotions that attach to and modify the meaning of abortion choice are 'straightening devices', recuperating aborting women with norms of conduct that are already 'lined up' (Ahmed 2010b: 91). The narrative of a 'difficult choice' presumes that by terminating a pregnancy, women go against their automatic and natural orientation towards their foetuses as 'happy objects'. The narrative of a difficult choice is usually joined by emphasis on the reasons women terminate their pregnancies—they haven't finished university, they don't have a good job, they are single, etc. These common justifications for abortion reify images of the 'good mother'— as being educated, economically self-sufficient and in a stable (heterosexual) relationship—while also imploring women to justify their abortions to others. Women who have abortions are represented as oriented towards their foetuses as happy objects, but as unable to offer their potential children the economic or social resources deemed necessary to ensure their happiness. The decision to terminate a pregnancy is thereby framed as a choice women make as maternal subjects caring for and protecting their potential children.

When foetuses are positioned invariably as happy objects for pregnant women, they become grievable objects upon abortion, and abortion carries with it the promise of grief. Grief dominates accounts of abortion across varied, and indeed seemingly opposite, perspectives on abortion; and the grief most frequently depicted presents women as perpetually mourning the death of their unborn children. Foetocentic grief

produces pregnant women as already mothers to the autonomous 'children' within their wombs, while also designating
abortion to be morally problematic and harmful to women.

Happiness and grief form an emotional economy structured by the presence or absence of a child; this economy
conveys the good and bad of pregnancy choices for women,
and directs women towards motherhood through their choices.
The emotional economy of abortion does not, however, map
easily onto women's experiences of abortion, where relief is the
most commonly reported emotion, and severe or prolonged
grief is rare. The emotional economy is, therefore, performative rather than descriptive. It works to reconcile conflicting
modes of femininity: on one hand, the postfeminist discourse
of women's freedom, as articulated through 'choice'; and, on the
other, heavily circumscribed norms of gender that fixate on
motherhood as a woman's anchoring point. The citation of
a 'difficult choice' and foetocentric grief restores aborting
women to cultural viability as maternal subjects.

Abortion shame and shaming compel women to remain
silent about their abortions, and the high rates of women who
conceal their abortions from others is one means by which
the emotional economy of abortion has achieved cultural
dominance in lieu of empirical validation. Because shame is
'unspeakable', it is difficult to measure in terms of women's
actual experiences of abortion. Shame and the related emotion
of guilt certainly form part of the cultural imagery of abortion;
these emotions mark their subjects as non-normative, and
thereby work alongside maternal happiness and abortion
grief to reify ideas and ideologies of femininity. Women's

silence and secrecy about their abortions may represent an internalisation of abortion shame and stigma. High rates of concealment determine that people who have not had abortions themselves—and, often, men who could never become pregnant let alone have abortions—generally author representations of abortion. Thus, expectations about how women should approach and experience abortion dominate the representational terrain, paving the way for gender stereotypes and images and ideals about 'good women' to predominate.

Abortion is rarely presented from the view of the pregnant woman who no longer wants to be pregnant and, instead of being represented as the cessation of an unwanted pregnancy, abortion is more often depicted as a procedure that destroys autonomous life. Of course, terminating a pregnancy does cease the development of an embryo/foetus that would otherwise, except in cases of miscarriage, transform into an autonomous human, and viewing abortion in these terms does not necessarily endorse an anti-abortion perspective (Ludlow 2008). When abortion is viewed solely as the destruction of embryonic or foetal life, however, attention focuses on the foetus rather than the pregnant woman. Getting pregnant is not always a willed, intentional act. Unwanted and unplanned pregnancies are a routine component of women's reproductive lives; and, for women who are unwillingly pregnant, abortion is the only guaranteed means by which to deliver them from this condition. When the foetus is the focal point of pregnancy (or abortion), then it is generally transformed into an autonomous entity and pregnant women are conceived of as already mothers. Within this schema, abortion is represented as, at

best, unpleasant albeit necessary and, at worst, morally repre-
hensible and dangerous for women. Anti-abortionists depict
women who have abortions as selfish mothers who refuse
to nurture their children to birth or as hapless and vulnerable victims who kill their children without full appreciation
of what abortion entails or its emotional and psychological
aftermath; those who support women's access to abortion, in
contrast, frequently highlight the economic and social circumstances that 'force' women to have abortions.

By interrogating the logic behind an incessant focus on
economic and other reasons for abortion, I am not suggesting
that such factors have no relevance when thinking about why
women have abortions. Lori Freedman and Tracy Weitz
argue that in the USA there has been a discernible shift in
the economic status of women seeking abortion: 'Whereas
middle-class women of the 1970s and 1980s more widely
fought for and used abortion to delay their fertility in order
to achieve their educational and occupational goals, it is more
often working-class women in the 1990s and 2000s who
used abortion to manage much harsher economic realities'
(2012: 40). The depiction of abortion as a liberatory experience, as an expression of freedom, can gloss over economic
and other costs of parenting. An obsession with economic and
other reasons for abortion, however, reifies a context where
women are expected to justify their abortions to others, and
paints abortion as a forced rather than voluntary under-
taking. I am calling for the celebration of abortion as an act
that allows unwillingly pregnant women to get what they want
and ensures that, for women of reproductive age, hetero-sex is

separated from reproduction. The position of the 'unwilling-ly pregnant woman' is discursive and material. Although not the focus of this book, I join those who believe that abortion needs to be fought for within an encompassing reproductive justice framework that provides pregnant women with the necessary economic and social support systems to ensure, as much as possible, that the only women who have abortions are the unwillingly pregnant, of which there are many (Ross 2006; Silliman et al. 2004).

Advocates for reproductive justice critique the concept of choice for obfuscating modes of privilege and disadvantage that stratify women, determine the resources that can facili-tate or hinder one's access to reproductive choices, and inflect understandings of effective and 'good' parenting. Reproduct-ive politics cannot be reduced to abortion politics, and abortion politics are not merely gender politics. Laws on abortion were liberalised at the same time as several social movements began to challenge identities that had previously been unmarked and were, as such, vestiges of privilege. Abortion quickly became a conduit through which conservatives have bemoaned the loss of traditional cultural and social life and aspire to re-establish the modes of privilege that existed before abortion laws were liberalised. Cultural representations of abortion are a means whereby the subject position of the 'good mother' is produced; as a subject position formed at the intersection of several vectors of identity—including those of gender, race, class and sexuality—she is a means whereby their formative power relations are reinforced and upheld. Representations of abortion are, in other words, a means of creating a fixed social order in response to challenges to fixity and the power relations that are naturalised therein. The figure of the 'aborting woman' is constructed as a threat to the social body through her association with other sources of intense social anxiety. Her connection to the figure of 'the feminist' has marked her as anti-children, anti-male and anti-family. The discussion of abortion alongside and through the figures of the 'teenage mother', the 'welfare dependent', and the 'sexually irresponsible' produces her as a reckless failure or 'loser'. The aborting woman's association with the figures of the 'divorcee', the 'homosexual', the 'lesbian parent', and 'single mother' pose her as a threat to the institution of the nuclear family.

Because motherhood holds a central role in nation building, abortion is also commonly presented as a threat to the nation. This threat is discernible through the attachment of the 'aborting woman' with others who are seen to threaten the security of the nation, including 'the communist' in the 1970s and, today, the 'asylum seeker'. The idea that abortion is a flood or swamp that threatens to erode the social or moral fabric of the nation from within promotes the idea that pregnant women's bodies need to be secured for the nation. The attachment of abortion to other issues posed as threats to the White Nation and the patriarchal nuclear family demonstrate that struggles over abortion represent much more than single-issue campaigns. Cultural imaginings of abortion position the aborting woman as a threat and also, at once, appease this threat through reconciling her with what she is perceived to threaten: the figure of the 'good mother' and her attendant responsibilities and privileges.

The representation of abortion as an exceptional experi-ence further aligns the fact that one in three women will have an abortion in her lifetime with the norm of motherhood for pregnant women. The commingling of choice with particular emotions allows for a rigid, normative identity to be regu-lated behind the illusion of freedom. Forms of regulation in the contemporary, neoliberal era can only be sustained when they are perceived to emanate from free subjects. Even in anti-abortion activism we have seen a turn towards 'choice' in policies advocating for 'informed choice' and rhe-toric such as 'real choices'; and concomitant policy goals do not explicitly seek to restrict women's freedom (although, of course, this is precisely their effect), but, rather, feign to protect women from making choices they will later regret.

A politics reduced to choice is fundamentally individual-ising, and the autonomous subject it references and produces is nothing less than fictitious. The entrepreneurial, self-directed subject of choice is completely dependent on and sustained through domestic and reproductive labour that remains thoroughly feminised. Yet the repeated presump-tion that women perform such labour because they choose to, because such labour makes them happy, removes it from the economic, political and socio-economic context. In order for there to be freedom in the realm of abortion we must move away from notions of freedom based on the autonomous (choosing) subject. We live in a community, and therefore, as Wendy Brown insists, 'there is no such thing as individual freedom … [H]uman freedom is finally, always a project of making a world with others' (Brown et al. 2006: 26). At present, the directed subject of choice—where women are positioned as having endless choices and, oriented towards children as happy objects, are perceived to choose mother-hood purely to realise desire—mediates the tension choice holds at the level of women's reproductive bodies. This is, however, a fragile balance. Autonomy and choice exist alongside constraint and dependency: personal choices are political.

Claims to freedom that are articulated through choice can disguise structural modes of inequality; a focus on the law as the means of ensuring reproductive justice can have a similar effect. The decriminalisation of abortion has undeni-able benefits: it removes the threat of legal prosecution from women and their doctors; on a symbolic level, it formally recognises women as subjects of decisions about abortion; and in jurisdictions where the law directly obstructs the provision of abortion care, decriminalisation can improve women's access to abortion (Baird 2017: 205). While impor-tant, the decriminalisation of abortion does not ensure that women can access abortion locally or affordably, nor does it make abortion culturally intelligible as a legitimate or normal choice. The 'intense legalism' characteristic of neoliberal feminisms more generally draws attention away from the cultural production of gender (Brown and Hadley 2002). The law on abortion is not the source of restrictions on abortion, but reflects and reinforces norms of gender, pregnancy and motherhood. In Australia, where abortion is decriminalised in many jurisdictions, these norms have outlived the laws that attempted to force conformity to their parameters. The emotional economy of abortion produces a self-surveilling subject who regulates her own conduct, making restrictive laws appear unnecessary.

A HAPPY ABORTION?

Alternative cultural narratives have always existed alongside the dominant script of anguish, grief and shame, meaning that my focus on dominant modes of representing abortion in this book may afford the representational terrain of abortion more uniformity than is apparent in the heterogeneous cultural landscape. Some pro-choice activists have, for instance, continually argued that abortion holds no inevitable psychological or emotional outcome for women (for example, Vick 2002).

The recent growth of anti-stigma activism also forms a counter-discourse to the emotional narrative of abortion that centres this book. This is especially true of the accompanying emergence of an 'unapologetic' narrative of abortion, which is discernible (in varying manifestations) across many sites, including the abortion stories of popular feminists (Ford 2016; West 2016), the viral Twitter campaign *#ShoutYourAbortion* (Fishwick 2015; West 2015), the mainstream press (Sanger 2017: 220), and online forums, including the 1 in 3 Campaign (2016). This narrative associates abortion with feelings of relief, gratitude and even happiness; accompanied by the political slogan 'Abortion on demand, without apology', it is clearly a retort to the unwritten contract examined in this book where, in exchange for having abortions, women are required to profess a degree of sadness and distress. The incitement to 'shout' about your abortion responds to abortion stigma and the cultural imperative to remain silent about one's abortion, attempting to reframe abortion as a normal and shared experience. In a classic statement of this alternative, unapologetic abortion narrative, 'Australia's go-to feminist' (Simic 2016) Clementine Ford (2009), for example, describes her abortions thus:

> I've had not one but two abortions. I know I'm supposed to grovel and grape my belly along the ground for all eternity begging the world's forgiveness. I'm supposed to kowtow and claim they were each the hardest decision I ever made, that I think about them every day, that I fall into violent pits of depression because I feel such intense agony over the fact I'm such a heartless, baby-killer. Bollocks to that. I feel no shame regarding either of them. I was acting in my own best interest, a fact I refuse to apologise for.

As a clearly discernible counter-discourse, the unapologetic narrative of abortion is a testament to the normative strength of the (apologetic) abortion narrative examined in this book while also signalling a rupture, we can hope, in its hegemonic grasp on cultural meanings of abortion.

Legal scholar Carol Sanger champions the proliferation of first-person abortion narratives, arguing that more women must share their experiences of abortion publicly in order to incite the legal and cultural change required to ensure women can access abortion readily, lawfully and without fear of stigma. Quoting the philosopher Bernard Williams, she asserts that 'their experiences are the only realistic and honest guide we have to what the unique phenomenon of abortion genuinely is, as opposed to what moralists, philosophers and legislators say it is. It follows that their experience is the only realistic guide to what the deepest consequences will be of our social attitudes to abortions' (Williams quoted in Sanger 2017: 49–50). Realising that her vision for change burdens the women who have abortions, Sanger notes that '[p]erhaps the personal risk would seem worth it if the connection between private talk, public discussion, and political decision making were better understood' (219). Sanger's focus on women's experiences draws attention to the gap between the representation and 'reality' of abortion, emphasising that stereotypes about how women should feel leading up to and after their abortions rationalise restrictive laws that portend to 'protect' women from abortion. The call to normalise abortion—evident in Sanger's politics and the unapologetic narrative of abortion— also recognises that the exceptionality of abortion can leave women fearful of the social consequences of their abortions and opens it up to endless political, legal and cultural contestation. A politics focused on individual experiences can, however, also hold each woman who has had an abortion responsible for the cultural and legal contexts of abortion, through either her silence or disclosure. The inference that individual experience signifies the truth of what 'abortion genuinely is' further produces an 'individualised' and 'responsibilised' subject, removed from the broader social and cultural contexts through which her experience of abortion has been forged (Scott 1990).

The hegemonic narrative of abortion that centres this book is fundamentally anti-abortion and needs to be dislodged. A politics of abortion fought through first-person narratives, however, runs the risk of further transforming abortion politics into a politics of individual experience. As I have shown in this book, this trend has been under way since the mid-1980s, and its recent intensification belongs to interlocking historical developments that are enmeshed with a depoliticised and depoliticising neoliberal worldview. There has been, in Bev Skeggs' words, an 'imperative to subjectivity', which eclipses a view of the self forged through 'structural issues of inequality', postulating instead that 'the world no longer has meaning unless grounded in the personal, the subjective, and the particular' (2004: 291). This imperative to subjectivity characterises a new form of mediated feminism, which, as Rosalind Gill (2016) identifies, reifies the principles of 'individualism, choice and agency' (613) and fuels a politics that is not based on social, cultural or structural change but, rather, an 'attitudinal pose of assertiveness and defiance' (623). Unapologetic abortion politics often bears the hallmarks of this type of feminism—it reifies the individual, both as the source of her experience and the grounds upon which abortion politics should be waged, celebrates the principle of choice, and 'assertiveness and defiance' characterise her experience of abortion.

The personal is political, but it is important to unpack and reflect on the politics of the personal—personal narratives cannot do this work in and of themselves. When it comes to cultural representations of the abortion experience, we need to think about the norms they rely on and reinforce, and the work these norms do in upholding categories of identity that are made to appear natural but are, in fact, 'effects of a specific formulation of power' (Butler 1990: ix). When the politics of abortion is reduced to how women feel leading to or after them, regardless of whether these feelings are positive or negative, broader social, structural and political issues are left unaddressed. These issues include the gendered division of labour and the class and race-based inequalities that can facilitate or hinder the decisions we make about parenting as well as how others judge and evaluate these decisions, historico-sociological questions relating to the separation of contraception from abortion and women's allotted responsibility for preventing unwanted pregnancies, and ontological questions pertaining to the condition of pregnancy.

Although I unpack the normative assumptions that underpin the emotional common sense of abortion in this book, I am certainly not arguing for an intensification of an abortion politics waged through recourse to a woman's emotions. The argument that abortion should be freely available to women because they feel nothing but relief afterwards shares a certain logic to the argument that abortion should be restricted in order to protect women from negative emotional consequences. Monolithic and uniform representations of the emotional experience of abortion produce a naturalised female subject, and this is no less true for positive than for negative emotions. The heterogeneity of women's lives and aspirations can never be captured in a single narrative of abortion. Thus, despite being titled *Happy Abortions*, I am not advocating for the singular representation of abortion as happy to replace the depiction of abortion as being inevitably difficult and unhappy occasions. The title comes from a leading question of the book: what makes the possibility of a happy abortion, at best, transgressive and, at worst, unspeakable? When abortion is viewed from the position of a pregnant woman who does not want to be pregnant, the repeated representation of the only means that can ensure she gets what she wants, and can ensure this in a relatively straightforward and painless way, as unhappy is rather absurd. From the perspective of the unwillingly pregnant woman, we can see abortion as something to be celebrated rather than a choice to be tolerated. While I have offered caution against supplanting an abortion politics focused on structural inequality with first-person abortion narratives, the unapologetic abortion narrative nevertheless holds value because it implies and validates the subject position of the unwillingly pregnant women for whom abortion is a beneficial and life-enhancing decision. The constant move to foreclose this subject position reveals that the idea that some pregnant women do not want to become mothers to their foetuses remains subversive. As long as motherhood remains the only authentic and 'happy' choice for pregnant women, abortion will manifest as a fundamentally unacceptable choice that women need to justify to or hide away from others. If negative emotions work to reify foetal motherhood, then other emotions hold the potential to pave the way for multiple pregnant subjectivities. Campaigning for legal and social recognition of the multiplicity of pregnant subjectivities is vital to pro-choice activism and scholarship.

Recognition of multiplicity involves reconceiving pregnancy as a subjective and variable condition, rather than an objective one, as it is most commonly described. Pregnant women are not automatically mothers, although some pregnant women may be mothers to children already born and some may assume this identity in relation to their developing foetuses. Foetuses are not autonomous subjects, but may nevertheless 'come to life' through the hopes, aspirations and material practices of pregnant women. Recognition of the contingent nature of pregnancy enables us to appreciate the multiplicity of experiences that accompany different forms of pregnancy loss or termination. The women who miscarry, those who terminate pregnancies that were at one stage wanted, and those who terminate unwanted pregnancies inhabit different pregnant realities, making these experiences incommensurate with one another, no matter how hard anti-abortionists attempt to bind them together through the singular representation of pregnancy as entailing a mother and her child.

Once we view pregnancy as a subjective rather than objective condition, then the emotional world of pregnant women becomes multiple and varied, rather than a fixed reflection of nature. Sara Ahmed argues that freedom involves the freedom 'to respond to the world, to what comes up, without defending oneself or one's happiness against what comes up' (2010b: 222). Recognition of the multiplicity of pregnant subjectivities, and the inclusion of the 'unwillingly pregnant women' amongst these, ascribes abortion, not with the strict feeling rules and emotional economies that circumscribe abortion today, but with potential. As potential, abortion would hold the possibility of multiple, perhaps contradictory emotions, and could be an occasion for happiness or hope just as easily and legitimately as grief or sadness. With no fixed norm to measure aborting women against, shame and guilt would disappear from the affective landscape of abortion. The dismantling of motherhood as the placeholder of women's happiness would reframe abortion as, unambiguously, a woman's choice, albeit not one made by an autonomous actor. This project involves a disruption to the emotions through which abortion is currently made intelligible.

NOTES

Introduction: An emotional choice

1 The Supreme Court Ruling in *Whole Women's Health v Hellerstedt* (2016) declared that the TRAP laws introduced in Texas were unconstitutional; while this Ruling will ensure that many such laws are rescinded and no further TRAP-style provisions introduced, it remains unclear whether clinics that were closed as a consequence of such laws will reopen (Sanger 2017: 34–6).

2 Abortion has, however, been repeatedly debated in the Canadian parliament since the Supreme Court ruling of 1988. From 1988 to 2013, 43 private members' bills with anti-abortion implications were introduced into the House of Commons. Most notably, in 1991, a bill seeking to re-criminalise abortion was narrowly defeated in the Canadian parliament (Saurette and Gordon 2013: 158).

1 The politics of choice

1 My main archive is the newsletters and pamphlets of these three activist organisations, which are held at the State Library of Victoria. The newsletter of RTL has had several titles since 1973: the *Newsletter of the Victorian Right to Life Association*, published at irregular intervals between 1973 and 1976; *Right to Life News*, published bi-monthly from 1977 to 2002; and *RTLA News*, published bi-monthly from 2002 onward. The Victorian Law Reform Commission published eleven newsletters between 1970 and 1972 and, upon being renamed the Victorian Law Repeal Association, it published newsletters at irregular intervals between 1972 and 1975. WAAC published twenty-one issues of its magazine *Abortion Is a Woman's Right to Choose* between 1973 and 1981. It was retitled *Right to Choose: A Woman's Health Magazine* in 1981, and published a further seven issues between then and 1986.

2 Legal scholar Karen Petersen (1984) suggests that the different outcomes may have been a result of two factors: removing Medicaid funding was a backlash against *Roe v Wade* (1973), which was a far more radical law than those introduced into Australian jurisdictions; Medicaid recipients in America were also generally poor and black, whereas white, middle-class women in Australia would have been affected if a similar law was introduced into Australia. In Australia, laws on abortion also construct abortion as a 'medical' issue, rather than a moral issue based on rights, and, when placed alongside the USA, Australia has a comparatively expansive medical benefits scheme (O'Connor et al. 1999: 4, 15).

3 This may have stemmed from the (probably misguided) belief that RTL held significant political influence and popular support (Gregory 2005: 299–300).

2 Happy choices

1 In recent years, feminism has arguably become a more attractive, even stylish, identifier for young women, although the feminism represented valorises the individual, emphasising empowerment, assertiveness and personal confidence, and thus reifies the postfeminist disavowal of the structural and normative weight of gender (Gill 2016). The parliamentary debates I examine in this chapter were from the mid-2000s, coming before this renewed mainstream interest in feminism.

2 According to my calculations, 78 per cent of female, compared to just 48 per cent of male, parliamentarians supported the bill decriminalising abortion in Victoria. 84 per cent of female compared to 56 per cent of male parliamentarians supported the Commonwealth bill to remove restrictions on medical abortion. Only 46 per cent of male senators supported the bill, however, so it would not have passed both houses if only the men present voted. Figures for the Commonwealth bill are approximate. The calculations for the House of Representatives are based on the second vote taken immediately before the final vote. Faced with a resounding defeat, then Prime Minister John Howard did not record the final vote, and the bill passed on a 'voice vote'.

3 The full names of these bills are the Therapeutic Goods Amendment (Repeal of Ministerial Responsibility for Approval of RU486) Bill 2005 and the Abortion Law Reform Bill 2008; I refer to them as the Commonwealth and Victorian bills respectively.

4 Racial categories are frequently subsumed to those of class and especially welfare dependency (Altman and Sanders 1995; Archer 2009).

5 A recent Ipsos (2015) Poll surveyed 17,030 adults across twenty-three countries and found that 43 per cent supported abortion whenever a woman wanted one, and only 5 per cent thought it should be completely prohibited. Those in between supported abortion only in specific circumstances. Sweden and France had the most progressive views towards abortion with, respectively, 78 per cent and 67 per cent of those surveyed supporting abortion whenever a woman wanted one. Unequivocal support for women's choice was lower in Great Britain (66%), Canada (54%), Australia (49%) and the USA (40%). Those disagreeing with abortion under all circumstances in these countries ranged from 7 per cent (France and the UK) to 12 per cent (Australia and the USA) and was highest in Japan (27%) and Russia (22%).

6 The idea that the criminalisation of abortion helps prevent men and the 'abortion industry' from coercing women into having abortions was a major argument used to oppose the 2017 motion to decriminalise abortion in the UK (Maria Caulfield, MP; United Kingdom 2017).

3 The grief of choice

1 The main source for my observations about Women Exploited by Abortion, renamed Women Hurt by Abortion in 1990, is its newsletter, which was published at irregular intervals from 1986 to 1998, and is held at the State Library of Victoria. Chapter 1 (Note 1) detailed the sources I used to trace the history of RTL.

2 I will expand on this argument in the conclusion to this book.

3 I focus on the representation of the experience of abortion in Melbourne's broadsheet newspaper *The Age* and tabloid the *Herald Sun* as well as, to a less extensive degree, the national broadsheet

The Australian. Newspaper sources prior to 1991 came from two archives: abortion papers held at the State Parliament of Victoria and the Papers of Bertram Wainer, held at the State Library of Victoria (MS 13436). Two tabloids, *The Herald* and *The Sun* merged in 1990 to become the *Herald Sun*. The major newspapers consulted for this project are fully digitalised after 1991. A search for 'abortion' in *The Age* from the years 1991 to 2008 in the Factiva database yielded 2664 results. These sources were supplemented by the coverage of abortion in the *Herald Sun* and *The Australian* around events that caused a surge of interest in the issue, such as parliamentary bills, the screening of programs about abortion on television, and the publication of popular books about abortion. This chapter focuses on trends within the articles that detailed women's experiences of abortion.

4   This is the first detailed account of abortion experience I could find in the Australian newspapers *The Herald, The Sun, The Age* and *The Australian*. At least the first two of Helen's abortions were performed before laws were liberalised. The newspaper article does not, however, explicate this point.

5 A nation's choice?

1   The important exception here is pregnant women who are coerced into childbearing or abortion by intimate partners or others (see Hayes 2016).

BIBLIOGRAPHY

1 in 3 Campaign. 2016. *The 1 in 3 Campaign: These Are OUR Stories* [online]. Available from: www.1in3campaign.org/about [accessed 17 January 2017].

Abbott, A. 2004. The ethical responsibilities of a Christian politician, lecture delivered to the Adelaide University Democratic Club, Adelaide University, 16 March [online]. Available from: www.tonyabbott.com.au/LatestNews/Speeches/tabid/88/articleType/ArticleView/articleId/3550/THE-ETHICAL-RESPONSIBILI-TIES-OF-A-CHRISTIAN POLITICIAN.aspx [accessed 13 March 2014].

Abigail, W., Power, C. and Belan, I. 2008. Changing patterns in women seeking terminations of pregnancy: A trend analysis of data from one service provider 1996–2006. *Australian and New Zealand Journal of Public Health*, 32(3), 230–237.

Abortion Campaign Committee. n.d. Free Abortion on Demand [online]. Available from: www.loc.gov/pictures/item/yan1996000520/PP/ [accessed 24 January 2017].

Abortion Law Reform Association. 1970a. *ABRA/ Abortion Law Reform Association* 1 (April 23).

———. 1970b. *ABRA/Abortion Law Reform Association* 2 (23 June).

———. 1970c. *ABRA/Abortion Law Reform Association* 3 (3 September).

———. 1970d. *ABRA/Abortion Law Reform Association* 4 (11 November).

———. 1971. *ABRA/Abortion Law Reform Association ABRA* 7 (17 August).

———. 1972a. *Newsletter (Abortion Law Reform Association)*, Winter.

———. 1972b. *Newsletter (Abortion Law Reform Association)*, August.

———. 1974a. *Newsletter (Abortion Law Reform Association)*, n.d.

———. 1974b. *Newsletter (Abortion Law Reform Association)*, January–February.

————. 1974c. Petition to Parliament. State Library of Victoria, Wainer Papers, MS134636, Box 17.

Adams, I. and Buttrose, I. 2005. *Motherguilt*. Camberwell, London: Viking.

The Age. 1970. 90,000 lost each year. *The Age*, 14 May.

The Age. 1973. Abortion is key issue: Cardinal. *The Age*, 25 April.

The Age. 2005. Editorial: The abortion issue and its many shades of grey. *The Age*, 5 February.

The Age. 2006a. Change law on funding abortion abroad. *The Age*, 10 September.

The Age. 2006b. Editorial: No place for politics in debate on abortion drug. *The Age*, 8 January.

Ahmed, S. 2004a. Affective Economies. *Social Text*, 22 (2), 117–139.

————. 2004b. *The Cultural Politics of Emotion*. New York: Routledge.

————. 2010a. Killing joy: Feminism and the history of happiness. *Signs: Journal of Women in Culture and Society*, 35(3), 571–694.

————. 2010b. *The Promise of Happiness*. Durham and London: Duke University Press.

Albury, R. 1979. Attacks on Abortion Rights: The Latest Round. *Scarlet Woman*, 9 (September), 23.

Allen, K. 2002. Abortion, and no regrets. *The Age*, 20 May.

Allison, L. 2008. Issue a personal one for Lyn Allison. *Herald Sun*, 1 June.

Altman, J. and Sanders, W. 1995. From exclusion to dependence: Aborigines and the welfare state in Australia. *In*: Dixon, J. and Scheurell, R. eds. *Social Welfare with Indigenous Peoples*. London and New York: Routledge, 206–229.

Altman, J. C. and Hinkson, M. eds. 2007. *Coercive Reconciliation: Stabilise, Normalise, Exit Aboriginal Australia*. Melbourne: Arena Publications.

Angus Reid. 2013. Canadians have mixed feelings about abortion, but shun a new debate [online]. Available from: http://angusreidglobal.com/wp-content/uploads/2013/01/2013.01.28_Abortion_CAN.pdf [accessed 16 December 2016].

Anonymous GP. 1972. A general practitioner's view of the law. *In*: McMichael, T. ed. *Abortion: The Unenforceable Law: The Reality of*

Unwanted Pregnancy and Abortion in Australia. North Carlton, VIC: ALRA, 45–46.

Anthias, F. and Yuval-Davis, N. 1989. *Woman-nation-state.* New York: Springer.

Archer, V. 2009. Dole bludgers, tax payers and the New Right: Constructing discourses of welfare in 1970s Australia. *Labour History,* 96, 177–190.

Astbury Ward, E., Parry, O. and Carnwell, R. 2012. Stigma, abortion, and disclosure: Findings from a qualitative study. *The Journal of Sexual Medicine,* 9(1), 1–11.

Austin, J. L. 1975. *How to Do Things with Words.* Cambridge: Cambridge University Press.

Australia. 1973. Parliamentary debates: House of Representatives: Official Hansard, 10 May.

———. 1979a. Parliamentary debates: House of Representatives: Official Hansard, 21 March.

———. 1979b. Parliamentary debates: House of Representatives: Official Hansard, 22 March.

———. 2006a. Parliamentary debates: Senate: Official Hansard, 8 February.

———. 2006b. Parliamentary debates: Senate: Official Hansard, 9 February.

———. 2006c. Parliamentary debates: House of Representatives: Official Hansard, 14 February.

———. 2006d. Parliamentary debates: House of Representatives: Official Hansard, 15 February.

———. 2006e. Parliamentary debates: House of Representatives: Official Hansard, 16 February.

Australian Bureau of Statistics. 2012. Year Book Australia: Population—Births, 24 May [online]. Available from: www.abs.gov.au/ausstats/abs@.nsf/Lookup/by%20Subject/1301.0~2012~Main%20Features~Births~51 [accessed 20 July 2017].

Australian Institute of Family Studies. 2017. Stay at home dads. [online]. Available from https://aifs.gov.au/publications/stay-home-dads [accessed 13 June 2017].

Bailey, A. and Zita, J. 2007. The reproduction of whiteness: Race and the regulation of the gendered body. *Hypatia*, 22(2), vii–xv.

Baird, B. 1996. 'The Incompetent, Barbarous Old Lady Round the Corner': The image of the backyard abortionist in pro-abortion politics. *Hecate*, 22(1), 7–26.

———. 1998a. The self-aborting woman. *Australian Feminist Studies*, 13(28), 323–337.

———. 1998b. *'Somebody Was Going to Disapprove Anyway': Rethinking Histories of Abortion in South Australia, 1937–1990*, PhD thesis. Adelaide, SA: Flinders University.

———. 2001. Abortion, questions, ethics, embodiment. *History Workshop Journal*, 52, 197–216.

———. 2004. Contexts for lesbian citizenships across Australian public spheres. *Social Semiotics*, 14(1), 67–84.

———. 2006a. The futures of abortion. *In:* McMahom, E. and Olubas, B. eds. *Women Making Time: Contemporary Feminist Critique and Cultural Analysis*. Crawley, Western Australia: University of Western Australia Press, 116–149.

———. 2006b. Maternity, whiteness and national identity: The case of abortion. *Australian Feminist Studies*, 21(50), 197–221.

———. 2013. Abortion Politics during the Howard years: Beyond liberalisation. *Australian Historical Studies*, 44(2), 245–261.

———. 2017. Decriminalization and Women's Access to Abortion in Australia. *Health and Human Rights*, 19(1), 197–208.

Baker, A. 1983. Abortion risk. *The Age*, 27 June.

Balibar, E. 1991. Is there a "neo-racism"? *In:* Balibar, E. and Wallerstein, I. eds. *Race, Nation, Class: Ambiguous Identities*. London: Verso, 17–28.

Bartky, S. L. 1990. *Femininity and Domination: Studies in the Phenomenology of Oppression*. New York: Routledge.

Bashford, A. and Strange, C. 2002. Asylum-seekers and national histories of detention. *Australian Journal of Politics & History*, 48(4), 509–527.

Bean, L., Gonzalez, M. and Kaufman, J. 2008. Why doesn't Canada have an American-style Christian right? A comparative framework for analyzing the political effects of evangelical subcultural identity. *Canadian Journal of Sociology*, 33(4), 899–943.

Beaumont, L. 2004. Fighting over the right to choose. *The Age*, 7 November.

Beck, U. 1992. *Risk Society: Towards a New Modernity*. London: Sage Polity.

Begun, S. and Walls, N. 2015. Pedestal or gutter: Exploring ambivalent sexism's relationship with abortion attitudes. *Affilia*, 30(2), 200–215.

Beisel, N. and Kay, T. 2004. Abortion, race, and gender in nineteenth-century America. *American Sociological Review*, 69(4), 498–518.

Berlant, L. 1997. *The Queen of America Goes to Washington City: Essays on Sex and Citizenship*. Durham, NC: Duke University Press.

———. 2004a. Critical inquiry, affirmative culture. *Critical Inquiry*, 30(2), 445–451.

———. 2004b. Introduction: Compassion (and withholding). *In:* Berlant, L. ed. *Compassion: The Culture and Politics of an Emotion*. London and New York: Routledge, 1–14.

———. 2007. Nearly utopian, nearly normal: Post-Fordist affect in La Promesse and Rosetta. *Public Culture*, 19(2), 273–301.

Berlant, L., Najafi, S. and Serlin, D. 2008. The broken circuit: An interview with Lauren Berlant. *Cabinet Magazine*, 31 [online]. Available from: www.cabinetmagazine.org/issues/31/najafi_serlin.php [accessed 20 July 2017].

Betts, K. 2001. Boat people and public opinion in Australia. *People and Place*, 9(4), 34–48.

———. 2004. Attitudes to abortion in Australia: 1972 to 2003. *People and Place*, 12(4), 22–28.

Beynon-Jones, S. M. 2013. 'We view that as contraceptive failure': Containing the 'multiplicity' of contraception and abortion within Scottish reproductive healthcare. *Social Science & Medicine*, 80 (March 2013), 105–112.

Birch, T. 2002. History is never bloodless: Getting it wrong after one hundred years of federation. *Australian Historical Studies*, 33(118), 42–53.

Birnbauer, W. 2006. Abortion drug a legal risk, says QC. *The Age*, 5 February.

Blanchard, D. A. 1996. *The Anti-abortion Movement: References and Resources*. New York: GK Hall.

Blaxland, M. 2010. Mothers and mutual obligation: Policy reforming the good mother. *In:* Goodwin, S. and Huppatz, K. eds. *The Good Mother: Contemporary Motherhoods in Australia.* Sydney: Sydney University Press, 131–152.

Boas, P. 1972. Judy. *In:* McMichael, T. ed. *Abortion, the Unenforceable Law: The Reality of Unwanted Pregnancy and Abortion in Australia.* North Carlton, VIC: ALRA, 85–86.

Bode, K. 2006. Aussie battler in crisis? Shifting constructions of white Australian masculinity and national identity. *Australian Critical Race and Whiteness Studies Association,* 2(1), 1–18.

Boonstra, H. D. and Nash, E. 2014. A surge of state abortion restrictions puts providers—and the women they serve—in the crosshairs. *Guttmacher Policy Review,* 17(1), 9–15.

Boyle, M. 1997. *Re-thinking Abortion: Psychology, Gender, Power and the Law.* London and New York: Routledge.

BPAS. 2015. *Abortion: Trusting Women to Decide and Doctors to Practise* [online]. Available from: www.abortionreview.org/images/uploads/Trusting_women_and_doctors_June_2015.pdf [accessed 3 January 2017].

Brison, S. 1999. Trauma narratives and the remaking of the self. *In:* Bal, M., Crewe, J. and Spitzer, L. eds. *Acts of Memory: Cultural Recall in the Present.* Hanover, NH: University Press of New England, 39–54.

British National Party. 2016. *2030 Deadline: New NHS Birth Figures Confirm Immigrant Births Will Be Majority within Two Decades* [online]. Available from: www.bnp.org.uk/news/2030-deadline-new-nhs-birth-figures-confirm-immigrant-births-will-be-majority-within-two-decade [accessed 15 December 2016].

Brookes, B. 1988. *Abortion in England: 1900–1967.* London, New York and Sydney: Croom Helm.

Brough, M. 2007. Social Security and Other Legislation Amendment (Welfare Payment Reform) Bill 2007: Second Reading Speech, 7 August [online]. Available from: www.formerministers.fahcsia.gov.au/malbrough/speeches/Pages/ss_amendment_7aug07.aspx [accessed 21 January 2016].

Brown, W. 1995. *States of Injury.* Princeton, NJ: Princeton University Press.

————. 2003. Neo-liberalism and the end of liberal democracy. *Theory & Event*, 7(1).

————. 2006. American nightmare: Neoliberalism, neoconservatism, and de-democratization. *Political theory*, 34(6), 690–714.

————. 2010. *Walled States, Waning Sovereignty*. New York: Zone Books.

Brown, W. and Hadley, J. 2002. Introduction. *In:* Brown, W. and Hadley, J. eds. *Left Legalism/Left Critique*. Durham, NC: Duke University Press, 1–37.

Brown, W. *et al.* 2006. Learning to love again: An interview with Wendy Brown. *Contretemps: An Online Journal of Philosophy*, 6, 25–42.

Bulbeck, C. 2010. Unpopularising feminism: 'Blaming feminism' in the generation debate and the mother wars. *Sociology Compass*, 4(1), 21–37.

Burgman, V. 2003. *Power, Profit and Protest: Australian Social Movements and Globalisation*. Crows Nest, NSW: Allen & Unwin.

Butler, J. 1990. *Gender Trouble: Feminism and the Subversion of Identity*. London and New York: Routledge.

————. 1993. *Bodies That Matter: On the Discursive Limits of 'Sex'*. Theatre Arts Books. London and New York: Routledge.

Cafarella, J. 1992. The heartache of abortion. *The Age*, 28 August.

Cameron, D. 2004. War on babies. *The Age*, 18 November.

Campo, N. 2005. "Having it all" or "had enough"? Blaming feminism in *The Age* and *The Sydney Morning Herald*, 1980–2004. *Journal of Australian Studies*, 28(84), 63–72.

————. 2009. *From Superwomen to Domestic Goddesses: The Rise and Fall of Feminism*. Bern: Peter Lang.

Cannold, L. 1995. Killing from care: A woman's sorrow. *The Age*, 1 November.

————. 1998. *The Abortion Myth: Feminism, Morality, and the Hard Choices Women Make*. St Leonards, NSW: Allen & Unwin.

————. 2000. The extended Australian report of 'The Johannesburg Initiative'. [online]. Available from: http://cannold.com/static/files/assets/6674fbe1/johannesburg-report-2000-11.pdf [accessed 22 August 2012].

————. 2002. Understanding and responding to anti-choice women-centred strategies. *Reproductive Health Matters*, 20(19), 171–180.

————. 2013. 'So, what are your plans for abortion, Mr Abbott'. *The Sydney Morning Herald*, 14 June [online]. Available from: www.smh.com. au/federal-politics/political-opinion/so-what-are-your-plans-for-abortion-mr-abbott-20130613-2o6u6 [accessed 4 November 2015].

Capello, A. 2002. Don't keep abortion grief a secret (letter). *The Age*, 16 May.

Caruth, C. 1996. *Unclaimed Experience: Trauma, Narrative, and History*. Baltimore, MD: Johns Hopkins University Press.

Catholic Archdiocese of Melbourne. 2016. *Abortion Resources: Life, Marriage and Family Office* [online]. Available from: www.cam.org. au/lifemarriagefamily/Resources/Abortion [accessed 13 December 2016].

Chan, A. and Sage, L. C. 2005. Estimating Australia's abortion rates 1985–2003. *The Medical Journal of Australia*, 182(9), 447–452.

Chan, A. *et al.* 2001. *Pregnancy Outcome in South Australia 2009* [online]. Available from: www.sahealth.sa.gov.au/ [accessed 7 March 2017].

Charles, V. E. *et al.* 2008. Abortion and long-term mental health outcomes: A systematic review of the evidence. *Contraception*, 78(6), 436–450.

Children by choice. 2016. Becoming a medical abortion provider [online]. Available from: www.childrenbychoice.org.au/forprofessionals/becoming-a-medical-abortion-provider [accessed 15 June 2017].

Chuck, E. and Silva, D. 2017. *Roe v. Wade* attorney: Trump is biggest threat yet to reproductive rights. *NBC News*, 22 January [online]. Available from: www.nbcnews.com/news/us-news/roe-v-wade-attorney-trump-biggest-threat-yet-reproductive-rights-n707871 [accessed 24 January 2017].

Clough, P. 2008. The affective turn: Political economy, biomedia and bodies, *Theory, Culture & Society*, 25(1), 1–22.

Cockrill, K. and Nack, A. 2013. 'I'm not that type of person': Managing the stigma of having an abortion. *Deviant Behavior*, 34(12), 973–990.

Cohen, S. 1972. *Folk Devils and Moral Panics: The Creation of the Mods and Rockers*. London: MacGibbon and Kee.

Coleman, K. 1998. The politics of abortion in Australia: Freedom, church and state. *Feminist Review*, 29(summer), 75–97.

Collier, M. 2012. Abortion is 27 percent of deaths in England, Wales: 189,000 babies terminated in 2010 in UK, *Christian Post*, 22 October [online]. Available from: www.christianpost.com/news/abortion-is-27-percent-of-deaths-in-england-wales-189000-babies-terminated-in-2010-83726/ [accessed 7 March 2017].

Community Affairs Legislation Committee. 2006. Therapeutic Goods Amendment (Repeal of Ministerial responsibility for approval of RU486) Bill 2005. Canberra: The Senate, Parliament House.

Condit, C. 1990. *Decoding Abortion Rhetoric: Communicating Social Change*. Chicago and Urbana, IL: University of Illinois Press.

Connors, L. 1976. Abortion: safer than pill? *The National Times*, 19–24.

Conor, L. 2016. *Skin Deep: Settler Impressions of Aboriginal Women*. Perth: University of Western Australia Publishing.

Cook, R. J. 2014. Stigmatized meanings of criminal abortion law. *In:* Cook, R. J., Erdman, J. N. and Dickens, B. M. eds. *Abortion Law in Transnational Perspective: Cases and Controversies*. Philadelphia: University of Pennsylvania Press, 347–369.

Crespigny, L. and Savulescu, J. 2004. Abortion: Time to clarify Australia's confusing laws. *Medical Journal of Australia*, 181(4), 201–203.

Cresswill-Myatt, N. 2000. Death of a lifetime. *Herald Sun*, 15 April.

Cunningham, S. 2002. Longing. *The Age*, 30 March.

Curtis, M. 1996. A matter of life or death: Inside story. *The Age*, 22 September.

Cutcher, L. and Milroy, T. 2010. Misrepresenting Indigenous mothers: Maternity allowances in the media. *In:* Goodwin, S. and Huppatz, K. eds. *The Good Mother: Contemporary Motherhoods in Australia*. Sydney: Sydney University Press, 153–175.

Dargan, F. 2000. The well of sorrow. *Herald Sun*, 30 April.

Davis, B. 2008. Shame, shame, shame. *The Age*, 20 August.

Daylight, P. and Johnstone, M. 1986. *Women's Business: Report of the Aboriginal Women's Taskforce*. Canberra: Australian Government Publishing Service.

De Costa, C. 2007. *RU-486: The Abortion Pill*. Salisbury: Boolarong Press.

Dieckhoff, M. *et al.* 2016. A stalled revolution? What can we learn from women's drop-out to part-time jobs: A comparative analysis of Germany and the UK. *Research in Social Stratification and Mobility*, 46(Part B), 129–140.

Dixon, S. C. *et al.* 2014. 'As many options as there are, there are just not enough for me': Contraceptive use and barriers to access among Australian women. *The European Journal of Contraception & Reproductive Health Care*, 19(5), 340–351.

Dogra, N. 2011. The mixed metaphor of 'third world woman': Gendered representations by international development NGOs. *Third World Quarterly*, 32(2), 333–348.

Donath, O. 2015. Regretting motherhood: A sociopolitical analysis. *Signs: Journal of Women in Culture and Society*, 40(2), 343–367.

Dubow, S. 2010. *Ourselves Unborn: A History of the Fetus in Modern America*. Oxford: Oxford University Press.

Duden, B. 1993. *Disembodying Women: Perspectives on Pregnancy and the Unborn*. Cambridge, MA: Harvard University Press.

Dunn, A. 2004. At the heart of a delicate issue. *The Age*, 20 March.

Dunn, A. *et al.* 2004. Soaring teen abortion rate revealed. *The Age*, 10 November.

Eksleman, G. 2004. My abortion: One woman's story. *The Age*, 16 July.

El-Murr, A. 2010. Representing the problem of abortion: Language and the policy making process in the Abortion Law Reform Project in Victoria, 2008. *The Australian Feminist Law Journal*, 33(1), 121–140.

Elgot, J. and McDonald, H. 2017. Northern Irish women win access to free abortions as May averts rebellion. *The Guardian*, 30 June [online]. Available from: www.theguardian.com/world/2017/jun/29/rebel-tories-could-back-northern-ireland-abortion-amendment [accessed 20 July 2017].

Evatt, E. 1977. *Final Report: Royal Commission on Human Relationships*. Canberra: Australian Government Publishing Service.

Ewing, S. 2005. *Women and Abortion: An Evidence Based Review*. Parramatta, ACT: Women's Forum Australia.

Faludi, S. 1991. *Backlash: The Undeclared War against Feminism*. New York: Three Rivers Press.

Feder, E. K. 2007. The dangerous individual('s) mother: Biopower, family, and the production of race. *Hypatia*, 22(2), 60–78.

Felman, S. and Laub, D. 1992. *Testimony: Crises of Witnessing in Literature, Psychoanalysis and History*. New York: Routledge.

Finch, L. and Stratton, J. 1988. The Australian working class and the practice of abortion 1880–1939. *Journal of Australian Studies*, 23(1), 45–64.

Finer, L. and Fine, J. B. 2013. Abortion law around the world: Progress and pushback. *American Journal of Public Health*, 103(4), 585–589.

Finer, L. B. and Zolna, M. R. 2014. Shifts in intended and unintended pregnancies in the United States, 2001–2008. *American Journal of Public Health*, 104(S1), S43–S48.

Fishwick, C. 2015, #ShoutYourAbortion: Women fight stigma surrounding abortions. *The Guardian*, 23 September [online]. Available from: www.theguardian.com/world/2015/sep/22/shoutyourabortion-women-fight-stigma-surrounding-abortions [accessed 10 March 2017].

Fitzgerald, P. 1976. Melbourne schoolgirl abortions: 1000 a year. *The Herald*, 3 April.

Flavin, J. 2008. *Our bodies, our crimes: The policing of women's reproduction in America*. New York: NYU Press.

Ford, C. 2009. Clementine Ford reveals her two no guilt, no shame abortions. *News Corp Australia Network*, 15 October [online]. Available from: www.news.com.au/news/my-no-guilt-no-shame-abortions/news-story/f38b7169c4c24ff8dcd075b2f776d9f3 [accessed 30 August 2017].

———. 2016. *Fight Like a Girl*. Crows Nest, NSW: Allen & Unwin.

Forell, C. 1978. Abortion: Rights as well as wrongs. *The Age*, 12 January.

Foster, D. G. *et al.* 2013. Effect of abortion protesters on women's emotional response to abortion. *Contraception*, 87(1), 81–87.

Foucault, M. 1990. *The History of Sexuality. Vol. 1. An Introduction.* London: Penguin Books.

———. 2008. *The Birth of Biopolitics: Lectures at the Collège de France, 1978–1979.* Basingstoke: Palgrave Macmillan.

Fournier, S. and Crey, E. 1997. *Stolen from Our Embrace: The Abduction of First Nations Children and the Restoration of Aboriginal Communities.* Vancouver, BC: Douglas & McIntyre Ltd.

Francis, C. 2002. Democracy's shame. *Herald Sun*, 10 February.

———. 2007. Abortion risk to women. *Herald Sun*, 31 July.

Francke, L. B. 1978. *The Ambivalence of Abortion*. New York: Random House.

Francome, C. 2004. *Abortion in the USA and the UK*. Farnham, UK: Ashgate.

Franklin, S. 2014. Rethinking reproductive politics in time, and time in UK reproductive politics: 1978–2008. *Journal of the Royal Anthropological Institute*, 20(1), 109–125.

Freedman, L. and Weitz, T. A. 2012. The politics of motherhood meets the politics of poverty. *Contemporary Sociology*, 41(1), 36–42.

Frenkel, J. 2006. Vale's Muslim threat blasted. *Herald Sun*, 15 February.

Freud, S. 1957. Mourning and melancholia. *In:* Strachey, J. ed. *The Standard Edition of the Complete Psychological Works of Sigmund Freud, Vol. 14*. London: Hogarth Press, 237–258.

———. 1961. New introductory lectures on psycho-analysis. Lecture 33: Femininity. *In:* Strachey, J. ed. *Standard Edition of the Complete Psychological Works of Sigmund Freud, Vol. 22*. London: Hogarth Press, 136–157.

Friedman, S. 2015. Still a 'stalled revolution'? Work/family experiences, hegemonic masculinity, and moving toward gender equality. *Sociology Compass*, 9(2), 140–155.

Gerrard, M. 1977. Sex guilt in abortion patients. *Journal of Consulting and Clinical Psychology*, 45(4), 708.

Gibson, S. 2004. The problem of abortion: Essentially contested concepts and moral autonomy. *Bioethics*, 18(3), 221–233.

Gill, R. 2008. Empowerment/sexism: Figuring female sexual agency in contemporary advertising. *Feminism & Psychology*, 18(1), 35–60.

———. 2016. Post-postfeminism?: New feminist visibilities in postfeminist times. *Feminist Media Studies*, 16(4), 610–630.

Gill, R. and Scharff, C. 2013. Introduction. *In:* Gill, R. and Scharff, C. eds. *New Femininities: Postfeminism, Neoliberalism and Subjectivity*. Basingstoke: Palgrave Macmillan, 1–20.

Gillespie, R. 2003. Childfree and feminine. *Gender & Society*, 17(1), 122–136.

Gilligan, C. 1993. *In a Different Voice: Psychological Theory and Women's Development*. Cambridge, MA: Harvard University Press.

Gilroy, P. 1991. *'There Ain't No Black in the Union Jack': The Cultural Politics of Race and Nation*. Chicago: University of Chicago Press.

———. 1993. *The Black Atlantic: Modernity and Double Consciousness*. Cambridge, MA: Harvard University Press.

Ginn, J. *et al.* 1996. Feminist fallacies: A reply to Hakim on women's employment. *The British Journal of Sociology*, 47(1), 167–174.

Girard, F. 2017. Implications of the Trump Administration for sexual and reproductive rights globally. *Reproductive Health Matters*, 25(49), 1–8.

Gleeson, K. 2011. Tony Abbott and abortion: Miscalculating the strength of the religious right. *Australian Journal of Political Science*, 46(3), 473–488.

Glendon, M. A. 1987. *Abortion and Divorce in Western Law*. Cambridge, MA: Harvard University Press.

Gold, S. 1972. A psychiatrist's view of the law. *In:* McMichael, T. ed. *Abortion, the Unenforceable Law: The Reality of Unwanted Pregnancy and Abortion in Australia*. North Carlton, VIC: ALRA, 44–45.

Goldbeck-Wood, S. 2017. Reforming abortion services in the UK: Less hypocrisy, more acknowledgment of complexity. *Journal of Family Planning Reproductive Health Care*, 43(1), 3–4.

Goodwin, P. and Odgen, J. 2007. Women's reflections upon their past abortions: An exploration of how and why emotional reactions change over time. *Psychology and Health*, 22(2), 231–248.

Granzow, K. 2007. De-constructing 'choice': The social imperative and women's use of the birth control pill. *Culture, Health & Sexuality*, 9(1), 43–54.

Grattan, M. and Wroe, D. 2004. Abortion out of control, says minister. *The Age*, 2 November.

Graves, L. Trump once said women should be punished for abortion. Now, he's making it happen. *The Guardian*, 24 January [online]. Available from: www.theguardian.com/commentisfree/2017/jan/24/trump-once-said-women-should-be-punished-for-abortion-t [accessed 24 January 2016].

Greer, G. 1972. Interview on ABC Radio, 22 March 1972. *In:* McMichael, T. ed. *Abortion, The Unenforceable Law: The Reality of Unwanted Pregnancy and Abortion in Australia.* North Carlton, VIC: ALRA, 50.

———. 1992. The feminine mistake. *The Sydney Morning Herald,* 9 May.

———. 2000. Though I have no child of my own, I still have pregnancy dreams. I'm a huge abdomen floating in the warm shallow sea of my childhood. I'm waiting with vast joy and confidence. But I'm waiting for something that will never happen. *Herald Sun,* 16 April.

Gregory, R. 2005. *Corrupt Cops, Crooked Docs, Prevaricating Pollies and 'Mad Radicals': A History of Abortion Law Reform in Victoria, 1959–1974,* PhD thesis. Melbourne: RMIT University.

Grove, N. J. and Zwi, A. B. 2006. Our health and theirs: Forced migration, othering, and public health. *Social Science & Medicine,* 62(8), 1931–1942.

Guthrie, C. 2007. Carhart, constitutional rights, and the psychology of regret. Vanderbilt Public Law Research Paper, Nashville, TN: Vanderbilt University Law School.

Guttmacher Institute. 2016a. Counselling and Waiting Periods for Abortion [online]. Available from: www.guttmacher.org/state-center/spibs/spib_MWPA.pdf [accessed 15 December 2016].

———. 2016b. Medicaid Funding of Abortion [online]. Available from: www.guttmacher.org/evidence-you-can-use/medicaid-funding-abortion [accessed 3 January 2017].

Hadley, J. 1997. The 'awfulisation'of abortion'. *Choices,* 26(1), 7–8.

Hage, G. 1998. *White Nation: Fantasies of White Supremacy in a Multicultural Society.* Annandale, NSW: Pluto Press.

———. 2003. *Against Paranoid Nationalism: Searching for Hope in a Shrinking Society.* Annandale, NSW: Pluto Press.

Hakim, C. 1995. Five feminist myths about women's employment. *The British Journal of Sociology,* 46(3), 429–455.

Halberstam, J. 2005. Shame and white gay masculinity. *Social Text,* 23(3–4), 219–233.

Hall, S. 1999. Un-settling 'the heritage', re-imagining the post-nation: Whose heritage? *Third Text,* 13(49), 3–13.

————. 2006. The West and the rest: Discourse and power. *In:* Maaka, R. and Anderson, C. eds. *The Indigenous Experience: Global Perspectives,* Toronto, ON: Canadian Scholars' Press, 165–173.

Hall, S. *et al.* 1978. *Policing the Crisis: Mugging, Law and Order and the State.* London: Macmillan.

Hanschmidt, F. *et al.* 2016. Abortion stigma: A systematic review. *Perspectives on Sexual and Reproductive Health,* 48(4), 169–177.

Harden, A. and Ogden, J. 1999. Young women's experiences of arranging and having abortions. *Sociology of Health & Illness,* 21(4), 426–444.

Hardon, A. and Posel, D. 2012. Secrecy as embodied practice: Beyond the confessional imperative. *Culture, Health & Sexuality,* 14(sup1), S1–S13.

Harris, L. H. *et al.* 2011. Dynamics of stigma in abortion work: Findings from a pilot study of the Providers Share Workshop. *Social Science & Medicine,* 73(7), 1062–1070.

Harrison, B. G. 1973. *Now That Abortion Is Legal.* New York: McGill.

Hartouni, V. 1997. *Cultural Conceptions: On Reproductive Technologies and the Remaking of Life.* Minneapolis and London: University of Minnesota Press.

Haussegger, V. 2002. The sins of our feminist mothers. *The Age,* 23 July.

————. 2005. *Wonder Woman.* Sydney: Allen & Unwin.

Hawkin, G. 1973. Will abortion open the floodgates? *The Australian,* 25 April.

Hayes, P. 2016. Reproductive coercion and the Australian state: A new chapter? *Australian Community Psychologist,* 28 (1), 90–100.

Hays, S. 1998. *The Cultural Contradictions of Motherhood.* New Haven, CT: Yale University Press.

Heath, S. 1996. Australia to outlaw abortion pill. *The Age,* 17 May.

Henderson, M. 2006. *Marking Feminist Times: Remembering the Longest Revolution in Australia.* Bern: Peter Lang.

Henshaw, S. K. and Morrow, E. 1990. Induced abortion: A world review, 1990. *Family Planning Perspectives,* 22(2), 76–89.

The Herald. 1976. Clinic team aborts 7500. 3 April.

————. 1978. Abortion: 50,000 last year. 18 November.

Herald Sun. 2005. Abortion issue ready to flare up. 7 August.

———. 2006. Editorial: No easy answers. 17 February.

Hill, E. 2006. Howard's 'choice': The ideology and politics of work and family policy 1996–2006'. *Australian Review of Public Affairs*, 23(February), 1–8.

———. 2007. Budgeting for work–life balance: The ideology and politics of work and family policy in Australia. *Australian Bulletin of Labour*, 33(2), 226–245.

Himmelweit, S. and Sigala, M. 2004. Choice and the relationship between identities and behaviour for mothers with pre-school children: Some implications for policy from a UK study. *Journal of Social Policy*, 33(3), 455–478.

Hindell, K. and Simms, M. 1971. *Abortion Law Reformed.* London: Peter Owen Limited.

Hirve, S. S. 2004. Abortion law, policy and services in India: a critical review. *Reproductive Health Matters*, 12(24), 114–121.

Hochschild, A. R. 1979. Emotion work, feeling rules, and social structure. *American Journal of Sociology*, 85(3), 551–575.

Hoggart, L. 2015. Abortion counselling in Britain: Understanding the controversy. *Sociology Compass*, 9(5), 365–378.

Hook, D. 2005. Affecting whiteness: Racism as technology of affect (1). *International Journal of Critical Psychology*, 16 [online]. Available from: http://eprints.lse.ac.uk/956/1/Affecting.pdf [accessed 1 April 2011].

Hopkins, N., Reicher, S. and Saleem, J. 1996. Constructing women's psychological health in anti-abortion rhetoric. *The Sociological Review*, 44(3), 539–564.

Houston, M. 2008. Knocked up—but the 'a' word is knocked back. *The Age*, 8 July.

Howard, J. 2005. The Prime Minister the Hon John Howard MP address to Federal Women's Council, Parliament House Canberra, 24 June [online]. Available from: http://parlinfo.aph.gov.au/parlInfo/download/media/pressrel/9QGG6/upload_binary/9qgg64.pdf;fileType=application/pdf [accessed 22 April 2012].

Huang, P. 2008. Anchor babies, over-breeders, and the population bomb: The reemergence of nativism and population control in anti-immigration policies. *Harvard Law and Policy Review*, 2(2), 385–406.

Hudson, P. 2004. G-G fuels abortion row: Jeffery urges target of 'zero terminations'. *The Age*, 7 November.

Hunt, K. and Rygiel, K. 2006. *(En)Gendering the War on Terror: War Stories and Camouflaged Politics*. Farnham, UK: Ashgate.

Hussein, S. 2016. *From Victims to Suspects: Muslim Women Since 9/11*. Coogee, NSW: New South Books.

Hutchinson, T. 2007. No story is the same, whatever the advice (opinion). *The Age*, 6 January.

Illsley, R. and Hall, M. H. 1976. Psychosocial aspects of abortion: A review of issues and needed research. *Bulletin of the World Health Organization*, 53(1), 83.

Imber, J. 1979. Sociology and abortion: Legacies and strategies. *Contemporary Sociology*, 8(6), 825–832.

Ipsos. 2015. Citizens in 23 countries polled: 43% support a woman having an abortion whenever she wants one [online]. Available from: www.ipsos.com/sites/default/files/2016-06/047.1-G%40-Abortion-july-2015.pdf [accessed 16 December 2016].

Irigaray, L. 1985. *Speculum of the Other Woman*. Ithaca, NY: Cornell University Press.

Jacobs, M. D. 2009. *White Mother to a Dark Race: Settler Colonialism, Maternalism, and the Removal of Indigenous Children in the American West and Australia, 1880–1940*. Lincoln and London: University of Nebraska Press.

Jensen, T. and Tyler, I. 2015. 'Benefits broods': The cultural and political crafting of anti-welfare commonsense. *Critical Social Policy*, 35(4), 470–491.

Joffe, C. 2017. What will become of reproductive issues in Trump's America? *Reproductive Health Matters*, 25(49), 1287826.

Johnson, C. 2003. Heteronormative citizenship: The Howard government's views on gay and lesbian issues. *Australian Journal of Political Science*, 38(1), 45–62.

Johnston, J. 2015. Irish women go public against abortion stigma. *Politico*, 12 October [online]. Available from: www.politico.eu/article/irish-women-go-public-against-abortion-stigma-x-ile-choice [accessed 4 March 2017].

Jones, C. 2013. 'Human weeds, not fit to breed'?: African Caribbean women and reproductive disparities in Britain. *Critical Public Health,* 23(1), 49–61.

Jones, R. K. and Kavanaugh, M. L. 2011. Changes in abortion rates between 2000 and 2008 and lifetime incidence of abortion. *Obstetrics & Gynecology,* 117(6), 1358–1366.

Jupp, J. 2002. *From White Australia to Woomera: The Story of Australian Immigration.* Cambridge, UK: Cambridge University Press.

Kaposy, K. 2010. Improving abortion access in Canada. *Health Care Analysis,* 18(1), 17–34.

Kelly, J. and Evans, M. D. R. 1999. Attitudes toward abortion: Australia in comparative perspective. *Australian Social Monitor,* 2(4), 83–90.

Kennedy, R. 2011. An Australian archive of feelings: The Sorry Books campaign and the pedagogy of compassion. *Australian Feminist Studies,* 26(69), 257–279.

Keogh, L. *et al.* 2017. Intended and unintended consequences of abortion law reform: perspectives of abortion experts in Victoria, Australia. *Journal of Family Planning and Reproductive Health Care,* 43(1), 18–24.

Keown, J. 1988. *Abortion, Doctors and the Law: Some Aspects of the Legal Regulation in England from 1803 to 1982.* Cambridge, UK: Cambridge University Press.

Kevin, C. 2005. Maternity and freedom: Australian feminist encounters with the reproductive body. *Australian Feminist Studies,* 20(46), 3–15.

———. 2009. Great expectations: Episodes in a political history of pregnancy in Australia since 1945. *In:* Kevin, C. ed. *Feminism and the Body: Interdisciplinary Perspectives.* Newcastle upon Tyne: Cambridge Scholars Publishing, 49–69.

———. 2011. "I did not lose my baby ... My baby just died": Twenty-First-Century Discourses of Miscarriage in Political and Historical Context. *South Atlantic Quarterly,* 110(4), 849–865.

———. 2012. Jayden's Law and the history of miscarriage. *Flinders Journal of History and Politics,* 28, 31.

Keys, J. 2010. Running the gauntlet: Women's use of emotion management techniques in the abortion experience. *Symbolic Interaction*, 33(1), 41–70.

Kirby, M. 1998. Western Australia's new abortion laws: Restrictive and reinforcing the power of the medical profession and the state over women's bodies and lives. *Australian Feminist Studies*, 13(28), 305–312.

Kirkman, M. *et al.* 2009. Reasons women give for abortion: A review of the literature. *Archives of Women's Mental Health*, 12(6), 365–378.

Kirkman, M. *et al.* 2010. Abortion is a difficult solution to a problem: A discursive analysis of interviews with women considering or undergoing abortion in Australia. *Women's Studies International Forum*, 34, 121–129.

Kissane, K. 1995. Abortion doubts redefine debate. *The Age*, October 25.

———. 1998. Abortion in the First Person. *The Age*, 4 April.

Kissling, F. 2005. Is there life after Roe?: How to think about the fetus. *Conscience: The News Journal of Catholic Opinion*, Winter 2004/2005, 11–18.

Klatch, R. E. 1988. *Women of the New Right*. Philadelphia, PA: Temple University Press.

Kline, M. 1993. Complicating the ideology of motherhood: Child welfare law and First Nation women. *Queen's Law Journal*, 18(2), 306–342.

Kumar, A., Hessini, L. and Mitchell, E. M. 2009. Conceptualising abortion stigma. *Culture, Health & Sexuality*, 11(6), 625–639.

Kuperberg, A. and Stone, P. 2008. The media depiction of women who opt out. *Gender & Society*, 22(4), 497–517.

Layne, L. 2003. *Motherhood Lost: The Cultural Construction of Miscarriage and Stillbirth in America*. New York and London: Routledge.

Leach, M. 2003. 'Disturbing practices': Dehumanizing asylum seekers in the refugee 'crisis' in Australia, 2001–2002. *Refuge*, 21(3), 25–33.

Lee, E. 2003. *Abortion, Motherhood, and Mental Health: Medicalizing Reproduction in the United States and Great Britain*. Hawthorne, NY: Aldine de Gruyter.

————. 2017. Constructing abortion as a social problem: 'Sex selection' and the British abortion debate. *Feminism & Psychology*, 27(1), 15–33.

Lentin, R. 2013. A woman died: Abortion and the politics of birth in Ireland. *Feminist Review*, 105(1), 130–136.

Leslie, C. 2010. The 'psychiatric masquerade': The mental health exception in New Zealand abortion Law. *Feminist Legal Studies*, 18(1), 1–23.

Little, M. O. 2003. The morality of abortion. *In:* Wellman, C. and Frey, R. eds. *A Companion to Applied Ethics.* Oxford: Blackwell Press, 313–325.

Lonergan, G. 2012. Reproductive justice and migrant women in Great Britain. *Women: A Cultural Review*, 23(1), 26–45.

Lorber, J. 1994. *Paradoxes of Gender.* New Haven, CT, and London: Yale University Press.

Lowe, P. 2016. *Reproductive Health and Maternal Sacrifice: Women, Choice and Responsibility.* London: Palgrave Macmillan.

Ludlow, J. 2008. Sometimes, it's a child and a choice: Toward an embodied abortion praxis. *NWSA Journal*, 20(1), 26–50.

Luibhéid, E. 2004. Childbearing against the state? Asylum seeker women in the Irish republic. *Women's Studies International Forum*, 27(4), 335–349.

Luker, K. 1984. *Abortion and the Politics of Motherhood.* Berkeley, Los Angeles and London: University of California Press.

Lupton, D. 2013. *The Social Worlds of the Unborn.* Hampshire, UK, and New York: Palgrave Macmillan.

MacCallum, M. 2002. *Girt by Sea: Australia, the Refugees and the Politics of Fear.* Melbourne: Black Inc.

Mackinnon, A. 2000. 'Bringing the unclothed immigrant into the world': Population policies and gender in twentieth-century Australia. *Journal of Population Research*, 17(2), 109–123.

Madeira, J. L. 2014. Aborted emotions: Regret, relationality, and regulation. *Michigan Journal of Gender and Law*, 21(1) [online]. Available from: http://repository.law.umich.edu/mjgl/vol21/iss1/1.

Maiden, S. 2006. Women 'aborting away the future'. *The Australian*, February 14.

Major, B. and Gramzow, R. H. 1999. Abortion as stigma: Cognitive and emotional implications of concealment. *Journal of Personality and Social Psychology*, 77(4), 735–745.

Major, B. *et al.* 2000. Psychological responses of women after first-trimester abortion. *Archives of General Psychiatry*, 57(8), 777–784.

Major, B. *et al.* 2009. Abortion and mental health: Evaluating the evidence. *American Psychologist*, 64(9), 863–890.

Manion, J. 2003. Girls blush, sometimes: Gender, moral agency, and the problem of shame. *Hypatia*, 18(3), 21–41.

Manne, A. 2005. *Motherhood: How Should We Care for Our Children?* Crows Nest, NSW: Allen & Unwin.

Manninen, B. A. 2013. The value of choice and the choice to value: Expanding the discussion about fetal life within prochoice advocacy. *Hypatia*, 28(3), 663–683.

Martin, L. A. *et al.* 2014. Abortion providers, stigma and professional quality of life. *Contraception*, 90(6), 581–587.

Martinot, S. 2007. Motherhood and the invention of race. *Hypatia*, 22(2), 79–97.

Mbembé, J.-A. 2003. Necropolitics, trans. L. Mintjes. *Public Culture*, 15(1), 11–40.

McBride, D. and Mazur, A. 2006. Measuring feminist mobilization: Cross-national convergences and transnational networks in Western Europe. *In:* Ferree, M. M. and Tripp, A. M. eds. *Global Feminism: Transnational Women's Activism, Organizing, and Human Rights*. New York: NYU Press, 219–246.

McCandless, J. and Sheldon, S. 2010. 'No father required'? The welfare assessment in the human fertilisation and embryology act 2008. *Feminist Legal Studies*, 18(3), 201–225.

McCudden, M. 2004. Letter to the editor. *The Age*, 17 July.

McCulloch, A. 2013. *Fighting to Choose: The Abortion Rights Struggle in New Zealand*. Wellington, NZ: Victoria University Press.

McCulloch, A. and Weatherall, A. 2017. The fragility of de facto abortion on demand in New Zealand Aotearoa. *Feminism & Psychology*, 27(1), 92–100.

McDonnell, K. 1984. *Not an Easy Choice: A Feminist Re-examines Abortion*. London, Sydney, Dover and New Hampshire: Pluto Press.

McGuire, F. 1982. Right to life grant gets axe. *The Herald*, 28 April.

McLaren, A. and McLaren, A. T. 1997. *The Bedroom and the State: The Changing Practices and Politics of Contraception and Abortion in Canada, 1880–1997*. Toronto, ON: Oxford University Press.

McMichael, M. and Wynn, S. 1972. Consequences of unwanted pregnancy and abortion: Woman and child. *In:* McMichael, T. ed. *Abortion, the Unenforceable Law: The Reality of Unwanted Pregnancy and Abortion in Australia*. North Carlton, VIC: ALRA, 61–66.

McMichael, T. 1972a. Attitudes toward the foetus. *In:* McMichael, T. ed. *Abortion, the Unenforceable Law: The Reality of Unwanted Pregnancy and Abortion in Australia*. North Carlton, VIC: ALRA, 39–40.

———. 1972b. Foreword. *In:* McMichael, T. ed. *Abortion, the Unenforceable Law: The Reality of Unwanted Pregnancy and Abortion in Australia*. North Carlton, VIC: ALRA.

McRae, S. 2003. Choice and constraints in mothers' employment careers: McRae replies to Hakim. *The British Journal of Sociology*, 54(4), 585–592.

McRobbie, A. 2007. Top girls? Young girls and the post-feminist sexual contract. *Cultural Studies*, 21, 718–737.

———. 2009. *The Aftermath of Feminism: Gender, Culture and Social Change*. London: SAGE Publications.

———. 2013. Feminism, the family and the new 'mediated' maternalism. *New Formations: A Journal of Culture/Theory/Politics*, 80(80–81), 119–137.

Michels, N. 1988. *Helping Women Recover from Abortion*. Minneapolis, MN: Bethany House.

Milkie, M. A., Pepin, J. R. and Denny, K. E. 2016. What kind of war? 'Mommy Wars' discourse in US and Canadian News, 1989–2013. *Sociological Inquiry*, 86(1), 51–78.

Mills, A. and Barclay, L. 2006. None of them were satisfactory: Women's experiences with contraception. *Health Care for Women International*, 27(5), 379–398.

Monagle, M. 2004. Good sex savvy is the way to cutting abortion rate. *The Age*, 14 November.

Moore, N. 1996. 'Me operation': Abortion and class in Australian women's novels, 1920s–1950. *Hecate*, 22(1), 27–46.

Moore, N. 2001. The politics of cliché: Sex, class, and abortion in Australian realism. *Modern Fiction Studies*, 47(1), 69–91.

Moreton-Robinson, A. 2000. *Talkin' Up to the White Woman: Aboriginal Women and Feminism*. St Lucia, QLD: University Of Queensland Press.

Mouw, T. and Sobel, M. E. 2001. Culture wars and opinion polarization: The case of abortion. *American Journal of Sociology*, 106(4), 913–943.

Munson, Z. W. 2010. *The Making of Pro-life Activists: How Social Movement Mobilization Works*. Chicago: University of Chicago Press.

Murdoch, A. K. 1994. The incalculable, unforgettable loss. *The Age*, 24 August.

Murrie, L. 1998. Changing masculinities: Disruption and anxiety in contemporary Australian writing. *Journal of Australian Studies*, 22(56), 169–179.

Nader, C. 2008. MP's emotional abortion story may help 'shatter taboo'. *The Age*, 19 August.

Nader, C. and Cooke, D. 2007. Health chief tells of abortion experience. *The Age*, 18 August.

Nader, C. and Rood, D. 2007. Conscience vote looms on abortion in Victoria. *The Age*, 19 July.

Nathanson, D. 1987. A timetable for shame. *In:* Nathanson, D. ed. *The Many Faces of Shame*. New York: Guilford, 1–63.

National Collaborating Centre for Mental Health. 2011. Induced Abortion and Mental Health: A Systematic Review of the Mental Health Outcomes of Induced Abortion, Including Their Prevalence and Associated Factors [online]. Available from: www.aomrc.org.uk/wp-content/uploads/2016/05/Induced_Abortion_Mental_Health_1211.pdf [accessed 1 March 2017].

National Population Summit. 2004. *Australia's Population Challenge: The National Population Summit, Parliament House, Adelaide, South Australia*. Hackney, SA: Australian Population Institute (SA).

Nelson, J. 2003. *Women of Color and the Reproductive Rights Movement*. New York: NYU Press.

Nickson, C., Smith, A. and Shelley, J. 2004. Intention to claim a Medicare rebate among women receiving private Victorian pregnancy termination services. *Australian and New Zealand Journal of Public Health*, 28(2), 120–124.

Noble, T. 2005. Abbott poses counsel rebate to cut abortions. *The Age*, 3 August.

Norman, W. V. 2012. Induced abortion in Canada 1974–2005: Trends over the first generation with legal access. *Contraception*, 85(2), 185–191.

O'Connor, J. S., Orloff, A. S. and Shaver, S. 1999. *States, Markets, Families: Gender, Liberalism and Social Policy in Australia, Canada, Great Britain and the United States*. Cambridge, UK: Cambridge University Press.

Orgad, S. and De Benedictis, S. 2015. The 'stay-at-home' mother, postfeminism and neoliberalism: Content analysis of UK news coverage. *European Journal of Communication*, 30(4), 418–436.

Overby, L. M., Tatalovich, R. and Studlar, D. T. 1998. Party and free votes in Canada: Abortion in the House of Commons. *Party Politics*, 4(3), 381–392.

Pardy, M. 2009. The shame of waiting. *In:* Hage, G. ed. *Waiting*. Melbourne: Melbourne University Press, 195–209.

Pavalko, E. K. and Wolfe, J. D. 2016. Do women still care? Cohort changes in US women's care for the ill or disabled. *Social Forces*, 94(3), 1359–1384.

Pearson, C. 2002. The silent tragedy of the population debate. *The Age*, 5 March.

Petchesky, R. 1981. Antiabortion, antifeminism, and the rise of the New Right. *Feminist Studies*, 7(2), 206–246.

———. 1984. *Abortion and Women's Choice: The State, Sexuality, and Reproductive Freedom*. New York: Longman.

———. 1987. Fetal images: The power of visual culture in the politics of reproduction. *Feminist Studies*, 263–292.

Petersen, K. 1984. The public funding of abortion services: Comparative developments in the United States and Australia. *International and Comparative Law Quarterly*, 33(1), 158–180.

———. 1993. *Abortion Regimes*. Aldershot and Brookfield: Dartmouth.

———. 2010. Early medical abortion: Legal and medical developments in Australia. *Medical Journal of Australia*, 193(1), 26–29.

Phillips, K. 2009. Provocative women in the border zone: Articulations of national crisis and the limits of women's political status. *Continuum: Journal of Media & Cultural Studies*, 23(5), 597–612.

Pocock, B. 2003. *The Work/Life Collision: What Work Is Doing to Australians and What to Do About It.* Annandale, NSW: Federation Press.

Pollitt, K. 2014. *Pro: Reclaiming Abortion Rights.* New York: Picador.

Population Research Institute. 1999. *Norplant Information* [online]. Available from: www.pop.org/content/norplant-background-a-pri-petition-888 [accessed 20 December 2016]

Prager, J. 2008. Healing from history. *European Journal of Social Theory*, 11(3), 405–420.

Prasad, S. 2015. There are still many barriers to abortion in Canada. *Huffington Post*, 27 September [online]: Available from: www.huffingtonpost.ca/sandeep-prasad/canadas-abortion-myth_b_8198478.html [accessed 4 March 2017].

Price, K. 2010. What is reproductive justice? How women of color activists are redefining the pro-choice paradigm. *Meridians: Feminism, Race, Transnationalism*, 10(2), 42–65.

Probyn, E. 2005. *Blush: Faces of Shame.* Minneapolis: University of Minnesota Press.

Purcell, C. 2015. The sociology of women's abortion experiences: Recent research and future directions. *Sociology Compass*, 9(7), 585–596.

Purcell, C., Hilton, S. and McDaid, L. 2014. The stigmatisation of abortion: A qualitative analysis of print media in Great Britain in 2010. *Culture, Health & Sexuality*, 16(9), 1141–1155.

Rankin, L. Not everyone who has an abortion is a woman: How to frame the abortion rights issue. *Truthout*, 31 July [online]. Available from: www.truth-out.org/opinion/item/17888-not-everyone-who-has-an-abortion-is-a-woman-how-to-frame-the-abortion-rights-issue [accessed 20 July 2017].

Raymond, E. and Grimes, D. 2012. The comparative safety of legal induced abortion and childbirth in the United States. *Obstetrics & Gynecology*, 119(2, Part 1), 215–219.

Reagan, L. J. 1997. *When Abortion Was a Crime: Women, Medicine, and Law in the United States, 1867–1973*. Berkeley, Los Angeles, London: University of California Press.

Real Choices Australia. 2016. *About Real Choices Australia* [online]. Available from: http://realchoices.org.au/about [accessed 15 December 2016].

Reardon, D. C. 1987. *Aborted Women: Silent No More*. Westchester, IL: Crossway Books.

Rebick, J. 2005. *Ten Thousand Roses: The Making of a Feminist Revolution*. Toronto, ON: Penguin Canada.

Rebouché, R. 2014. A functionalist approach to comparative abortion law. *In:* Cook, R. J., Erdman J. N. and Dickens, B. M. eds. *Abortion Law in Transnational Perspective: Cases and Controversies*. Philadelphia: University of Pennsylvania Press, 98–120.

Redden, M. 2016. Quarter of US abortion clinics have closed over last five years, report says. *The Guardian*, 25 February [online]. Available from: www.theguardian.com/world/2016/feb/24/us-abortion-clinics-closing-report [accessed 3 February 2017]

Reddy, W. M. 2001. *The Navigation of Feeling: A Framework for the History of Emotions*. Cambridge, UK: Cambridge University Press.

Reekie, G. 1997. History and the bodies of the illegitimately pregnant woman. *Australian Feminist Studies*, 12(25), 77–89.

———. 1998. *Measuring Immorality: Social Inquiry and the Problem of Illegitimacy*. Cambridge, UK: Cambridge University Press.

Regan, P. 2002. Secret life's moral vacuum. *The Age*, 16 May.

Reist, M. T. 2000. *Giving Sorrow Words: Women's Stories of Grief After Abortion*. Sydney: Duffy & Snellgrove.

———. 2002. The secret lives of loss for women after abortion. *The Age*, 16 May.

Richters, J. *et al.* 2003. Sex in Australia: Contraceptive practices among a representative sample of women. *Australian and New Zealand Journal of Public Health*, 27(2), 210–216.

Riddle, J. M. 1999. *Eve's Herbs: A History of Contraception and Abortion in the West*. Cambridge, MA: Harvard University Press.

Right to Life. 1976a. *Newsletter of the Victorian Right to Life Association*, July–August.

———. 1976b. *Newsletter of the Victorian Right to Life Association*, November–December.

———. 1977a. *Right to Life News*, January–February.

———. 1977b. *Right to Life News*, March–April.

———. 1977c. *Right to Life News*, July–August.

———. 1979. *Right to Life News*, September–October.

———. 1980a. *Right to Life News*, January–February.

———. 1980b. *Right to Life News*, July–August.

———. 1981a. *Right to Life News*, March–April.

———. 1981b. *Right to Life News*, November–December.

———. 1982. *Right to Life News*, March–April.

———. 1983. *Right to Life News*, March–April.

———. 1984. *Right to Life News*, July–August.

———. 1993. *Right to Life News*, July.

———. 1994. *Right to Life News*, February.

———. 1995. *Right to Life News*, September.

———. 1999. *Right to Life News*, October.

———. 2001. *Right to Life News*, December.

Right to Life of Michigan. 2017. Life notes: A risk to avoid [online]. Available from: www.rtl.org/prolife_issues/LifeNotes/AbortionsLinktoBreastCancer.html [accessed 4 March 2017].

Riordan, M. 2006. Monday: A child who should be born. *Herald Sun*, 27 November.

Roberts, D. 1997. *Killing the Black Body: Race, Reproduction, and the Meaning of Liberty*. Boston: Vintage.

Robjant, K., Hassan, R. and Katona, C. 2009. Mental health implications of detaining asylum seekers: systematic review. *The British Journal of Psychiatry*, 194 (4), 306–312.

Rocca, C. H. *et al.* 2015. Decision rightness and emotional responses to abortion in the United States: A longitudinal study. *PlOS ONE*, 10(7), e0128832.

Romans-Clarkson, S. E. 1989. Psychological sequelae of induced abortion. *Australasian Psychiatry*, 23(4), 555–565.

Rose, N. 1991. Governing by numbers: Figuring out democracy. *Accounting, Organizations and Society*, 16(7), 673–692.

————. 1999. *Powers of Freedom: Reframing Political Thought.* Cambridge, UK: Cambridge University Press.

Rosen, R. H. and Martindale, L. J. 1980. Abortion as "deviance". *Social Psychiatry*, 15(2), 103–108.

Rosenwein, B. 2002. Worrying about emotions in history. *American Historical Review*, 107(3), 821–845.

Ross, L. 2006. Understanding reproductive justice: Transforming the pro-choice movement. *Off Our Backs*, 36(4), 14–19.

Rowe, H. J. *et al.* 2009. Considering abortion: A 12-month audit of records of women contacting a Pregnancy Advisory Service. *The Medical Journal of Australia*, 190(2), 69–72.

Rowlands, S. 2014. Introduction. *In:* Rowlands, S. ed. *Abortion Care.* Cambridge, UK: Cambridge University Press, 1–5.

Royal College of Obstetricians and Gynecologists. *The Care of Women Requesting Induced Abortion: Evidence Based Clinical Guideline Number 7.* London: RCOG Press [online]. Available from: www. rcog.org.uk/globalassets/documents/guidelines/abortion-guide-line_web_1.pdf [accessed 20 July 2017].

Ruhl, L. 2002. Dilemmas of the will: Uncertainty, reproduction, and the rhetoric of control. *Signs: Journal of Women in Culture and Society*, 27(3), 641–663.

Russo, N. F. 2000. Understanding emotional responses after abortion. *In:* Joan Chrisler, C. G., Patricia R. eds. *Lectures on the Psychology of Women.* New York: McGraw-Hill, 129–143.

Ryan, L., Ripper, M. and Buttfield, B. 1994. *We Women Decide: Women's Experience of Seeking Abortion in Queensland, South Australia and Tasmania, 1985–92.* Bedford Park, SA: Women's Studies Unit, Faculty of Social Sciences, Flinders University.

Salecl, R. 2008. Society of choice. *Differences: A Journal of Feminist Cultural Studies*, 20(1), 157–180.

Salmon, A. 2011. Aboriginal mothering, FASD prevention and the contestations of neoliberal citizenship. *Critical Public Health*, 21(2), 165–178.

Sanger, C. 2017. *About abortion: Terminating pregnancy in twenty-first century America.* Cambridge, MA: Harvard University Press.

Saurette, P. and Gordon, K. 2013. Arguing abortion: The new anti-abortion discourse in Canada. *Canadian Journal of Political Science*, 46(1), 157–185.

———. 2016. *The Changing Voice of the Anti-abortion Movement: The Rise of 'pro-woman' Rhetoric in Canada and the United States*. Toronto, ON: University of Toronto Press.

Saxton, M. 2006. Disability rights and selective abortion. *In:* Davis, L. ed. *The Disability Studies Reader: Second Edition*. London and Milton Park: Routledge, 105–116.

Scharping, T. 2013. *Birth Control in China 1949–2000: Population Policy and Demographic Development*. New York and London: Routledge.

Scheff, T. J. 2003. Shame in self and society. *Symbolic Interaction*, 26(2), 239–262.

Schnookal, D. 1974. Excerpt from public meeting. In WAAC, Open letter, 28 November. State Library of Victoria, Wainer Papers, MS134636, Box 46.

Scott, J. W. 1991. The evidence of experience. *Critical Inquiry*, 17(4),773–797.

Sedgh, G. *et al.* 2016. Abortion incidence between 1990 and 2014: Global, regional, and subregional levels and trends. *The Lancet*, 388(10041), 258–267

Sethna, C. and Doull, M. 2013. Spatial disparities and travel to free-standing abortion clinics in Canada. *Women's Studies International Forum*, 38(May–June), 52–62.

Shanahan, A. 2004. In praise of a truly Christian politician. *The Age*, 19 March.

Shankar, M. *et al.* 2017. Access, equity and costs of induced abortion services in Australia: A cross-sectional study. *Australian and New Zealand Journal of Public Health*, 41(3), 309–314.

Shaver, S. 2002. Australian welfare reform: From citizenship to supervision. *Social Policy & Administration*, 36(4), 331–345.

Shaw, M. 2004. Abortion rate a tragedy, says Abbott. *The Age*, 17 March.

Shaw, M. and Farouque, F. 2004. Keeping baby bonus in check. *The Age*, 13 May.

Sheldon, S. 1993. 'Who is the mother to make the judgment?': The constructions of woman in English abortion law. *Feminist Legal Studies*, 1(1), 3–23.

———. 1997. *Beyond Control: Medical Power and Abortion Law*. London: Pluto Press.

———. 2014. The medical framework and early medical abortion in the UK: How can a state control swallowing? *In:* Cook, R. J., Erdman, J. N. and Dickens, B. M. eds. *Abortion Law in Transnational Perspective*. Philadelphia: University of Pennsylvania Press, 189–209.

———. 2015. The decriminalisation of abortion: An argument for modernisation. *Oxford Journal of Legal Studies*, 36(2), 334–365.

———. 2017. Abortion law reform in Victoria: Lessons for the UK. *Journal of Family Planning and Reproductive Health Care*, 43(1), 25–25.

Sheldon, S. and Wilkinson, S. 2001. Termination of pregnancy for reason of foetal disability: Are there grounds for a special exception in law? *Medical Law Review*, 9(2), 85–109.

Shellenberg, K. M. *et al.* 2011. Social stigma and disclosure about induced abortion: Results from an exploratory study. *Global Public Health*, 6(sup1), S111–S125.

Shrage, L. 2003. *Abortion and Social Responsibility: Depolarizing the Debate*. New York: Oxford University Press.

Siegel, R. B. 2008. Dignity and the politics of protection: Abortion restrictions under Casey/Carhart. *Yale Law Journal*, 117(8), 1694–1800.

———. 2014. Abortion and the woman question: Forty years of debate. *Indiana Law Journal*, 89(4), 1365–1380.

Silliman, J. M. *et al.* eds. 2004. *Undivided Rights: Women of Color Organize for Reproductive Justice*. Cambridge, MA: South End Press.

Simic, Z. 2010. Fallen girls? Plumpton High and the 'problem' of teenage pregnancy. *Journal of Australian Studies*, 34(4), 429–445.

———. 2016. First Person Feminism. *Sydney Review of Books* [online]. Available from: http://sydneyreviewofbooks.com/fight-like-a-girl-clementine-ford-review [accessed 10 March 2017].

Simpson, A. 2016. Whither settler colonialism? *Settler Colonial Studies*, 6(4), 438–445.

Singh, S., Sedgh, G. and Hussain, R. 2010. Unintended pregnancy: Worldwide levels, trends, and outcomes. *Studies in Family Planning*, 41(4), 241–250.

Skeggs, B. 2004. Uneasy alignments, resourcing respectable subjectivity. *GLQ: A Journal of Lesbian and Gay Studies*, 10(2), 291–298.

Smart, C. 1990. Law's power, the sexed body, and feminist discourse. *Journal of Law and Society*, 17(2), 194–210.

———. 1992. Disruptive bodies and unruly sex: The regulation of reproduction and sexuality in the nineteenth century. *In*: Smart, C. ed. *Regulating Womanhood: Historical Essays on Marriage, Motherhood and Sexuality*. London: Routledge, 7–32.

Smith, A. 2005. Beyond pro-choice versus pro-life: Women of color and reproductive justice. *NWSA Journal*, 17(1), 119–140.

Smith, C. 2004. Confront the reality of abortion. *The Age*, 17 July.

Smith, L. 2003. 'Suitable mothers': Lesbian and single women and the 'unborn' in Australian parliamentary discourse. *Critical Social Policy*, 23(1), 63.

Smyth, H. 2000. *Rocking the Cradle: Contraception, Sex, and Politics in New Zealand*. Wellington, NZ: Steele Roberts.

Solinger, R. 2001. *Beggars and Choosers: How the Politics of Choice Shapes Adoption, Abortion, and Welfare in the United States*. New York: Hill and Wang.

Solomon, R. C. 2003. Emotions, thoughts and feelings: What is a 'cognitive theory' of the emotions and does it neglect affectivity? *Royal Institute of Philosophy Supplement*, 52(1), 1–18.

Somerville, J. 2000. *Feminism and the Family: Politics and Society in the UK and USA*. Basingstoke, UK: Palgrave MacMillan.

Spoonley, P. 2015. New diversity, old anxieties in New Zealand: The complex identity politics and engagement of a settler society. *Ethnic and Racial Studies*, 38(4), 650–661.

Stark, J. 2008. Unplanned pregnancy study sparks call for safe-sex campaign. *The Age*, 30 January.

Stephens, A. 1986. Booklet tells youngsters how to get abortions. *The Sun*, 12 November.

———. 1987a. Abortion decision remains a dilemma. *The Sun Living Supplement*, 27 January.

————. 1987b. Teenagers Express Confusion and Fear. *The Sun Living Supplement*, 27 January.

Stephenson, N., Mills, C. and McLeod, K. 2017. 'Simply providing information': Negotiating the ethical dilemmas of obstetric ultrasound, prenatal testing and selective termination of pregnancy. *Feminism & Psychology*, 27(1), 72–91.

Stoler, A. L. 2011. Colonial aphasia: Race and disabled histories in France. *Public Culture*, 23(1), 121–156.

Stote, K. 2012. The coercive sterilization of aboriginal women in Canada. *American Indian Culture and Research Journal*, 36(3), 117–150.

Stratton, J. 2011. *Uncertain Lives: Race and Neoliberalism in Australia*. Newcastle upon Tyne, UK: Cambridge Scholars.

String, G. 2001. Where ritual passes for vigile. *The Age*, 18 July.

Stringer, R. 2006. Fact, fiction and the foetus: Violence against pregnant women and the politics of abortion. *Australian Feminist Law Journal*, 25(1), 99–117.

The Sun. 1979. Teen abortion worry. 22 September.

Suk, J. 2010. The trajectory of trauma: Bodies and minds of abortion discourse. *Columbia Law Review*, 110(5), 1193–1252.

Sullivan, J. 1982. What do you tell a pregnant 15-year-old? *The Age*, 8 May.

Swain, S. and Howe, R. 1995. *Single Mothers and Their Children: Disposal, Punishment and Survival in Australia*. Cambridge: Cambridge University Press.

Sweeny, K. and Vohs, K. D. 2012. On near misses and completed tasks: The nature of relief. *Psychological Science*, 23(5), 439–445.

Symonds, M. 1996. *...And Still They Weep: Personal Stories of Abortion*. London: SPUC Educational Research Trust.

Tangney, J. P. *et al*. 1996. Are shame, guilt, and embarrassment distinct emotions? *Journal of Personality and Social Psychology*, 70(6), 1256–1269.

Tarica, E. 2002. The agonising life of Alex. *The Age Green Guide*, 9 May.

Tatalovich, R. 1997. *The Politics of Abortion in the United States and Canada: A Comparative Study*. Armonk, NY: M.E. Sharpe.

Tebbel, C. 2004. 'My abortion': A woman affirms her decision. *The Age*, 22 July.

Terry, J. and Urla, J. 1995. *Deviant Bodies: Critical Perspectives on Difference in Science and Popular Culture*. Bloomington: Indiana University Press.

Tomkins, S. 1995. Shame–humiliation and contempt–disgust. *In:* Frank, A. and Sedgwick, E. K. eds. *Shame and Its Sisters: A Silvan Tomkins Reader*. Durham, NC: Duke University Press, 33–74.

Too Many Aborted. 2017. Number one killer. Too many aborted [online]. Available from: www.toomanyaborted.com/numberonekiller [accessed 7 March 2017].

Toy, M. A. 2000. Sell the pill in schools: Expert. *The Age*, 13 October.

Treas, J. and Lui, J. 2013. Studying housework across nations. *Journal of Family Theory & Review*, 5(2), 135–149.

Tribe, L. 1990. *Abortion: The Clash of Absolutes*. New York: Norton & Company.

Trioli, V. 1998. Don't stir a sleeping dog. *The Age*, 21 March.

Turnbull, M. 2003. *It's the Birthrate, Stupid! Facing Up to Fertility*, Paper presented at the National Population Summit (Adelaide), 21 November [online]. Available from: www.apop.com.au/SAconfNOV03/M%20Turnbull.pdf [accessed 20 December 2016].

Tyler, I. 2007. The selfish feminist: Public images of Women's Liberation. *Australian Feminist Studies*, 22(53), 173–90.

———. 2008. Chav mum chav scum. *Feminist Media Studies*, 8(1), 17–34.

———. 2013. Revolting subjects. *Social Abjection and Resistance in Neoliberal Britain*. London and New York: Zed Books.

United Kingdom. 2017. Parliamentary debates: House of Commons: Official Hansard, 13 March [online]. Available from: https://hansard.parliament.uk/Commons/2017-03-13/debates/D76D740D-2DDD-4CCB-AC11-C0DBE3B7D0D8/ReproductiveHealth (AccessToTerminations) [accessed 13 June 2017].

United Nations. 2014. *International Conference on Population and Development Programme of Action: Twentieth Anniversary Edition* [online]. United Nations Population Fund. Available from: www.unfpa.org/sites/default/files/pub-pdf/programme_of_action_Web%20ENGLISH.pdf [accessed 4 March 2017].

Vale, D. 2006. My comments were clumsy. *The Age*, 25 February.

Vashti Collective. 1973. *Vashti's Voice: A Newsletter of the Women's Liber-ation Movement*, 3(March).

Vick, L. 2002. Anti-choice, pro-choice. *The Age*, 7 March.

Victoria. 2008a. Parliamentary debates: Legislative Assembly: Official Hansard, Book 12, 9 September.

———. 2008b. Parliamentary debates: Legislative Assembly: Official Hansard, Book 12, 10 September.

———. 2008c. Parliamentary debates: Legislative Council: Official Hansard, Book 13, 7 October.

———. 2008d. Parliamentary debates: Legislative Council: Official Hansard, Book 13, 8 October.

———. 2008e. Parliamentary debates: Legislative Council: Official Hansard, Book 13, 9 October.

Vizard, S., Martin, H. and Watts, T. eds. 2003. *Australia's Population Challenge*. Camberwell, VIC: Penguin.

Vogel, L. 2017. Doctors, pharmacists push back on medical abortion rules. *Canadian Medical Association Journal*, 189(12), 480–481.

Volscho, T. W. 2011. Racism and disparities in women's use of the Depo-Provera injection in the contemporary USA. *Critical Soci-ology*, 37(5), 673–688.

Vucetic, S. 2011. *The Anglosphere: A Genealogy of a Racialized Identity in International Relations*. Stanford, CA: Stanford University Press.

Wacquant, L. 2009. *Punishing the Poor: The Neoliberal Government of Social Insecurity*. Durham, NC, and London: Duke University Press.

Wainer, B. 1969. To the editor. *The Age*, 12 September.

Wainer, J. 1975. *Pathways to Abortion*. Burwood, VIC: La Trobe University.

———. 2008. Abortion and the struggle to be good in the 1970s. *Austral-asian Psychiatry*, 42(1), 30–37.

Wakefield, S. 1982. Names of family advice clinics cause confusion. *The Age*, 22 April.

Walker, D. 1999. *Anxious Nation: Australia and the Rise of Asia, 1850–1939*. Brisbane: University of Queensland Press.

Warhurst, J. 2008. Conscience voting in the Australian Federal Parlia-ment. *Australian Journal of Politics and History*, 54(4), 579–596.

Waters, L. 2016. Australians need abortion laws for 2016 not 1899. *The Sydney Morning Herald*, 11 May.

Watkins, E. S. 2010. From breakthrough to bust: The brief life of Norplant, the contraceptive implant. *Journal of Women's History*, 22(3), 88–111.

Weinbaum, A. E. 2004. *Wayward Reproductions: Genealogies of Race and Nation in Transatlantic Modern Thought*. Durham, NC: Duke University Press.

Weisstein. N. 1993. Power resistance and science: A call for a revitalized feminist psychology. *Feminism & Psychology*, 3(2), 239–245.

Weitz, T. A. 2010. Rethinking the mantra that abortion should be 'safe, legal, and rare'. *Journal of Women's History*, 22(3), 161–172.

West, L. 2015. I set up *#ShoutYourAbortion* because I am not sorry, and I will not whisper. *The Guardian*, 23 September [online]. Available from: www.theguardian.com/commentisfree/2015/sep/22/i-set-up-shoutyourabortion-because-i-am-not-sorry-and-i-will-not-whisper [accessed 20 July 2017].

———. 2016. *Shrill*. London: Quercus.

West, R. 1984. A 23-year search for peace. *The Age*, 14 November.

Westmore, A. 1976. The tragedy and the joy of the gymslip mums. *The Sun*, 13 September.

Williams, B. A. O. 1993. *Shame and necessity*. Berkeley: University of California Press.

Winikoff, B. 2014. Is one of these things not just like the Other: Why abortion can't be separated from contraception. *Conscience: The Newsjournal of Catholic Opinion*, 35(3), 27–29.

Wolf, N. 1995. Our bodies, our souls: Re-thinking pro-choice rhetoric. *The New Republic*, 17 October.

Wolfe, P. 1994. Nation and miscegenation: Discursive continuity in the post-Mabo era. *Social Analysis*, 36(October), 93–152.

Women Exploited by Abortion. 1986. *Women Exploited by Abortion (Newsletter)* 1 (Autumn).

———. 1987–1988. *Women Exploited by Abortion (Newsletter)* 2(Spring/Summer).

———. 1988a. *Women Exploited by Abortion (Newsletter)* 3(3).

————. 1988b. *Women Exploited by Abortion (Newsletter)* 3(4).

————. 1988c. *Women Exploited by Abortion (Newsletter)* 4(1).

————. 1988d. *Women Exploited by Abortion (Newsletter)* 4(2).

Women Hurt by Abortion. 1990a. *Women Hurt by Abortion (Newsletter)* 5(1).

————. 1990b. *Women Hurt by Abortion (Newsletter)* 5(2).

————. 1991. *Women Hurt by Abortion (Newsletter)* 6(1).

————. 1992. *Women Hurt by Abortion (Newsletter)* 21.

————. 1993. *Women Hurt by Abortion (Newsletter)* 22.

————. 1995. *Women Hurt by Abortion (Newsletter)* 2(1).

————. 1997. *Women Hurt by Abortion (Newsletter)* 7(1).

————. 1998. *Women Hurt by Abortion (Newsletter)* Winter.

Women's Abortion Action Campaign. n.d. Answers to common right to life arguments about abortion. State Library of Victoria, Wainer Papers, MS134636, Box 46.

————. 1973. *Right to Choose!* 1.

————. 1974a. Open letter. 28 November. State Library of Victoria, Wainer Papers, MS134636, Box 46.

————. 1974b. *Right to Choose!* 2 (early 1974).

————. 1974c. *Right to Choose!* 5 (December).

————. 1975a. *A Woman's Guide to Abortion: Why, How, Where.* Glebe, NSW: D. Whelan.

————. 1975b. *Right to Choose!* 6 (February–March).

————. 1975c. *Right to Choose!* 7 (mid-year).

————. 1975d. *Right to Choose!* 8 (September–October).

————. 1976a. *Right to Choose!* 10 (March).

————. 1977. *Right to Choose!* 14 (Autumn).

————. 1978a. *Right to Choose!* 15 (Summer).

————. 1978b. *Right to Choose!* 16 (Winter).

————. 1978c. *Right to Choose!* Extra (July).

————. 1978d. *Right to Choose!* 17 (Spring).

————. 1979. *Right to Choose!* 18 (February–March).

————. 1980–1981. *Right to Choose!* 21 (Summer).

————. 1981–1982. *Right to Choose!* 24 (Summer).

————. 1986. *Right to Choose!* 1 (Summer/Autumn).

Women's Electoral Lobby. 1975. Open submission to the human relations commission. University of Melbourne Archives, Women's Electoral Lobby Papers, AN92/85.

Woodcock, S. 2011. Abortion counselling and the informed consent dilemma. *Bioethics*, 25(9), 495–504.

World Health Organization. 2012. *Unsafe Abortion: Global and Regional Estimates of the Incidence of Unsafe Abortion and Associated Mortality in 2008*. Geneva: World Health Organization [online]. Available from: http://apps.who.int/iris/bitstream/10665/44529/1/9789241 501118_eng.pdf [accessed 20 July 2017].

Wyatt, D. and Hughes, K. 2009. When discourse defies belief: Anti-abortionists in contemporary Australia. *Journal of Sociology*, 45(3), 235–253.

Yallop, R. 1982. $400,000 for anti-abortion groups. *The Age*, 6 March.

YouGov. 2011. *YouGov Survey Results*, 2–5 September [online]. Availablefrom:http://cdn.yougov.com/today_uk_import/yg-archives-yougov-abortions-060911.pdf [accessed 16 December 2016].

Yusuf, F. and Siedlecky, S. 2002. Legal abortion in South Australia: A review of the first 30 years. *The Australian and New Zealand Journal of Obstetrics and Gynaecology*, 42(1), 15–21.

Zavella, P. 2016. Contesting structural vulnerability through reproductive justice activism with Latina immigrants in california. *North American Dialogue*, 19(1), 36–45.

Ziegler, M. 2013. Roe's race: The Supreme Court, population control, and reproductive justice. *Yale Journal of Law & Feminism*, 25(1), 1–50.

INDEX

#ShoutYourAbortion campaign, 2, 16, 186, 273

1 in 3 campaign, 184, 185, 273

Abbott, Tony, 129–32, 197, 211, 213, 238, 240, 250, 254, 257
abnormalities of foetus, justification for abortion, 114
Aboriginal peoples: life expectancy of, 255–6; treatment of, 109
Aboriginal women, activism of, 70
aborting woman, 38, 74, 76, 84, 115, 120, 130, 158, 178, 201, 265; as new subjectivity, 33; as sociological type, 20–1; as subject of own pregnancy, 24–5; as threat, 270 (to family, 255; to nation, 241); as victim, 59–61, 67; attached to other figures of shame, 40; becomes a feared object, 258; cast as affect alien, 132, 263; conduit for fears, 224; constituted as national object, 47; designated as outsider, 218; economic status of, 268; false consciousness of,

147; framed as mother, 161; illegitimate, 127; internalising sense of failure, 207; legitimate, 127; norms governing, 210, 217; realigned with normative femininity, 90; regulation of, 41; representation of, 19–29, 187; self-punishment of, 127; voice of, absent in debates, 208; white, 217, 235–6; *see also* desperate aborting woman; selfish aborting woman; and silence regarding abortion
abortion: ambivalence regarding, 94–6; among women on welfare, 214; as a 'choice to kill', 71–6, 161; as a desperate measure, 112; as a right, 50, 57, 96, 121, 196, 202; as act of maternal sacrifice, 98, 152; as act of self-determination, 50; as benign, 42; as blameworthy, 201; as causing psychological damage, 176; as choice not to mother, 182; as common experience, 271; common sense, 41; as complex decision, 206–7; as conduit for restoring privileges, 269; as contrary to

ZED

Zed is a platform for marginalised voices across the globe.

It is the world's largest publishing collective and a world leading example of alternative, non-hierarchical business practice.

It has no CEO, no MD and no bosses and is owned and managed by its workers who are all on equal pay.

It makes its content available in as many languages as possible.

It publishes content critical of oppressive power structures and regimes.

It publishes content that changes its readers' thinking.

It publishes content that other publishers won't and that the establishment finds threatening.

It has been subject to repeated acts of censorship by states and corporations.

It fights all forms of censorship.

It is financially and ideologically independent of any party, corporation, state or individual.

Its books are shared all over the world.

www.zedbooks.net
@ZedBooks